The Political Economy of
U.S. Militarism

The Political Economy of U.S. Militarism

Ismael Hossein-zadeh

THE POLITICAL ECONOMY OF U.S. MILITARISM
© Ismael Hossein-zadeh, 2006.

All rights reserved. No part of this book may be used or reproduced in any manner whatsoever without written permission except in the case of brief quotations embodied in critical articles or reviews.

First published in hardcover in 2006 by
PALGRAVE MACMILLAN™
175 Fifth Avenue, New York, N.Y. 10010 and
Houndmills, Basingstoke, Hampshire, England RG21 6XS.
Companies and representatives throughout the world.

PALGRAVE MACMILLAN is the global academic imprint of the Palgrave Macmillan division of St. Martin's Press, LLC and of Palgrave Macmillan Ltd. Macmillan® is a registered trademark in the United States, United Kingdom and other countries. Palgrave is a registered trademark in the European Union and other countries.

ISBN-13: 978-0-230-60228-1 paperback
ISBN-10: 0-230-60228-2 paperback

Library of Congress Cataloging-in-Publication Data

Hossein-zadeh, Ismael.
    The political economy of U.S. militarism / Ismael Hossein-zadeh.
    p. cm.
    Includes bibliographical references.
    ISBN 1-4039-7285-0 (hardcover) ISBN 0-230-60228-2
    1. Military—industrial complex—United States. 2. United States—Military policy—Economic aspects. I. Title: Political economy of United States militarism. II. Title.

HC110.D4H67 2006
338.4'735500973—dc22   2006041583

A catalogue record for this book is available from the British Library.

Design by Newgen Imaging Systems (P) Ltd., Chennai, India.

First PALGRAVE MACMILLAN paperback edition: July 2007

10 9 8 7 6 5 4 3 2 1

Printed in the United States of America.

Transferred to digital printing in 2007.

Contents

Introduction

While they may have been immoral, external military operations of past empires often proved profitable and, therefore, justifiable on economic grounds. Military actions abroad usually brought economic benefits not only to the imperial ruling classes, but also (through "trickle-down" effects) to their citizens. This was the case with both precapitalist empires of the distant past and the capitalist imperial powers of Europe. Thus, for example, imperialism paid significant dividends to Britain, France, the Dutch, and other European powers of the eighteenth, nineteenth, and early twentieth centuries. As the imperial economic gains helped develop their economies, they also helped improve the living conditions of their working people and elevate the standards of living of their citizens.

The United States too has often used military power as a means for economic and territorial gains. These include not only the expansion of its territory from the Atlantic to the Pacific, but also the considerable non-territorial economic gains abroad, especially in the immediate aftermath of Word War II. Whether external economic advantages were pursued through policies of "benign imperialism" (i.e., through free trade and multilateral institutions such as the World Bank and the IMF), or through combinations of military and covert operations of overthrowing elected governments (e.g., in Iran, Chile, and Ecuador), the fact remains that the resulting economic gains significantly contributed to the long cycle of economic expansion of the immediate postwar years. Gross national product in real terms, that is, adjusted for inflation, more than doubled between 1950 and 1970, and real earnings of both businesses and working people followed accordingly. Poverty was drastically reduced by the early 1970s and, for the most part, the American people enjoyed a degree of economic security and a level of material amenities that seemed impossible barely three decades earlier.

This pattern of economic gains flowing from imperial military operations, however, seems to have somewhat changed in recent years, especially in the post–Cold War world. Moralities aside, U.S. military expeditions and operations of late are not justifiable even on imperialistic economic grounds. Indeed, escalating U.S. military expansions and aggressions have become ever more wasteful and cost-inefficient in the post–Cold War era. As shown in chapter 6 of this study, even the widely held claim that such expansions and aggressions are driven largely by concerns for fossil fuels seems increasingly dubious. Not surprisingly, official justifications for the post–Cold War military actions have become increasingly fuzzy: humanitarian concerns, international drug trafficking, global terrorism, militant Islam, or democratic ideals. The fact that external U.S. military operations of late have become economically burdensome has also undermined traditional or classical theories of imperialism that tend to explain imperial military expeditions and operations in terms of economic gains and objectives.

So, if it is not economic (or classic) imperialism, how are, then, the escalating military aggressions of the United States in recent years to be characterized? What are the driving forces behind these military expansions, expeditions, and operations?

Critics have offered a number of explanations. One of the most popular explanations attributes the rise of unilateral U.S. military adventures to the ascendance to power of the cabal of the so-called neoconservative militarists: the small but influential cabal of starry eyed ideologues, bent on spreading the U.S. economic and political system, along with American power and influence, has effectively managed to drive the country to the path of war and militarism. A second popular theory attributes the increasing militarization of U.S. foreign policy to political and intellectual inadequacies of George W. Bush as president, his near-missionary approach to politics, his political need to maintain his 9/11-induced strong status as commander in chief, and his tendency to cherish the status of a "war president." A widely shared third view, especially outside of the United States, attributes the recent rise of U.S. militarism, especially the invasion of Iraq, to the geopolitical imperatives of Israel and the concomitant influence of the Zionist lobby. Some of the proponents of this view go so far as to argue that the U.S. foreign and/or military policies in the Middle East are made by leading forces or figures of militant Zionism. The fourth, and perhaps the most widely held, view of the surge in U.S. military expansions in the Middle East and central Asia is that the recently heightened military activities in those regions are prompted by U.S. designs to gain access to more and cheaper sources of gas and oil.

Without denying the contributory roles of these factors, *The Political Economy of U.S. Militarism* points to a more crucial force behind the drive to war and militarism: the powerful beneficiaries of military expansion and war dividends, or the military-industrial complex and related influential interests that are vested in the business of war and military expansion. Drawing on a number of preeminent theories and empirical accounts on imperialism and militarism,[1] this study makes a clear distinction between "classical" or economic imperialism, on the one hand, and militaristic, cost-inefficient, or parasitic imperialism, on the other.

Historically, parasitic military imperialism has almost always evolved out of a higher stage of economic or classical imperialism: a prolonged reliance on military power for economic, territorial, or geopolitical gains gradually creates a dynamic out of which evolves a large standing military apparatus that tends to perpetuate itself—and develop into a bureaucratic military empire. Though military force in the economic sense of imperialism is usually a means for economic, territorial, or geopolitical gains, under parasitic military imperialism it becomes an end in itself. Accordingly, under parasitic imperialism, military adventures abroad are often prompted not necessarily by a desire to expand the empire's wealth beyond the existing levels but by a desire to appropriate the lion's share of the existing wealth and treasure for the military establishment. It is at such stages—as when Julius Caesar crossed the Rubicon—that military operations abroad tend to tip the scales in the direction of cost inefficiency and drain a national economy.

In a similar fashion, as the U.S. military establishment has grown in size, it has also evolved in quality and character: it is no longer just a means for economic or geopolitical gains but, perhaps more importantly, an end in itself. Accordingly, rising militarization of U.S. foreign policy in recent years is driven not so much by some general or abstract national interests, or by the interests of big oil, as it is by the special interests vested in the military-industrial complex and related business that need an atmosphere of war and militarism in order to justify their lion's share of the public money. Indeed, as shown in chapter 8 of this study, most nonmilitary transnational corporations, including big oil, no longer welcome global U.S. military adventures.

Viewed in this light, militaristic tendencies to war abroad can be seen largely as reflections of the metaphorical fights over allocation of the public finance at home, of a subtle or insidious strategy to redistribute national resources in favor of the wealthy, to cut public spending on socioeconomic infrastructure, and to reverse the New Deal reforms by expanding military spending. Increased military adventures abroad can also be seen, in part, as reflections of the conflict between the two major competing factions within the ruling elite at home: multilateralist proponents of neoliberalism, representing primarily the interests of nonmilitary transnational capital, on the one hand, and unilateralist advocates of nationalism and militarism, who tend to represent the interests of military industries and of the internationally noncompetitive businesses, on the other. As the former faction has been effectively outmaneuvered and marginalized in recent years by the latter faction, and as the pressure from *below*, that is, from potential opponents of war and militarism, has been successfully dissipated to negligible levels for the last three decades or so, military expansion and aggression has escalated accordingly.

Although *The Political Economy of U.S. Militarism* has drawn inspiration and information from a number of major scholarly works on militarism and imperialism, it differs from, and goes beyond, these important works in a number of significant ways—adding a unique perspective to the ongoing debate on the issue.

To begin with, it challenges and documents a case against the dominant view that the surge in U.S. military expansions in the Middle East and central Asia is driven mainly by oil interest. The study suggests that although oil is indubitably a concern, and that the United States has used military force in the past for energy purposes, these precedents fail to explain the recently heightened U.S. military operations abroad. As shown in chapter 6 of the study, there is strong evidence that major oil companies no longer favor war in the Middle East or other sources of energy, because they prefer stability and predictability to periodic spikes in the oil price that result from war and political convulsion. There is also strong evidence that the powerful interests vested in war and militarism might be using oil as a pretext to justify military adventures in order to derive higher dividends from the business of war.

Second, unlike most critics, this study cautions against attributing all the power and influence of the neoconservative militarists in and around the Bush administration to pure ideology, political persona, or the role of individual politicians; that is, against the widely circulated conspiracy theories that attribute the rise of U.S. militarism to a political coup d'etat by the cabal of neoconservative warmongers.[2] Instead, it focuses on the larger, but mostly submerged, picture: the powerful institutional and politico-economic interests that lie behind the façade of the cabal of neoconservative figures. Professional records of the key neoconservative players in the administration show that, for example, "32 major administration appointees . . . are former executives with, consultants for, or significant shareholders of top defense contractors."[3] (This issue is discussed in chapter 6, under the subheading "The Role of the Cabal of Neoconservatives.")

Third, this study also cautions against the view that tends to paint all the recently heightened militaristic tendencies as an exclusive product of the Bush administration. It suggests that such views need to be tempered against the evidence that the evolution of the military-industrial complex in the direction of an imperial military machine began long before George W. Bush arrived in the White House. Accordingly, major components of the neoconservative agenda, which is essentially the agenda of the beneficiaries of war and militarism, were designed long before George W. Bush's presidency. Undoubtedly, the Bush administration played a major role in the further growth of militarism. But the roots of militarism descend far back into the past. The old cliché that Rome was not built in one day is quite relevant here—and just as Rome was not built in a day, it won't be demolished in one day either. (Discussion of this issue is provided in chapter 3, under the subheading "Decline of 'Benign Imperialism' and the Rise of Military Imperialism," and in chapter 6, under subheadings "The Role of the Military-Industrial Complex" and "Defining the President's Mission.")

Fourth, *The Political Economy of U.S. Militarism* also cautions against simplifications and exaggerations of the power and influence of the Zionist lobby over the U.S. policy in the Middle East. It is true that most of the neoconservative militarists who have been behind the recent U.S. military expansion and aggression, and who played an instrumental role in the invasion of Iraq and Afghanistan, have long been active supporters of Israel's right-wing politicians and/or leaders. It is also no secret that there is a close collaboration over issues of war and militarism between militant Zionism, neoconservative forces in and around the Bush administration, and jingoistic think tanks of the military-industrial complex. It does not follow, however, that, as some critics argue, the U.S.–Israeli relationship represents a case of "tail wagging the dog," that is, the U.S. foreign policy in the Middle East is shaped by the Israeli/Zionist leaders. While, no doubt, the powerful Zionist lobby exerts considerable influence over U.S. foreign policy in the Middle East, the efficacy and the extent of that influence depend, ultimately, on the real economic and geopolitical interests of U.S. foreign policy makers. In other words, U.S. policy makers in the Middle East would go along with the desires and demands of the radical Zionist lobby only if such demands also tend to serve the special interests that those policy makers represent or serve, that is, if there is a convergence of interests over those demands. Aggressive existential tendencies of the U.S. military-industrial empire to war and militarism are shaped by its own internal or intrinsic dynamics. Conjunctural or reinforcing factors such as the horrors of 9/11, or the Zionist lobby, or the party in power, or the resident of the White House will, no doubt, exert significant influences. But, as shown in chapter 6 of this study, such supporting influences remain essentially contributory, not defining or determining.

Fifth, *The Political Economy of U.S. Militarism* examines the expansion of military spending as an integral part of the development of U.S. economy and, accordingly, studies the rise of militarism in the context of both conflicting and converging group and/or class interests over military expenditures. This stands in sharp contrast to a number of studies that tend to explain the surge in U.S. militarism by some abstract and ahistorical patterns of the rise of militarism in general—for example, by cultural fascinations with military power as a measure of national greatness, or by inherent tendencies in the ranks of military hierarchies to build bureaucratic military empires.[4] Surely, disposition to build bureaucratic empires have almost always existed in the ranks of military hierarchies. By itself, this is not what makes the U.S. military-industrial complex unique or more dangerous than the military powers of the past. What makes it distinctive and more dangerous is the "industrial" part of the complex. In contrast to the military industry of the United States, arms industries of past empires were not subject to capitalist market imperatives. Furthermore, those industries were often owned and operated by imperial governments, not by market-driven giant corporations. Consequently, as a rule, arms production was dictated by war requirements, not by market or profit imperatives. Thus, private ownership and the market-driven character of the United States arms industry have drastically modified the conventional relationship between the supply of and demand for arms: it is now often the supply (or profit) imperatives that drive demand for arms. In other words, imperial wars and demand for arms are nowadays precipitated more by sales and/or profit prerequisites than the other way around, as was the case with imperial powers of the past. President Eisenhower's warnings near the end of his second term against the potential dangers of the military-industrial complex seem to have been prompted by this intrinsic tendency of the complex to war and militarism.

Sixth, following Paul Kennedy's groundbreaking work on the destructive effects of overextended military establishments, *The Rise and Fall of the Great Powers*, most of the recently published critical books of U.S. militarism tend to draw very close parallels between the post-Rubicon, old or declining Roman Empire, on the one hand, and the currently militaristic imperial status of the United States, on the other. Specifically, these critics argue that the widespread power and influence of the U.S. military establishment may well have transformed the Unites States from a republic to a military empire with irreversible consequences, that is, decline and decay after the model of the post-Rubicon Rome. This study argues, by contrast, that while the possibility that U.S. imperialism may follow the historical trajectory of Old Rome cannot be ruled out altogether, it is nonetheless more likely that the decline or contraction of the U.S. military-imperial apparatus would take a different pattern, a pattern more in tune with the decline of an advanced capitalist or market structure than a precapitalist formation. Theories and actual developments that can serviceably be employed to explain the rise and fall of precapitalist imperial powers cannot easily be extended or extrapolated to explain the rise and fall of capitalist empires. Capitalism, like other "modes of production" before it, has its own "historically-specific laws of motion," as Karl Marx put it. Accordingly, the fate of the U.S. military-imperial power is more likely to resemble the pattern of the British Empire than that of the Roman Empire; that is, a cyclical pattern of ebbs and flows, of expansions and retrenchments, depending on both economic (budgetary) constraints and social challenges from *below*—for example, a widespread and effective challenge similar to the antiwar movement of the 1960s and early 1970s. This is not to subscribe to Francis Fukuyama's theory of the "end of history" (i.e., of the permanent or endless capitalism), but to point out that there is no automatic collapse for capitalism either. The future of the U.S. military-imperial power (and of capitalism in general) depends ultimately on the balance of social forces and the outcome of class struggle. (For a detailed discussion of this issue please see chapters 2 and 9 of this study.)

Seventh, a careful study of both the market forces behind and economic consequences of military spending is another distinguishing feature of this book. Some of the economic effects of military spending that the book examines are as follows: stimulating versus retarding effects; employment, demand-management, and investment effects; technological "spin-off" and innovation effects; "crowding-out" effects, or the opportunity costs of military spending in terms of social spending; redistributive, or income distribution, effects; waste, inefficiency, and corrupting effects; and the economic or financial limits of military spending, which are crucial to the limits of militarism. Most of the recently published books on U.S. militarism do not adequately discuss the contradictory economic effects of military spending. By vaguely and sporadically highlighting the long-term draining economic effects of military spending, they tend to overlook the fact that military spending can have short-term stimulating effects, especially during periods of high unemployment and economic contraction; and that, therefore, this stimulus property of military spending, known as military Keynesianism, has played an important role in the expansion of military expenditures. (This issue is discussed in some detail in chapter 8.)

Eighth, most of the recent books on the rise of U.S. militarism fail to take account of the long and important debate between the two major factions within the U.S. ruling class over military spending and international relations; that is, the debate between proponents of neoliberal multilateralism, or free trade imperialism, on the one hand, and those of neoconservative unilateralism, or military imperialism, on the other. Consequently, they seem to argue that the forces or economic interests that once advocated neoliberalism are now advocating unilateral militarism, and that the forces of unilateral militarism may well have irrevocably replaced those of neoliberalism.[5] Yet, for example, the change from the neoliberal multilateralism of the 1990s to the unilateral militarism that has replaced it is obviously the result of the victory of one faction of the ruling class over the other. Furthermore, as pointed out in chapter 3 of this study, the history of the leading capitalist countries shows that, depending on the degree of their economic competitiveness in global markets, world capitalist powers always tend to alternate policies of economic liberalism/ neoliberalism with those of unilateral militarism.

Ninth, *The Political Economy of U.S. Militarism* fills yet another gap in the ongoing discussions and critiques of U.S. militarism: the complex relationship between military expansion, economic interests (both domestic and international), and the long waves of economic expansion and contraction. It shows how, for example, long periods of economic slowdown and high unemployment are more conducive to military expansion than those of economic prosperity, because during such times of sluggish sales competition in global markets tends to intensify, which will then induce the internationally noncompetitive capitalists to call for protection and military muscle flexing. Furthermore, to help stimulate such lackluster economic conditions, increases in military spending are often used as fiscal policy tools to contain or reverse those recessionary cycles. Thus, the military-industrial complex handsomely benefits from this symbiotic relationship between fiscal policy needs of the ruling elite to stimulate the economy by increasing military spending and the protectionist needs of the internationally noncompetitive industries. Not surprisingly, the drastic increases in military spending in the early 1950s, the early 1980s, and the early 2000s all came about on the heels of the respective recessionary cycles of those times. By contrast, during periods of long expansionary cycles and economic prosperity, economic nationalism and unilateral militarism tend to recede to the background while economic liberalism and multilateralism will appear as preferred economic policy. For during periods of economic expansion, of strong demand, and of brisk sales all or most businesses (both domestic and transnational) would prefer stability and predictability to international political convulsions and military adventures. (Discussion of these issues is provided in chapters 3 and 8.)

Finally, this study is unique not only for its examination of the factors and forces that have been directly behind the U.S. drive to war and militarism but also for its careful analysis of a series of closely related topics that may appear as digressions but, in fact, help shed more light on the main journey. For example, it provides a distinct perspective on the roots of conflict between the Muslim world and the West. It also presents a rare viewpoint on religious fundamentalism, both Islamic and Judeo-Christian fundamentalisms, and its role in the expansion of war and militarism in the United States. The study further offers an uncommon analysis of the theory of *the clash of civilizations* and its subtle impact on the rise of U.S. militarism. (These issues are discussed in chapter 5.)

In sum, by focusing primarily on the intrinsic dynamics of the military-industrial complex as an internally driven juggernaut to war and militarism, *The Political Economy of U.S. Militarism* provides a welcome challenge to most of the prevailing critiques that attribute the rising militarization of U.S. foreign policy to big oil, to the ideological power of the neoconservatives, to the Zionist lobby, to the cultural or attitudinal fascination of the United States with military might as a sign of national greatness, to America's idealism to spread democracy, or to George W. Bush's near-missionary approach to presidency and his desire to be a war president.

By highlighting the critical influences of special economic interests and of market imperatives over the dynamics of the U.S. military-industrial complex, the study examines the escalating appropriations of the Pentagon largely as a roundabout way of cutting public spending on socioeconomic infrastructure, as an insidious strategy to reverse the New Deal and other social safety net programs, and as a regulatory mechanism to redistribute national income/resources in favor of the wealthy—especially of the beneficiaries of war dividends.

CHAPTER 1

The Military-Industrial Giant: An Empire in Itself

The conjunction of an immense military establishment and a huge arms industry is new in the American experience. The total influence—economic, political, and even spiritual—is felt in every city, every state house, and every office of the federal government. . . . In the councils of government, we must guard against the acquisition of unwarranted influence, whether sought or unsought, by the military-industrial complex.

—President Dwight D. Eisenhower,
Farewell Address, January 17, 1961

President Eisenhower's warning that "we must guard against the acquisition of unwarranted influence" of the military-industrial complex is more relevant today than when it was issued nearly half a century ago. The steadily rising—and now perhaps overwhelming—power and influence of the complex over both domestic and foreign policies of the United States is testament to President Eisenhower's felicitous advice.

Concern over the corrupting and destabilizing influences of a large military establishment was also a major reason why the Founding Fathers, despite their expansionist tendencies, opposed the idea of maintaining large standing armies during peacetimes. As George Washington put it, a large peace-time military establishment "hath ever been considered dangerous to the liberties of a country." This antimilitarist tradition should not be confused with pacifism. What the earlier U.S. leaders opposed was not military, but militarism—not military force as a means to achieve economic and/or territorial gains but military establishment as an end in itself. Indeed, they frequently used military force in pursuit of economic, territorial, and geopolitical gains. But at the end of each conflict they scaled back the expanded war-time military force to its prewar level out of concerns that "standing armies in time of peace are inconsistent with the principles of republican governments, dangerous to the liberties of a free people, and generally converted into destructive engines for establishing despotism."[1]

With varying degrees, this antimilitarist tradition was maintained until World War II. Although during that period of nearly 150 years the United States engaged in many wars—6 major ones and 104 minor ones—and the military force was expanded during each war, demobilization at the end of each conflict reduced the armed forces to their prewar size. Not surprisingly then, despite the fact that this antimilitarist tradition was somewhat weakened in the late nineteenth and early twentieth centuries, the size of the regular armed forces on the eve of World War II stood at only 139,000.[2]

Today more than ten times as many military forces literally span the entire globe. According to the Defense Department's annual "Base Structure Report," the Pentagon currently deploys nearly 1.5 million military personnel in 6,000 domestic bases and 702 overseas bases in 130 countries. Prior to the invasion of Iraq, the military high command deployed some 253,288 uniformed personnel to overseas bases, plus an equal number of dependents and Department of Defense (DoD) civilian officials and various functionaries such as technicians, spies, teachers, and civilian contactors. The Pentagon also deploys about a dozen carrier task forces in the oceans and seas of the world.

The actual number of military bases and installations abroad, however, is much higher than 702. For one thing, this number does not include foreign posts with a plant replacement value (PRV) of less than $10 million because the military documents only the bases with a PRV larger than $10 million. Second, DoD's annual Base Structure Report fails to include in this figure the many military installations that have in recent years been built or rented in Kosovo, Afghanistan, Iraq, Israel, Kuwait, Kyrgyzstan, Qatar, and Uzbekistan. Nor does the report include the many military and espionage installations in Britain which, as Chalmers Johnson points out, "have long been conveniently disguised as Royal Air Force bases." After carefully exposing the various omissions from the report's account of the U.S. military bases abroad, Johnson concludes, "If there were an honest count, the actual size of our military empire would probably top 1,000 different bases in other people's countries, but no one—possibly not even the Pentagon—knows the exact number for sure, although it has been distinctly on the rise in recent years."[3]

At the heart of the military-industrial complex lies the Pentagon itself. The military establishment's decision-making structure is sometimes called the "Iron Triangle." On one side of the triangle are the "civilian" agencies that formally shape U.S. military policy. These include the Office of the President, the National Security Council, the Senate and House Armed Services Committees, and agencies such as the CIA and NASA. A second side of the triangle consists of the military institutions. These include the Joint Chiefs of Staff, the top brass of the Air Force, Army, Marines, and Navy; the powerful "proconsul" regional commands, known as "NICS"; and, in a supporting role, veterans' organizations such as the American Legion and the Veterans of Foreign Wars. At the base of the triangle "are the 85,000 private firms that profit from the military contracting system, and that use their sway over millions of defense workers to push for ever-higher military budgets."[4]

In addition, the military-industrial complex has steadily spawned a vast web of other entities and organizations around itself. These include a considerable number of both DoD-financed and private research, consulting, and lobbying organizations such as the Rand Corporation and Hoover Institution, popularly known as think tanks. They also include a large number of service providers as a result of recent years' increasing outsourcing of many of the traditional military tasks and responsibilities. Furthermore, they include major research institutions of higher education such as the Massachusetts Institute of Technology and Harvard University. The Association of American Universities (AAU) reported in 2002 that almost 350 colleges and universities conduct Pentagon-funded research, that universities receive more than 60 percent of funding for defense-based basic research, and that the DoD is the third largest federal funder of university research (after the National Institutes of Health and the National Science Foundation).[5]

The official Pentagon budget for the 2005 fiscal year, which does not include the cost of war in Iraq and Afghanistan, stands at $419 billion. Taking into account a number of supplemental appropriations for the costs of wars in Iraq and Afghanistan and war-related operations such as Homeland Security will easily raise this figure to the tune of $700 billion, which represents 31.8 percent of the total federal budget of nearly $2,200 billion. While this is obviously a large portion of the national treasure, it nonetheless grossly understates the real magnitude of the Pentagon budget. A major reason for this understatement is the inclusion of the Social Security Trust Fund, nearly $520 billion for the 2005 fiscal year, in the federal budget. The Social Security Fund is a trust fund and should not be integrated with the regular government budget. So, if it is excluded from the federal budget, as it should be, the 2005 federal budget would be $1,680 billion, not $2,200 billion. This means that the true share of the Pentagon of the national tax dollars would be 41.6 percent, not 31.8 percent.[6]

Even without the enormous cost of war, the Pentagon now spends more money than all other discretionary budget items combined. (Broadly speaking, budget items are classified as either mandatory or discretionary. Mandatory items, also called entitlements, legally obligate the government to make payments to any person or program that meets the legal criteria for eligibility. Examples include Social Security, Medicare, and Medicaid. Discretionary budget items are decided by the president and the Congress through a number of annual appropriations bills. They include both military and nonmilitary expenditures. Nonmilitary discretionary budget items include education, health, housing assistance, international affairs, natural resources and environment, justice, veterans' benefits, science and space, transportation, training/employment and social services, economic development, and a few more items.)[7] According to Carlton Meyer, editor of *G2mil, The Magazine of Future Warfare*, the Pentagon now appropriates more money in real (inflation adjusted) terms than it did at the peak of the Vietnam War when some 500,000 GIs were in combat, and more than its annual average budget of the Cold War era when it was competing with the Soviet Union.[8] And according to the Stockholm-based SIPRI Group, "The United States leads the world in defence spending, accounting for 47 percent of the total, followed by Japan with five percent and Britain, France and China with four percent each."[9]

The massive amounts of military spending have over time led to the dependence of millions of U.S. citizens on that spending. Due to this economic dependence, many of the citizens who might be against militarism on philosophical or ideological grounds often find themselves promoting local military spending. Accordingly, all members of the Congress, regardless of their political orientation, vigorously compete with each other to attract defense contracts to their districts. It might be interesting to note that this dependence on and competition over military spending sometimes leads to a bigger appropriation than the Pentagon's original request! For example, the two Washington State senators, Patty Murray and Maria Cantwell, "voted to include in the fiscal year 2003 defense budget some $30 billion to be spent over a decade to lease Boeing 767 aircrafts and modify them to serve as aerial tankers for refueling combat aircraft in flight, a project not even listed by the air force in its top sixty priorities or among its procurement plans for the next six years. . . . Boeing, of course, builds the planes at factories in Washington State."[10] Because a bigger Pentagon budget creates further dependence on military spending, and further dependence on military spending generates more demand for that spending, the mutually reinforcing process has over time turned into a vicious circle with no end in sight.

Fighting against the Pentagon's perennial waste and mismanagement of taxpayers' money some 35 years ago, the late Senator J. William Fulbright described this perverse economic dependence of numerous U.S. citizens on military spending as follows: "Millions of Americans whose only interest is in making a decent living have acquired a vested interest in an economy geared to war. Those benefits, once obtained, are not easily parted with. Every new weapons system or military installation soon acquires a constituency."[11] Not only has military spending become vital to the livelihood of many people and the profits of many businesses, it has also become a major cushion that props up aggregate demand in times of economic recession when private-sector spending dwindles. It is not surprising, then, that proponents of large military spending have been most successful in increasing the Pentagon budget during periods of economic slowdown, as during such periods they find it easier to justify military spending as a fiscal instrument that would prevent aggregate demand (and hence the economy) from collapsing. For these reasons, the powerful beneficiaries of the Pentagon budget and partisans of militarism, as well as many economists, argue that there is no need to lament over the large military spending, and that the continued rise in military spending is a positive development that must be maintained and continued.

Critics of the inordinately large military spending argue, by contrast, that the massive allocation of national resources to the production of armaments or war-related goods and services is an unfortunate outcome of the gradual rise of militarism of the past 55 years that needs to be curtailed in favor of the production of more socially beneficial products. While acknowledging the importance of military spending for jobs and businesses, they argue that this is a sad development—like a bad habit, an addiction—that needs to be reversed. The unfortunate addiction to the disproportionately large doses of military spending needs to be remedied not only because it produces too many guns and too little butter but also because, perhaps more importantly, a top-heavy military apparatus will be unviable in the long run as it tends to undermine the economic base it is supposed to nurture. Furthermore, control of the massive amounts of national resources by the military-industrial complex tends to undermine democratic values, pervert republican principles, and curtail civil liberties. It also tends to corrupt both policy and politics at home and abroad.

A salient hallmark of militarism is the rise of the power and influence of the military establishment at the expense of representational government and democratic rule. The pernicious penetration of military ways into civilian affairs tends to gradually curtail civil liberties and influence national policies both at home and on the international level. The rising political marriage between military and civilian authority also slowly undermines the traditional division of responsibility between elected officials and military professionals who advised elected officials and executed their policies. Militarism often wields influence in subtle and indirect ways, as when, for example, the military-industrial complex places its priorities on the national agenda through key congressional committees, or through its network of influential lobbying think tanks. But militarization of civilian affairs also takes place in direct and open ways, such as formal assignment of military officers and representatives to high government positions. For example, the administration of President George W. Bush has filled many of the chief American diplomatic posts with military men or civilian militarists, including Secretary of State General Colin Powell, and the Deputy Secretary of State Richard Armitage, who was undersecretary of Defense in the Reagan administration. At the Pentagon, President Bush appointed Peter B. Teets, the former president and chief operating officer of Lockheed Martin Corporation, as undersecretary of the Air Force; former brigadier general and Enron Corporation executive Thomas E. White as secretary of the Army; Gordon England, a vice president of General Dynamics, as secretary of the Navy; and James Roche, an executive with Northrop Grumman and a retired brigadier general, as secretary of the Air Force. Lockheed Martin, General Dynamics, and Northrop Grumman are, of course, major Pentagon contractors.[12]

As the rising influence of the military-industrial complex curtails democratic rule, it also undermines accountability for public finances appropriated by the Pentagon. For example, the investigative reporter Kelly O'Meara of *Insight* magazine has reported that in May 2001 the deputy inspector general at the Pentagon "admitted that $4.4 trillion in adjustments to the Pentagon's books had to be cooked to compile . . . required financial statements and that $1.1 trillion . . . was simply gone and no one can be sure of when, where or to whom the money went."[13] Another example: in an article titled "Military Waste Under Fire: $1 Trillion Missing," Tom Abate of the *San Francisco Chronicle* reported on May 18, 2003, that "the Department of Defense, already infamous for spending $640 for a toilet seat, once again finds itself under intense scrutiny, only this time because it couldn't account for more than a trillion dollars in financial transactions, not to mention dozens of tanks, missiles and planes." Circulation of the "wheeling and dealing" elites between and within the Pentagon, its contractors, the military brass, and government officials has become an ominously efficient vehicle for the waste and plunder of the citizens' tax dollars appropriated by the Pentagon. William Hartung and Michelle Ciarrocca of the World Policy Institute's Arms Trade Resource Center estimate that, for example, 32 major Bush policy makers have significant ties to the arms industry.[14] Powerful beneficiaries of military spending have extensive ties and considerable influence within the Defense Department, the National Security Council, the State Department, the White House, and the key congressional committees.

Congressional collaboration with the Pentagon and its contractors is, of course, not limited to key committees of the Congress; it includes most members of the Congress as they have grown increasingly addicted to generous contributions from the military-industrial complex to their reelection. They have also grown increasingly dependent on the Pentagon "pork projects" in their home states that help create jobs and improve the local economy. It is not surprising, then, that most elected officials with an input or voting power in the process of the appropriation of the Pentagon budget find themselves in the pocket of defense contractors, so to speak. Five of the top six donors to the House Armed Services Committee were nuclear weapons and missile defense contractors in 2001. Lockheed Martin, the largest Pentagon contractor, ranked number one in donations to Senate Appropriations Committee and the Senate Committee on Governmental Affairs. The giant contractor more than doubled its spending on campaign financing from $4.2 million in 1999 to $9.7 million in 2000.

Major defense contractors are rewarded handsomely for their contributions to the election of their favorite politicians. The three largest contractors—Boeing, Northrop Grumman, and Lockheed Martin—enjoyed a combined $50 billion in contracts in 2003. The $21.9 billion going to Lockheed exceeds the largest single welfare program in the United States, the Temporary Assistance to Needy Families (TANF). The Pentagon's generous contracts are, however, not reciprocated with efficiency, accountability, or responsibility. Pentagon contractors' waste and inefficiency are no longer a secret. Budgets on proposed arms acquisitions routinely run well over the original estimates, and the often belatedly delivered products frequently fail the tests of quality standards. A large part of this waste and inefficiency is due to a lack of competitive bidding. Sadly, however, such failures of the Pentagon contractors are often covered up in classified documents to hide their waste and inefficiency. (This issue is further elaborated on in chapter 7 of this study.)

Another salient hallmark of militarism is its constant need to invent (or manufacture, if necessary) external "threats to the national security of the United States" in order to justify continued expansion of military spending. The military-industrial complex has frequently invoked the specter of "external threats" in order to justify its lion's share of the nation's treasure. Expansion of the Pentagon budget during the Cold War era was not a difficult act to perform as the explanation—the "communist threat"—seemed to conveniently lie at hand. Justification of increased military spending in the post–Cold War period, however, has required the military-industrial interests to be more creative in concocting "new sources of danger to U.S. interests." This perennial need for international conflicts is what makes U.S. military imperialism more dangerous than the imperialist powers of the past ages.

War profiteering is, of course, not new. Nor are bureaucratic tendencies in the ranks of military hierarchies to build parasitic, ceremonial military empires. By themselves, such characteristics are not what make the U.S. military-industrial complex more dangerous than the military powers of the past. What makes it more dangerous is the "industrial" part of the complex: the extent to which war has become big business. In contrast to the arms industry of the United States, arms industries of the past empires were not market-driven giant corporations. Furthermore, those industries were often owned and operated by imperial governments, not by private corporations. Consequently, as a rule, arms production was dictated by war requirements, not by market or profit imperatives of arms manufacturers, which is often the case with today's U.S. arms industry. As far as this industry is concerned, instigation of international conflicts, or invention of external "threats to national security," is a lucrative proposition that will increase both their profits by expanding their sales markets and their share of national tax dollars by increasing the Pentagon's budget.

Thus, private ownership and the market-driven character of the arms industry of the United States have drastically changed the conventional relationship between the supply of and demand for arms: imperial wars and demand for arms are nowadays precipitated more by sales and/or profit imperatives than the other way around, as was the case with the imperial powers of the past. This has had dire consequences for world peace and stability. Under the rule of past military empires, the subjugated peoples or nations could live in peace—imposed peace, to be sure—if they respected the geopolitical interests and economic needs of those imperial powers and simply resigned to their political and economic ambitions. Not so with the U.S. military-industrial empire: the interests of this empire are nurtured through "war dividends." Peace, imposed or otherwise, would mean sales stagnation for the giant arms manufacturers. It would also mean that the powerful beneficiaries of war dividends would find it difficult to justify their inordinately large share of national resources, or tax dollars.

For the old precapitalist military empires the mere perception of external "threats to national interests," or the mere specter of war, was sufficient to maintain the elite status of the military establishment and its bureaucratic privileges. Indeed, the bureaucratic hierarchies of those early military empires were often more interested in the preservation of the status quo—as this meant peaceful enjoyment of their parasitic positions—than in war and bloodshed. Again, not so with the U.S. military-industrial empire: international peace and harmony is not good for the business of this empire. Perhaps this is why the military side of the Pentagon was not as eager to wage war on Iraq as the civilian side, which is primarily a front for powerful corporate interests, especially those vested in war industries. Contrary to the cases of the earlier, precapitalist military empires, mere perception of external "threats" is not sufficient for the prosperity of the U.S. military-industrial empire. Actual, shooting wars—at least, occasionally—are needed not only for the expansion but, indeed, for the survival of this empire. Arms industries need occasional wars not only to draw down their stockpiles of armaments, and make room for more production, but also to display the "wonders" of what they produce: the "shock– and awe"–inducing properties of their products, and the "laser-guided, surgical operations" of their smart weapons. In the era of tight and contested budget allocations, arms producers need such "displays of efficiency" to prove that they do not waste taxpayers' money. Such maneuvers are certain to strengthen the arguments of militarist politicians against those (few) who resist huge military appropriations. Sadly, however, the incentive for the military industry to prove its efficiency is often measured, though not acknowledged, in terms of actual or potential death and destruction.

As noted, not all militarists don military uniform. In fact, business and ideological beneficiaries and promoters of war, who do not have to face direct combat and death, tend to be more jingoistic and trigger-happy than professional military personnel who will have to face the horrors of warfare. Calling such business and/or ideologically driven warmongers "civilian militarists," military historian Alfred Vagts points to a number of historical instances of how the eagerness of civilian militarists to use military force for their nefarious interests often led "to an intensification of the horrors of warfare." For example, he points out how in World War II "civilians not only anticipated war more eagerly than the professionals, but played a principal part in making combat . . . more terrible than was the current military wont or habit."[15] The 2003 U.S. invasion of Iraq serves as an even more blatant example of civilian militarists' instigation of war in pursuit of economic gains. It is no longer a secret that the neoconservative civilian militarists in and around the Bush administration, while lacking the knowledge or experience of military service, "dictated strategies, force levels, and war aims to the generals and admirals. Older, experienced senior officers denigrated them as 'chicken hawks.' "[16]

A number of recently surfaced documents reveal that not only were the civilian militarists, representing powerful (but largely submerged) business and geopolitical interests, behind the invasion of Iraq, but they also advocated a prolonged occupation of the country in order to avail their legal and economic "experts" the time needed to overhaul that country's economy according to a restructuring plan that they had drawn up long before the invasion. One such document, titled "Moving the Iraqi Economy from Recovery to Growth," was unearthed from the State Department in early 2003 by investigative reporter Greg Palast. The document, also called the "Economy Plan," was part of a largely secret program called "The Iraq Strategy." Here is how Palast describes the plan:

> The Economy Plan goes boldly where no invasion plan has gone before: the complete rewrite, it says, of a conquered state's "policies, laws and regulations." Here's what you'll find in the Plan: a highly detailed program . . . for imposing a new regime of low taxes on big business, and quick sales of Iraq's banks and

bridges—in fact, "ALL state enterprises"—to foreign operators. . . . And when it comes to oil, the Plan leaves nothing to chance—or to the Iraqis. Beginning on page 73, the secret drafters emphasized that Iraq would have to "privatize" (i.e., sell off) its "oil and supporting industries." The Plan makes it clear that— even if we didn't go in for the oil—we certainly won't leave without it. . . . If the Economy Plan reads like a Christmas wish-list drafted by U.S. corporate lobbyists, that's because it was. From slashing taxes to wiping away Iraq's tariffs (taxes on imports of U.S. and other foreign goods), the package carries the unmistakable fingerprints of the small, soft hands of Grover Norquist.[17]

Grover Norquist, once registered as a lobbyist for Microsoft and American Express, is one of many corporate lobbyists who helped shape the Economy Plan for the "new" Iraq. In fact, in an interview with Palast, Norquist boasted of moving freely at the Treasury, Defense, and State Departments and in the White House, "shaping the post-conquest economic plans—from taxes to tariffs to the intellectual property rights." Palast further points out that the oil section of the plan "calls for Iraqis to sell off to 'IOCs' (international oil companies) the nation's 'downstream' assets—that is, the refineries, pipelines and ports."[18]

The Economy Plan's "Annex D" laid out "a strict 360-day schedule for the free-market makeover of Iraq." But General Jay Garner, the initially designated ruler of Iraq, had promised Iraqis they would have free and fair elections as soon as Saddam was toppled, preferably within 90 days. In the face of this conflict, civilian militarists of the Bush administration, representing powerful special interests, overruled General Garner: elections were postponed—as usual, on grounds that the local population and/or conditions were not yet ready for elections. The real reason for the postponement, however, was that, as Palast points out, "[i]t was simply inconceivable that any popularly elected government would let America write its laws and auction off the nation's crown jewel, its petroleum industry." When Palast asked lobbyist Norquist about the postponement of the elections, he responded matter of factly: "The right to trade, property rights, these things are not to be determined by some democratic election." The troops would simply have to wait longer.[19]

General Garner's resistance to the plan to postpone the elections was a major factor for his sudden replacement with Paul Bremmer who, having served as managing director of Kissinger Associates, better understood the corporate culture. Soon after assuming power in Saddam Hussein's old palace, Bremmer canceled Garner's scheduled meeting of Iraq's tribal leaders that was called to plan national elections. Instead, he appointed the entire "government" himself. National elections, Bremmer pronounced, would have to wait until 2005. "The delay would, incidentally, provide time needed to lock in the laws, regulations and irreversible sales of assets in accordance with the Economy Plan. . . . Altogether, the leader of the Coalition Provisional Authority issued exactly 100 orders that remade Iraq in the image of the Economy Plan."[20] Most of Bremmer's restructuring decrees, however, remain on paper for now as they are fiercely resisted by the majority of the Iraqi people. The extent to which they could be put into effect depends largely on the political outcome of the power struggle that is raging in Iraq today.

As foreign policy is often a reflection of domestic policy, the recently heightened tendency of the United States to war and aggression also seems to be a reflection of the metaphorical domestic fight over allocation of national resources, or tax dollars. This is an indication of a corrupt relationship between domestic and foreign policies: the destructive power of money to debauch domestic policy is bound to affect foreign policy in the same destructive direction. This also helps explain why, for example, the Department of Defense has been gradually but surely "obscuring and displacing the Department of State as the primary agency for making and administering foreign policy," or why the United States "now stations innumerably more uniformed military officers than civilian diplomats, aid workers, or environmental specialists in foreign countries." By the same token, but more importantly, it also helps explain why since World War II beneficiaries of the Pentagon budget have almost always reacted negatively to discussions of international cooperation and tension reduction, or détente.[21]

Thus, for example, in the late 1940s and early 1950s, the Korean War and the "communist threat" were used as pretexts by the proponents of military buildup to overrule those who called for limits on military spending following the end of World War II. Representatives of the military-industrial complex, disproportionately ensconced in the State Department, succeeded in having President Truman embark on his famous overhaul of the U.S. foreign policy, which drastically increased the Pentagon budget and expanded the military-industrial establishment.

Likewise, in the face of the 1970s' tension-reducing negotiations with the Soviet Union, representatives of the military-industrial complex rallied around Cold Warrior think tanks such as the Committee on the Present Danger and successfully sabotaged those discussions. Instead, once again, by invoking the "communist threat," they managed to reinforce the relatively weakened tensions with the Soviet Union to such new heights that it came to be known as the Second Cold War—hence, the early 1980s' dramatic "rearming of America," as President Reagan put it.

Similarly, when the collapse of the Soviet system and the subsequent discussions of "peace dividends" in the United States threatened the interests of the military-industrial complex, representatives of the complex invented "new external sources of danger to U.S. interests" and successfully substituted them for the "threat of communism" of the Cold War era. These "new sources of threat" are said to stem from the "unpredictable, unreliable regional powers of the Third World," from the so-called rogue states, and more recently from "global terrorism" and Islamic fundamentalism.

This tendency of the beneficiaries of *war dividends* to foment international convulsions in order to justify the continuous hemorrhaging of the Pentagon budget also helps explain why the Bush administration, under the heavy influence of the Defense Department, viewed the 9/11 tragedy as an opportunity for further militarization. The monstrous attacks of 9/11 were treated not as crimes—requiring law enforcement, international police, intelligence gathering, and public diplomacy efforts and operations—but as war on America. Once it was thus established that the United States was "at war," military buildup followed logically.

To make its aggressive foreign policy, and the concomitantly huge Pentagon appropriations, acceptable to the American people, the military-industrial complex works assiduously to influence their way of thinking. This strategy is designed to inculcate militaristic ethos into the cultural and/or intellectual outlook of the society. Such values include glorification of the military and its ideals, unquestioning loyalty, adherence to faith and tradition, male bonding, strong sense of patriotism, military discipline, and an uncanny readiness to act—in short, "a John Wayne view of the world,' " as Chalmers Johnson put it.[22] While pacifism is frowned upon as something bordering treason, patriotism is touted as simply meaning a readiness to go to war. The military and its ideals have become so sacrosanct in the United States that candidates for government office, especially presidential candidates, fiercely compete with each other to prove stronger commitment to militarism than their rivals. This was clearly in evidence in the 2004 presidential race between George W. Bush and John Kerry who persistently tried to prove that he could out-Bush Bush when it came to strengthening the armed forces. Thus, as Tom Engelhardt observed long before the election date, "By the time John Kerry is finished with his obligatory tough-guy routine some six-plus months down the road, even if George Bush loses, the Pentagon will essentially be assured a slice of the budget no less grandiose than at present."[23]

Most Americans will probably feel offended by a judgment that their culture is imbued with considerable doses of militaristic values. But even a cursory look at the number of military expressions or terminology that have become part of the English language of the United States, or the degree of violence and gun fighting in the film and entertainment industries, will clearly indicate that such a judgment would not be really unfair or inappropriate. Just consider this small sample of everyday colloquial expressions: "fighting" for this or that program or policy; "victorious" in pursuit of his or her goal; something or someone is on "target"; involved in an election "campaign"; team so and so is "battling back"; that election race has become a "war"; conducting "war" on social problems such as poverty or drug abuse; "lock, stock, and barrel," meaning the whole of the thing, or completely; and many more. Even the American national anthem is a war song based on a poem written during the War of 1812. Many television stations, when they sign off, run a film of military jets flying above the flag.[24]

The military establishment focuses heavily on news media and entertainment industries to infuse public opinion with the ethos of militarism. It uses these effective culture-molding vehicles to justify, sanitize, and glorify wars. For example, during the preparation for and invasion of Iraq the media consistently glorified the war as if the whole and only purpose of the government and the country were to fight wars. The news media have been instrumental in the success of the Bush administration's strategy of sanitizing war as an electronic game devoid of torn flesh, mangled limbs, spilled blood, twisted intestines, ruined faces, body bags, and coffins. Of course, the underlying concern for this strategy is the fear that if the American people are shown a realistic picture of all the unnecessary death and destruction, they might not support the war—a prospect that would threaten the business interests of both the military-industrial complex and the corporate media![25]

The relatively successful infusion of the ethos of militarism into the civilian culture has been neither fortuitous nor altogether spontaneous. As noted above, the military-industrial complex has systematically pursued a vigorous strategy of cultivating militarism into the civilian ways of thinking. That strategy has included active enlistment of support and collaboration of veterans' organizations, of trade associations and chambers of commerce, of some of the fundamentalist wings of the church, of the news media, of the entertainment industry and of the institutions of education, especially of higher education. A thorough account of this strategy is beyond the purview of this study.[26] Suffice it to say that, for example, the number of colleges and universities that conduct Pentagon-funded research has in recent years increased to almost 350, according to a 2002 report of the Association of American Universities (AAU). The Massachusetts Institute of Technology and Johns Hopkins University alone raked in a combined total of $842,437,294 in military contracts in 2003. The AAU further notes that the Department of Defense accounts for 60 percent of federal funding for university-based electrical engineering research, 55 percent for the computer sciences, 41 percent for metallurgy/materials engineering, and 33 percent for oceanography. "With the DoD's budget for research and development skyrocketing, so to speak, to $66 billion for 2004—an increase of $7.6 billion over 2003— it doesn't take a rocket scientist to figure out that the Pentagon can often dictate the sorts of research that get undertaken and the sorts that don't."[27]

It was this tendency of the research departments of academic institutions to become increasingly dependent on military funding that prompted the late Senator J. William Fulbright to caution against the militarization of academia, warning that "in lending itself too much to the purposes of government, a university fails its higher purposes." The senator prophetically warned against the inauspicious development of what he called the "military-industrial-academic complex."[28]

In addition to utilizing the expertise and research services of the traditional civilian universities, the military-industrial empire also has its own system of military colleges and training institutions that are designed to formally meld higher education and the art of warfare, including the many schools of the National Defense University system (NDU). A sample of these schools includes the National War College, the Industrial College of the Armed Forces, the School for National Security Executive Education, the Joint Forces Staff College, the Information Resources Management College, the Defense Acquisition University, the Joint Military Intelligence College, the Defense Language Institute Foreign Language Center, the Naval Postgraduate School, the Naval War College, Air University, the Air Force Institute of Technology, the Marine Corps University, and the Uniformed Services University of the Health Sciences, among others. According to Chalmers Johnson's *The Sorrows of Empire*, there are currently about 150 military-educational institutions in the United States. The military-industrial-academic complex, however, is only one of the relatively more noticeable examples of the increasing militarization of American society. "While the Pentagon has long sought to exploit and exert influence over civilian cultural institutions," points out Nicholas Turse, "today's massive budgets make its power increasingly irresistible."[29]

The relentless and out-of-control growth of military spending since the late 1940s and early 1950s has led to a number of ominous social, economic, and political consequences: a disproportionately large (and often wasteful) spending of national resources on military buildup at the expense of more socially gainful or desirable programs; a cozy and corrupt relationship between government authorities and the military-industrial establishment; an unfortunate and perverse dependence of many people, businesses, and communities on military spending; a tainting of civilian culture and republican principles of government with the ethos and values of militarism; a steady weakening of civil liberties at home and increasingly aggressive policies abroad. As the late Sidney Lens put it in his classic book on the subject, *The Military-Industrial Complex*, "All this represents a qualitative change in the American way of Life. It has concentrated too much unchecked power in too few hands. It has corrupted the process of 'government by consent of the governed.'"[30]

Under the bipolar world of the Cold War era, one might have argued that regrettable as these consequences of militarism may have been they were necessary to "save us from communism." Even assuming that such an explanation was justified at the time, it has since the end of the Cold War become meaningless. Neither the alleged new, post–Cold War threats such as rogue states, or global terrorism, or Al-Qaedeh justify the size of the military-industrial colossus. Therefore, there must be an explanation of the gigantic growth of the military-industrial complex that goes beyond the issue of "national security." I have tried in this chapter and in the introduction to the book to lay down, in broad outlines, an analytical foundation toward such an explanation. The following chapters, building and elaborating on this foundation, will show that there is a built-in dynamics of the self-expanding military-industrial complex that transcends issues of national security.

CHAPTER 2

Imperial Militarisms: Past and Present

There is an unmistakably common pattern to the logic and development of imperial militarisms: a protracted reliance on military power in pursuit of economic, ideological, or geopolitical gains tends to create a dynamic out of which evolves a large standing military apparatus that tends to perpetuate itself—and to lead gradually to militarism. Although militarism thus evolves out of the military, the two are different in character. The military is usually a means to meet certain ends: to maintain national security or to gain economic, territorial, or geopolitical advantages. Militarism, on the other hand, represents a bureaucratized permanent military establishment as an end in itself; or as Chalmers Johnson, author of *The Sorrows of Empire*, puts it, "a phenomenon by which a nation's armed services come to put their institutional preservation ahead of achieving national security or even a commitment to the integrity of the governmental structure of which they are a part."[1]

Militarism is sometimes manifested in open or direct military rule: generals and other top military brass, donning military uniform, formally occupy all the major decision-making positions of power of a nation. More often, however, the power and influence of militarism is exercised indirectly, that is, through the formally civilian organs of the state structure. Whether open and direct or disguised and indirect, militarism tends to pervert social, economic, and political structures of a society in order to appropriate and control the lion's share of national resources and justify its overextended apparatus and parasitic role.

In the context of a major world power, destructive effects of militarism go beyond such distortions of domestic structures; in addition, such effects also tend to threaten international peace and stability as militarism often resorts to instigation of international conflicts in order to justify its parasitic existence by inventing "external threats to national interests or security." When an inordinately large military establishment of a world power reaches such high levels of influence that it can manipulate the foreign policy of that superpower for its own ends, militarism can be called military imperialism—or parasitic imperialism. Under the sway of military imperialism, instigation of international conflicts and military adventures abroad are often prompted not so much by territorial or economic gains for the empire or the nation as a whole—that is, not by a desire to expand the empire's wealth beyond the existing levels—but by a desire to appropriate the lion's share of the existing wealth and treasure for the military establishment. It is at such stages of imperial degeneration—as when Julius Caesar crossed the Rubicon—that military operations abroad tend to tip the scales in the direction of cost inefficiency and drain a national economy. When global military operations, combined with the costs of maintaining a huge military apparatus abroad, exceed the economic gains from such operations, the top-heavy and costly military apparatuses tend to undermine the thus-burdened economic base. Today U.S. militarism seems to be headed in this direction.

A number of historical developments tend to support this argument. In his prominent historical study, *The Rise and Fall of the Great Powers*, Paul Kennedy carefully describes a number of instances of how military empires grew out of the womb of great civilizations, gradually weakened those civilizations, and eventually supplanted and drowned them altogether. Focusing on the "proper" extent to which national resources should be used for military purposes, the book shows how out-of-control military empires "became increasingly wasteful, arrogant, and corrupt. Leaders focused on foreign adventures rather than domestic issues while telling their citizens that sacrifices and high levels of military spending were needed to protect them from foreign demons. Each empire died after they ran up so much debt from foreign adventures that no one would loan them more money, causing a rapid collapse."[2]

The Roman Empire is a classic example of this historical pattern of the rise and fall of the great powers. Before Julius Caesar crossed the Rubicon (49 BC), which marked the superpower's historical transition from republicanism to militarism, Rome ruled through the electoral system of representational government for nearly two centuries. Despite the fact that the pre-Rubicon Roman Republic was the world's major superpower for a long time, and it used extensive military force to control and extort payments from vast regions outside of Italy, it nonetheless could not be called a military empire because during that period the military was used primarily as a means to achieve economic, territorial, and geopolitical ends. In other words, although the pre-Rubicon superpower was an economic, territorial, and geopolitical empire, it was not a military empire because during that period the military was under the control of the civilian government. Protracted dependence on military force to control vast territories and extensive resources, however, led to the proliferation of multiple sources of power and prestige within the extended military establishment that gradually undermined the republican principles of the civilian government and eventually emerged as the fully fledged military empire of the post-Rubicon period.

Although the military dictatorship that supplanted the Roman democracy destroyed its system of elections, rendered the Roman senate powerless, and terminated the popular assemblies and legislative comitia that were crucial to the republican system, Roman armies continued to claim that they were simply serving "the senate and the Roman people"; they "paraded under banners emblazoned with the Latin initials SPQR (*Senatus Populusque Romanus*)."[3] But the military rule did more than destroy the Roman democracy. In so doing, it also precipitated its own demise: as the military establishment lavishly helped its colossal apparatus to the lion's share of the empire's treasury, the economic base that was supposed to sustain the large military spending suffered. All the while it spread the seeds of bitterness and enmity, both at home and abroad. The continuing top-heavy military apparatus upon a weakening economic base, combined with a world of enemies determined to defy the military rule, gradually overwhelmed and eventually drowned the military empire.

The rise of the huge military establishment in the United States since World War II represents another example of how militarism can evolve out of a continued reliance on the military as a means to pursue economic, ideological, or geopolitical ends. After the war, the United States relied on the military power to fight the "threat of communism," to keep foreign markets open to trade and investment, and to safeguard global markets. Continued reinforcement of the armed forces in pursuit of these objectives has gradually led to the proliferation of a large military apparatus whose further growth seems to have acquired an autonomous, self-expanding dynamic that tends to be increasingly at odds not only with international peace and stability but also with broader national interests. The powerful military-industrial complex (the combination of the U.S. armed forces, arms industry, and associated economic and political interests) has effectively transformed the defense apparatus into a militarist, imperial establishment whose primary claim to the lion's share of national resources rests on instigation of wars and conflicts that, aside from moral issues, are not justifiable even on economic or geopolitical grounds for the imperium. This explains why, for example, official justifications of the U.S. military expansions and aggressions since the collapse of the Berlin Wall have become increasingly fuzzy: fighting against "rogue states," global terrorism, international drug trafficking, and militant Islam; or fighting for human rights and democratic values.

The gigantic growth of the military-industrial complex has affected the "American way of life" in a number of fundamental ways: the disproportionately large (and often wasteful) spending of national resources on military buildup at the expense of more socially desirable programs such as health and education, the cozy and corrupt relationship between government authorities/institutions and the military-industrial complex, the steadily weakening civil liberties at home, and increasingly confrontational policies abroad.

These developments have led some observers to argue that the United States might have already crossed its own metaphorical Rubicon, the watershed between republicanism and militarism. Accordingly, these observers maintain that the out-of-control expansion of the military-industrial complex is leading the overstretched military empire in a direction that, if not checked, is headed toward decay and decline a la Old, post-Rubicon Rome.[4]

While the theory that paints the future of U.S. military imperialism after the pattern of post-Rubicon Rome is used to explain the "rise and fall of great powers," as Paul Kennedy puts it, and while the possibility that the U.S. military empire may follow that historical trajectory cannot be ruled out altogether, nonetheless it is highly likely that the decline or contraction of this imperial power would take a different pattern, a pattern more in tune with an advanced capitalist economic structure than precapitalist formations. Theories and actual developments that can serviceably be employed to explain the rise and fall of precapitalist imperial powers cannot necessarily be extended or extrapolated to explain the rise and fall of capitalist empires. Capitalism, like other modes of production before it, has its own "historically-specific laws of motion," to borrow Karl Marx's felicitous words.

For example, conflict of interests and power struggles within capitalist ruling circles are usually resolved through a politico-juridical and institutional framework of what is called bourgeois democracy—a framework that has been molded over time by market imperatives, or the requirements of the economic system. By contrast, conflicts and power struggles within precapitalist formations often led to civil wars, territorial conquests, or physical annihilation of one side or the other of the conflict. Indeed, such physical destruction of political or economic adversaries within an imperial, dynastic, or feudal structure seems to have been, more often than not, the only way to end or to resolve irreconcilable interests or hostilities. This is how, for instance, Roman *imperators* (military commanders), provincial governors, and various other contending sources of power resolved their political and economic claims against each other, or against the senate and/or nobility that was ensconced in the city-state of Rome, after Julius Caesar illegally crossed the Rubicon and thrust the country into civil war (49 BC). (Although the official date of the demise of the Republic of Rome, or the birth of the Roman Empire, is said to be 27 BC, when the Senate effectively delegated all the powers to Octavian, the grandnephew of Julius, in practice the Republic had been dying since 133 BC, with the killing of the Gracchi brothers. Their deaths signaled the end of legal procedure and the beginning of heavy-handed, extra-legal, or violent methods of settling claims or conflict of interests.)

Under advanced and well-integrated capitalist economies, on the other hand, antagonistic social forces and conflicting interests within the ruling circles usually cannot afford to engage in military civil wars or armed struggles because, while conflicting, their interests are also vested in a unified market system. The need to respect and preserve the health and integrity of the market structure induces and/or compels the various factions of the capitalist class to avoid any kind of violent factional or sectarian fight that might disrupt or paralyze the market, as this would be tantamount to economic suicide: everybody would lose if the market is disrupted or paralyzed. Guided, or disciplined, by this economic imperative of market mechanism, contending or conflicting interests within the ruling circles are obliged to play by the rules and regulations that are suitable to the market system, that is, to fight within the legal and political framework tolerable by market imperatives: the rules of bourgeois democracy.

This helps explain why violent factional fights or civil wars within the ruling circles are nowadays rare or nonexistent in countries with advanced, well-integrated market economies. By the same token, it also helps explain why in the lesser-developed countries, where various economic interests are not yet fully vested in an integrated market, such violent clashes are still visible. More starkly yet, it helps explain why under precapitalist formations military civil wars and armed struggles were quite normal as the way to settle economic and political claims: to militarily or physically vanquish the opponents and appropriate their territory, their economic interests, or their political authority. Perhaps more importantly, the historically specific forms or methods of settling conflicting economic and political disputes help explain that, contrary to the claims of some pundits, there is nothing inherent, racial, genetic, or Western in the fact that today's economically advanced countries enjoy more stable socioeconomic and political structures. Instead, the determining factor seems, once again, to be economics, or as the cliché goes, *it is the economics, stupid*!

It follows that, for example, had the economies of the northern and southern states that became part of the United States of America been as developed, integrated, and interdependent in the mid-nineteenth century as they are today, the devastating American Civil War would most probably have been avoided. To put it differently, it is very unlikely that today's highly integrated economy and, therefore, interdependent economic interests would allow such violent methods of resolving conflicts and disagreements within the capitalist class. Perhaps the controversial presidential election of 2000 can go some way to clarifying this point. As the election results were contested with no clear winner between the Democratic candidate Al Gore and the Republican candidate George W. Bush, the stock market first stagnated and then began a downward slide. To avoid an economic crisis and a catastrophic Wall Street reaction, the heatedly contested claims were soon resolved without any physical violence or without a shot being fired. Instead, the invisible (but real) U.S. establishment *peacefully* resolved the stand-off in favor of George W. Bush by means of a U.S. Supreme Court verdict. And nobody within the ruling elite challenged the court ruling because the subtle understanding was that if the election stalemate continued for a longer time, or if violent clashes erupted, and the stock market crashed, everybody would lose.

What are the implications of this discussion for the question at hand: the future and limits of escalating U.S. militarism; or more specifically, the implications for the relevance of the theory of the Old Rome to the expansion and/or decline of the U.S. military empire?

The answer seems to be that, barring a social upheaval from *below*, it is highly unlikely that the U.S. imperial military power would follow the pattern of the decline or decay of the Roman Empire, or that of any other precapitalist empires. Instead, the decline of the U.S. military-industrial empire (in due time, of course) would more likely be akin to the pattern of the decline of the British and other European colonial/imperial powers than to that of the Roman Empire. An overview of the experience of British imperialism and the pattern of expansion and contraction of its armed forces can be instructive here.

Before achieving international market superiority in the second half of the eighteenth century, England relied heavily on its military power for economic gains in global markets. Mercantilist policies were instrumental in the early stages of industrialization in England. The essence of mercantilism was that the British government played an active role in mobilizing and channeling both domestic and external economic resources toward industrialization and development of the country. Colonial policies of territorial conquest and transfer of their economic resources to England was a major part of the mercantilist theory of industrialization. So were the strict policies of protection of British industries against their international rivals, especially against the Dutch manufacturers who were originally more efficient than the British. More than two centuries of mercantilist policies helped England achieve international economic superiority by the second half of the eighteenth century. Consequently, Britain's ability to dominate international markets by virtue of its competitive market forces made most of its huge colonial military-administrative forces redundant. The costs of defending and/or subduing colonies thus came to be increasingly viewed as a costly trade-off as British traders gained a competitive edge in foreign markets:

> The military expenses attendant on Britain's overseas ventures, especially the costs of holding and defending its American colonies, had become so large that these colonies were now tapping the wealth of the center. This prompted [Josiah] Tucker to make his famous complaint in 1783 that America "was a Millstone hanging about the Neck of this country [Britain], to weigh it down. And as we ourselves had not the Wisdom to cut the Rope, and to let the Burthen fall off, the Americans have kindly done it for us."[5]

International industrial superiority, combined with the disproportionately high cost of maintaining a gigantic colonial apparatus, led many of the leading British elite, representing largely the internationally competitive industrialists, to suggest in the late eighteenth and early nineteenth centuries an alternative to mercantilism in pursuit of international economic gains. The alternative view, which was most effectively expounded by Adam Smith, the putative father of modern economics, maintained that Britain's ability to dominate international markets by virtue of its competitive market forces made most of its colonial military and administrative apparatus superfluous. The new vision, which came to be known as classical liberalism, or laissez-faire doctrine, further upheld that what England needed was not occupation of others' lands by military and administrative means, which had become very costly, but economic utilization of those lands by market means, by virtue of its superior international productivity.

The question the British manufacturers and their political representatives in the British parliament were grappling with at this time was how to end the formal colonial ties, and cut its enormous costs, without disturbing the existing pattern of trade specialization that England had methodically established as a result of two centuries of successful mercantilist policies. The essence of that pattern of trade specialization, also called international division of labor, consisted of Britain supplying its satellites of trading partners with manufactured products in exchange for their minerals and raw material products. Proponents of transition to free trade and economic liberalism argued that, once having achieved economic superiority, England's continued support of protectionist policies of mercantilism could actually undermine its economic leadership, as such policies provided other countries the opportunity to achieve what England had accomplished as a result of pursuing those policies for two centuries. On the other hand, if England switched its trade policies from mercantilism to free trade and, more importantly, prevailed in having its trading partners adopt such policies, it could thereby deter them from nurturing their own industrial independence, that is, from adopting protectionist polices vis-à-vis superior British industries.

Having achieved worldwide industrial superiority by virtue of more than two centuries of mercantilism and colonialism, England then moved to impose free trade policy on world markets so that it could maintain the existing international division of labor, and hence its industrial leadership, through market mechanism instead of colonial-military force. England, of course, still needed military power but just enough to keep foreign lands and markets open to free trade, not to conquer and keep them occupied.

Whereas proponents of the new doctrine called it laissez-faire, or economic liberalism (as always, portraying it as freedom and/or democracy

in general), critics called it "free trade imperialism,"[6] signifying a prefer-
ence by the economically superior to use its market power for economic
gains instead of military power. Other terms have since been coined to convey the doctrine: ultra-imperialism, neocolonialism, benevolent or benign
or progressive imperialism, and neoliberalism. Today's neoliberal theory of
international trade, promoted largely by the internationally competitive
economic powers through World Trade Organization and other multilateral institutions, derives its laissez-faire economic philosophy, hence the
liberal part of its name, from that classical liberalism.

The rise of economic liberalism posed a serious threat to the traditional
military-administrative apparatus of British colonialism. Not surprisingly,
the powerful interests vested in militarism and/or colonialism put up a vigorous resistance. The result was a lively theoretical debate and long political
struggle between proponents of free trade imperialism and those of
military-colonial imperialism, which lasted several decades. Proponents of
the laissez-faire doctrine eventually gained the definitive upper hand in
1848 as they succeeded in dismantling the last of the Corn Laws. From
then on England moved more vigorously to impose free trade policies on
its trading partners.

England's gradual utilization of free trade and economic liberalism
(instead of military power) for international economic gains, however, did
not mean that it had permanently abandoned militarism and/or economic
protection. Eschewing economic protection and the use of military power
to enforce such protectionist polices, if or when necessary, lasted only as
long as England remained unrivaled in international markets. Once the
newly rising economic powers such as Germany and France began to
threaten that hitherto unrivaled British position by the late nineteenth and
early twentieth centuries, England resorted, once again, to economic protection, military power, and colonialism. The ensuing fierce rivalry over
global markets and resources eventually led to the eruption of World War I.

From a long historical perspective, military policies of British capitalism, including both the imperial/colonial and postcolonial eras, signify a
pattern of expansion and retrenchment: expanding to protect its global
markets when threatened by international rivals, and retrenching when it
enjoyed international economic superiority, or when external military
operations became too taxing or burdensome to nonmilitary capital
and/or the overall national economy. The pattern also serves as a more general, capitalistic mechanism or dynamics than exclusively British: depending on the degree of their international economic competitiveness (or lack

thereof), all world capitalist powers tend to alternate free trade imperialism with military imperialism. For example, when the U.S. economy virtually faced no international competition in the immediate post–World War II years, U.S. leaders and policy makers promoted free trade and multilateralism—just as the United Kingdom had done for most of the nineteenth century. But since the early 1970s, when that unrivaled international economic status came to an end, it has behaved increasingly unilateralist, disregardful or sometimes even resentful of multilateral institutions and, in recent years, blatantly militaristic—again, similar to the military muscle flexing of the British imperial power in late nineteenth and early twentieth centuries when it faced the rise of the United States, Germany, and other European rival powers. Indeed, as Timothy Garton Ash of *The Guardian* newspaper points out,

> If you want to know what London was like in 1905, come to Washington in 2005. Imperial gravitas and massive self-importance. That sense of being the centre of the world, and of needing to know what happens in every corner of the world because you might be called on—or at least feel called upon—to intervene there. Hyperpower. Top dog. And yet, gnawing away beneath the surface, the nagging fear that your global supremacy is not half so secure as you would wish. As Joseph Chamberlain, the British colonial secretary, put it in 1902: "The weary Titan staggers under the too vast orb of his fate". . . . The United States is now that weary Titan.[7]

Ash's comparisons are not based on simple or simplistic impressions; they are based on a number of specific similarities between the U.S. imperial power of today and British imperialism of a hundred years ago. For example, the United States has the insurgency guerrilla warfare in Iraq as the nemesis of its imperial military power; the United Kingdom had the Boer guerrilla war. (Although British imperialism eventually crushed the Boers by pouring some 450,000 British and colonial soldiers there and herding "roughly a quarter of the Boer population into concentration camps, where many died," nonetheless the protracted and costly war against a relatively small insurgent force helped undermine the myth of the invincible British imperial power.) Furthermore, as Ash further points out, "China and India are to the United States today what Germany and America were to Britain a hundred years ago." The rapid transformation of China into a global economic powerhouse, and the likelihood that India will follow its footsteps, means an increasing narrowing of the U.S. economic and military spheres of influence in global arena. China is already the world's second largest energy user, after the United States. It also possesses the world's second largest foreign currency reserves, after Japan—the United States ranks only ninth, following Singapore.[8]

This is not to suggest that the decline or demise of the U.S. military-imperial power is imminent—by no means. After all, British imperialism lasted for another 40 years after the Boer War ended in the early twentieth century. Nor does it mean that the U.S. military imperialism will peacefully recede or retreat to the rank of other leading countries without a fight—no imperial power has done so. (For example, it took two devastating world wars to reduce British imperialism to the fold of other industrialized countries.) It is rather to point out that, as Ash suggests, "whether the 'American century' that began in 1945 will last until 2045," longer or shorter, "its end can already be glimpsed on the horizon." It is to further point out that, barring a radical and widespread social upheaval from below, the U.S. military-imperial power, having once reached its limits, would more likely follow the pattern of the decline of the British Empire than that of the Roman Empire; that is, America is more likely to become the next Old Europe than the next Old Rome, as most critics of U.S. militarism contend. (A detailed account of those limits, that is, the limits of U.S. militarism, and their restraining potential in terms of the curtailment of the U.S. military-imperial power, is offered in chapter 9 of this study. Indeed, chapter 9 picks up the discussion that is left off here in this chapter. Therefore, interested readers can move directly from here to chapter 9 without loss of continuity.)

CHAPTER 3

The Rise of U.S. Militarism

We should avoid those overgrown military establishments, which under any form of government are inauspicious to liberty, and which are to be regarded as particularly hostile to Republican Liberty.

—President George Washington, Farewell
Address, September 17, 1796

Expansion of the U.S. military establishment since the late 1940s and early 1950s clearly reversed its previous antimilitarist tradition of over 150 years. At the end of each war before World War II—and the United States fought many of them—demobilization of war-time armed forces reduced them to their prewar size. This took place even at the end of World War II, but only for a brief period of time (from mid- to late 1940s). The subsequent remilitarization that started in the late 1940s under President Truman has continued unabated to this day. Continued reliance on the armed forces to "contain the Soviet threat," and to keep world markets and resources open to U.S. capital, has led to the gradual evolution of military power from a means in the service of economic and geopolitical gains to an end in itself. The resulting military empire, better known as the military-industrial complex, has had momentous effects not only on domestic politics, economics, and republican traditions of the United States, but also on international relations, on global war and peace issues, and on the lives of many people worldwide. This chapter is devoted to a brief exposition of the developments that led to the rise of militarism in the United States. Before that, I will offer an overview of the elaborate imperial and/or custodial plans that the U.S. ruling class designed during World War II for the postwar world in order to supplant the waning

British Empire, to check the further advances of the forces of fascism, and to rescue the badly shaken capitalist system.

Designing a "Benign" Empire: How the U.S. Imperial Power Supplanted British Imperialism

Rationalist philosophers of the Enlightenment had believed that the more educated people became the more tolerant and peaceful they would be. The impressive development of Western capitalism in the late nineteenth and early twentieth centuries, and its rapid expansion to most parts of the world, also led many to believe that capitalism was capable of perpetual self-adjustment and continuous growth without any need of government intervention. Such hopes, however, proved to be as utopian as those of the old messianic fantasies. The international economic and geopolitical rivalry among Western imperialist powers during that period, which eventually led to the two devastating world wars of the first half of the twentieth century, coupled with the no less devastating ravages of the Great Depression of the 1930s, created onerous living conditions for numerous citizens of our planet. The misery and devastation of war and depression shook many people's faith in capitalism as a self-adjusting, humane system. The emergence of the rival system of the Soviet Union, despite its bureaucratic and dictatorial character, further undermined the credibility and the appeal of market mechanism because while the capitalist West was suffering from economic depression, unemployment, and poverty in the 1930s, the Soviet economy was enjoying impressive rates of growth, with no unemployment, homelessness, or hunger.

Not surprisingly, many of the colonial and other less-developed areas of the world combined their anticolonial and anti-imperial national liberation struggles with demands for government-sponsored models of socialist-oriented or "noncapitalist" development. In the core capitalist countries of the West, too, demands for reform and voices of revolution were frequently heard during the widespread protest demonstrations of the 1930s by the poor and working classes. Anticapitalist sentiments and demands to harness or to do away with the skittish, unreliable, and, at times, brutal forces of market mechanism in favor of regulating and/or managing national economies were heard not only among the Left and working classes but also in the ranks of the middle and lower middle classes and the small business. Spokespersons of these strata openly debated the wisdom of trusting vital social issues with an economic system that periodically led to devastating outcomes such as war and depression. The rise of fascism and the outbreak of World War II further heightened the need for government intervention in national economic affairs.

Predictably, these developments created anxiety among the ruling elites of the capitalist West as they tended to undermine the credibility and viability of market mechanism. Although the United States was not directly involved in the war until late 1941, its policy makers were nonetheless alarmed by Hitler's swift occupation of continental Europe and the prospects of his forces cutting off the United States from its international markets. The U.S. ruling elite moved swiftly to both check the further advances of the forces of fascism and to rescue the badly shaken capitalist system.

The most urgent questions that concerned the U.S. business and government leaders in the face of the rapid advances of German forces centered on the issue of economic self-sufficiency should the war interrupt foreign trade. Could the United States be self-sufficient within the Western hemisphere, or did it require trade with other world areas? How self-contained was the Western hemisphere compared to German-controlled Europe? How much of the world's resources and territory did the United States require to meet its economic needs?[1]

Combined with the lingering insecurity and anxiety from the Great Depression, these questions made business and government leaders uncomfortable, especially the leaders of big business with high stakes in international trade and investment. In response, they set out to defeat sentiments of economic nationalism and/or "isolationism" in favor of globalization, to restore trust in market mechanism and international trade, and to replace the British Empire as the dominant economic and political power in the world.[2]

In pursuit of these objectives, the leading figures of what is sometimes called the U.S. "establishment" worked closely with the government of President Roosevelt. Operating through the institutional umbrella of the Council on Foreign Relations, leaders of the establishment provided both theoretical advice and intellectual justification for major foreign policy overhauls during and immediately after the war. A brief look at the social status and class composition of the council can help a better understanding of the imperial origins and objectives of the U.S. foreign policy since World War II. It can also be instructive on grounds that it provides some interesting insights into how the ruling class often shapes major government policies from behind the scenes.

The Council on Foreign Relations, which continues to operate by the same name, had begun in 1918 as "a dinner club which gave those residents of New York City who were interested in international affairs—and who could afford expensive meals—an opportunity to hear speeches by distinguished foreign visitors." Its handbook for 1919 expresses its objectives as follows:

> The object of the Council on Foreign Relations is to afford a continuous conference on foreign affairs, bringing together at each meeting international thinkers so that in the course of a year several hundred expert minds in finance, industry, education, statecraft and science will have been brought to bear on international problems. It is a board of initiation—a board of invention. It plans to cooperate with the government and all existing international agencies to bring all of them into constructive accord.[3]

In their revelatory book on the origins, objectives, and operations of the council—aptly titled, *Imperial Brain Trust*—Laurence Shoup and William Minter show how the organization is composed of wealthy, influential, and largely global-oriented corporate leaders, with networks and ties to major industrial, financial, and trading corporations, as well as with elite academic and legal experts in Ivy League schools and Wall Street law firms. They show that, for example, in 1971 fourteen out of nineteen members of the Board of Trustees of the Rockefeller Foundation were also members of the council. These numbers for six other leading foundations in the same year were as follows: ten out of seventeen for the Carnegie Corporation, seven out of sixteen for the Ford Foundation, six out of eleven for the Rockefeller Brothers Fund, five out of seventeen for A. P. Sloan Foundation, four out of nine for the Commonwealth Fund, and three out of thirteen for C. F. Kettering Foundation. Comparable numbers of trustees for major research organizations were as follows: seven out of twenty-two for Brookings Institution in 1966, nine out of twenty for RAND Corporation in 1969, nine out of twenty-two for Defense Analysis in 1969, and eight out of fourteen for Hudson Institute in 1970.

Shoup and Minter further show that council members also work as governing board members of the major universities. For example, the number of council members who also served as members of the board of governors of nine major universities in 1973 were as follows: twelve (Harvard), ten (Yale), ten (Princeton), eight (MIT), seven (Columbia), seven (Johns Hopkins), six (Chicago), five (New York University), and five (Cornell). The authors also provide a list of major industrial, commercial, and financial firms with four or more council members as directors or partners for the 1969–1970 period: U.S. Steel, Mobil Oil, Standard Oil (later became Exxon, now Exxon-Mobil), IBM, ITT, GE, du Pont, Chase Manhattan Bank, J. P. Morgan and Co., City Bank, Chemical Bank, Bank of New York, Morgan Stanley Bank, Lehman Brothers Bank, Equitable Life Insurance, New York Life Insurance, Metropolitan Life Insurance, and Mutual of New York Insurance. The list also includes a number of other investment banks or companies as well as a number of major law firms.[4]

In light of this socioeconomic background, it is not surprising then that the council has almost always advocated a globalist foreign policy. Accordingly, it has consistently strived to expand external markets and investment opportunities for U.S. capital. By the same token, it vehemently opposed views of economic nationalism and self-sufficiency, which were occasionally discussed during the two world wars and the Great Depression. With the outbreak of World War II in September 1939, however, those views of economic self-sufficiency gained a fresh currency; and the council set out to quell such visions in favor of international trade and economic globalization. This globalist perspective underpinned the overall war objectives of the United States—which meant not only preparations for the war but also for a new postwar world.

To this end, the council began in the summer of 1940 a wide-range study of the war-time economic needs of the United States. The study was carried out by a group of the council's economic experts called the Financial and Economic Experts. Top on the their study agenda was to examine the viability of a possible U.S.-Western hemisphere economic self-sufficiency should the unpredictable war developments make such a potential scenario a reality. The Council noted that at the time the world was divided into four major economic blocs or areas: continental Europe dominated by Germany, the U.S.-Western hemisphere, the United Kingdom and the remnants of its empire and commonwealth countries, and the Far East-Pacific area, which included Japan, China, and the Dutch East Indies.[5]

The study collected and set up a comprehensive list of each area's exports and imports. It then divided the tradable products of various countries and regions into "competing" and "complementary" products. Competing products, also called substitutes, are similar or identical products of which both trading partners have a surplus and wish to export. Complementary products are those products of which one trading partner has a surplus and wishes to export while the other needs and wishes to import them. A trading area was considered to have the ability to be self-sufficient in a particular product, let us say in aluminum, if it exported as much aluminum to other areas as it imported from them; because this meant that if the war conditions prevented that area from trading with other areas, it could rechannel its own aluminum within its area. Implicit in the discussion of a trading area or an economically self-sufficient bloc was government intervention and economic planning should the war necessitate such actions. This was what the Soviet Union had to do to become self-sufficient as the capitalist world imposed economic sanctions on that country following the Bolshevik Revolution in 1917. This was also a prospect that frightened the Council on Foreign Relations, the "imperial brain trust" of the globalist U.S. capital.

The council completed the study by the fall of 1940. It then sent its findings, conclusions, and policy recommendations to President Roosevelt and the Department of State in two separate memoranda, numbered Memorandum E-B19 (mid-October 1940) and Memorandum E-B34 (July 24, 1941). The major points of these memoranda, which were largely accepted and implemented by the government, can be summarized as follows. First, as things stood in late summer and early fall of 1941, that is, before the U.S. entry into the war, "the self-sufficiency of the German-dominated Continental European bloc was . . . much higher than that of the Western hemisphere as a whole." Second, the U.S.-Western hemisphere was not self-sufficient largely because the United States needed wider export markets for its manufactured products. As Winfield W. Riefler, the council head at the time, put it, the United States needed "elbow room" or "living space" beyond the Western hemisphere in order to prevent major readjustments or alterations in the U.S. economic structure. Third, to become self-sufficient, the U.S.-Western hemisphere needed trade and "economic integration" with the other two non-German blocs, the British Empire and the Far East.

The degree of self-sufficiency of such an expanded region—initially called "Western hemisphere, British Empire, and Far East bloc," later called the "Grand Area"—would be "substantially greater than that of any other feasible union." It was estimated that for the new, U.S.-led Grand Area "the inter-area trade was 79 percent of total trade in the case of imports and 86 percent for exports. This self-sufficiency was greater than that of Continental Europe, whose inter-area trade figures were 69 percent and 79 percent respectively." The council thus concluded that "as a minimum, the American 'national interests' involved the free access to markets and raw materials in the British Empire, the Far East, and the entire Western hemisphere."[6]

The council and government planners also discussed some of the major economic, political, and military prerequisites for the success of the projected U.S.-led, non-German Grand Area. For one thing, it was pointed out that effective economic cooperation within the Grand Area required certain multilateral institutions and "appropriate measures in the fields of trade, investment, and monetary arrangements" so that the friendly trading partners could conduct their international business smoothly and effectively.[7] Second, it was indicated that in order to prevent the German forces from penetrating into the Grand Area, the British resistance to German pressure in the Atlantic and elsewhere must be supported and maintained. The third (implicit) condition for the success of the non-German free trade Grand Area was that all countries within the area, including Japan, accepted and/or submitted to the U.S. designs and conditions for the projected area.

To meet these conditions, the council suggested a complementary requirement, a safeguarding or insuring measure: "military . . . supremacy for the United States within the non-German world." In its E-B19 memorandum to the president and the State Department in mid-October 1940, the council recommended the following: "The foremost requirement of the United States in a world in which it proposes to hold unquestioned power is the rapid fulfillment of a program of complete re-armament." Council planners acknowledged that the new and expanded military role "necessarily will involve increased military expenditures and other risks." But they reasoned that such expenditures and risks would be more than offset by long-term economic gains: "Since the loss of outside markets and raw materials would force serious economic readjustments within the smaller region of the Western hemisphere, such an enlargement of the United States' economic domain, with the attendant increase of necessary military commitments and costs, would be essential over the course of time."[8] These recommendations, which were largely accepted and implemented by President Roosevelt's government, turned out to be the initial plans and projections of the United States' new global or imperial role.

Although the Grand Area was designed as a war-time economic and military framework in reaction to Germany's expansionist policies, the United States also simultaneously made tentative plans for beyond the war: to expand the Grand Area to include continental Europe once the Axis Alliance was defeated, thereby making the Grand Area global:

> The Grand Area, as the United States-led non-German bloc was called during 1941, was only an interim measure to deal with the emergency situation of 1940 and early 1941. The preferred ideal was even more grandiose—one world economy dominated by the United States. The Economic and Financial Group [of the Council] said in June 1941, "the Grand Area is not regarded by the Group as more desirable than a world economy, nor as an entirely satisfactory substitute." Because the Group thought it unrealistic to plan at that time for a British or Anglo-American victory, it suggested that blueprints for integrating the existing Grand Area under American leadership should be worked on as a short-range war or defense measure. This area would then be an organized nucleus for building an integrated world economy after the war.[9]

As it turned out, however, plans for building an integrated world economy did not wait until after the war. Soon after these projections were made in mid-1941, the balance of power in war fronts developed in ways that presaged the doom of the Axis powers. The effective resistance of the Soviet army to Hitler's military force in the late summer of 1941, followed by the United States' effective repulsion of the Japanese attack on Pearl Harbor in the late fall of that year, shattered the myth of the invincibility of the Axis powers. Soon after these setbacks of Germany and its allies, the United States began to draw plans for the postwar period. As it turned out, the blueprints for the postwar era of a one-world capitalist economy—and most of the attendant international institutions such as the International Monetary Fund, the World Bank, and the United Nations—were drawn during, not after, the war.

A major premise of the U.S. plan of the non-German Grand Area was that all the countries of the projected area, including Japan, would (or would have to) accede to the designs of the plan. But Japan had its own imperial plans for the Far East region. It was called the Greater East Asia Co-Prosperity Sphere, and it included China, Indochina, Thailand, the Philippines, Malaya, and certain Pacific Islands. The U.S. planners, of course, took account of the likelihood that Japan's imperial ambitions might threaten their own imperial plans for the Grand Area. But they resolved that this threat "will have to be dissipated through peaceable means if possible, or through force," if necessary. The U.S. planners "were thus ready to go to war with Japan if that nation threatened American control of the world outside of Continental Europe."[10]

Thus, the United States reacted forcefully when it learned in the late summer and early fall of 1941 that Japan had planned to send its military forces into southern Indochina in pursuit of controlling Southeast Asia. It immediately imposed a total economic embargo on Japan and froze its assets in the United States. These measures were followed by a November 26, 1941, memorandum to Japan in which the United States stipulated further conditions for the lifting of the trade embargo: "This memorandum took a hard-line, visualizing a return to the status quo of 1939 by demanding a Japanese withdrawal from China and Indochina in return for resumption of trade relations. With its oil supplies getting low because of the trade embargo, Japan had to choose between submission and war."[11]

Not expecting submission, the United States prepared for war. This involved not so much military preparation as it did preparation of public opinion for the war: convincing the American people that an attack on British and Dutch colonies in the South Pacific was tantamount to an attack on U.S. economic frontiers. Thus, on November 28, 1941, the War Council "decided that Roosevelt should inform Congress and the American people that if Japan attacked Singapore or the East Indies, the security of the United States would be endangered and war might result." The War Council then drafted a message, designed to be addressed to the nation by the president, which maintained that the situation created by Japan "holds unmistakable threats to our interests, especially our interest in peace and in peaceful trade, and to our responsibility for the security of the Philippine Archipelago. The successful defense of the United States, in a military sense, is dependent upon supplies of vital materials which we import in large quantities from this region of the world." The message further maintained: "To permit Japanese domination and control of the major sources of world supplies of tin and rubber and tungsten would jeopardize our safety in a manner and to an extent that cannot be tolerated."

Although the president himself favored the thus-crafted message of the War Council, he nonetheless "faced the difficult task of persuading Congress and the American people that war for these ends was justified." But Japan's preemptive attack on Pearl Harbor on December 7, 1941, "which came because the Japanese had correctly calculated that the United States was likely to declare war when they moved further into Southeast Asia, made the whole problem moot." It is clear, therefore, that the Japanese attack came as no surprise as the alternative would have been surrender without a fight.[12]

Successful repulsion of the Pearl Harbor attack, coupled with the Soviet army's effective resistance against Hitler's forces, led the U.S. policy makers to conclude in late 1941 that the defeat of the Axis powers was merely a matter of time. Accordingly, they expanded the hitherto non-German Grand Area to "include the entire globe. A new world order with international political and economic institutions was projected, which would join and integrate all of the earth's nations under the leadership of the United States. The Unification of the whole world was now the aim of the Council [on Foreign Relations] and government planners."[13] A week after the entry of the United States into the war, Isaiah Bowman of the council on Foreign Relations wrote that the council and the American government now had to "think of world-organization in a fresh way. To the degree that the United States is the arsenal of the Democracies it will be the final arsenal at the moment of victory. It cannot throw the contents of that arsenal away. It must accept world responsibility. . . . The measure of our victory will be the measure of our domination after the victory."[14]

To this effect, the Department of State created (in late December 1941) a committee, the Advisory Committee on Postwar Foreign Policy, to plan for the postwar world. At the heart of the Advisory Committee's task was to reestablish market mechanism and restore trust in capitalism on a global level. As noted earlier, the two world wars, combined with the Great Depression, had shattered many people's faith in market mechanism. From the mid-nineteenth century until the Great Depression of the 1930s, the so-called neoclassical economics, the ideological counterpart of today's neoliberal economics, dominated not only the economic "science" and textbooks but also the official propaganda and the popular ideology of how capitalism worked. It was believed that, by virtue of the proverbial invisible hand of the market mechanism, capitalism is capable of automatic self-adjustment without any need for government intervention.

The cataclysmic crash of the market in 1929 and its inability to rebound on its own, which prompted governments to rush to the rescue of the market through various kinds of reforms and stimulus packages, exposed the myth of the market's perpetual ability to self-adjust. Government intervention, prompted in response to the market collapse, was further heightened in the face of war-time economic imperatives. By the end of the war, the role of government in regulating and, in some countries, even managing national economic affairs had become a well-established norm. The need for rebuilding the war-battered economies in the postwar period called for an even bigger economic role for the

government. While the increased economic role of the government provided a sense of economic security for many people (largely through
employment and various relief programs that had started in the fight
against the Great Depression), it made the capitalist elite uncomfortable.
The uneasiness of the ruling class was further reinforced by the fact the
planned economy of the Soviet Union had weathered both the war and the
depression much better than the market economies of the West; indeed, it
remained totally immune to the depression.

Starting with late 1941, the U.S. ruling elite set out to tackle the challenges that would face the world capitalist system at the end of the war.
This was a monumental task: to help rebuild many of the war-torn
economies of the world, to reestablish the paralyzed international trade
system, and to curtail and roll back the extensive government involvement
in the economic life of many countries that had taken root since the Great
Depression—in short, to rehabilitate and restore trust in world capitalism.
Amazingly, the U.S. ruling class, working largely through the Council on
Foreign Relations and the state apparatus, was keenly aware of the enor-
mity of the task they had resolved to accomplish. It was acutely conscious
that the task ahead was fraught with all kinds of dangers, not only on social
and political grounds but also on purely economic grounds: deconstruct-
ing the war-time economic structures in which governments played leading roles in both production and distribution could lead to economic
disruptions of crisis proportions. This was a major concern of the postwar
planners.

Thus, the first document produced by the economic subcommittee of
the Advisory Committee on Postwar Foreign Policy "stressed the danger of
another world depression and the need to provide confidence in world economic stability." This required that, at a minimum, "the United States had
to be involved with the internal affairs of the key industrial and raw mate-
rials-producing countries." Early in 1942 Herbert Feis, a council member
and State Department economic advisor, expressed the concern that most
world economies faced the danger of crisis and unemployment and so
needed foreign markets to avoid "drastic internal adjustments as a result of
changes in external markets." At the same time, Leo Pasvolsky, another
member of the postwar planning team, pointed out that the "relation
between international trade and investment on the one hand and the
domestic recovery program of the United States on the other" was especially significant. In early March of the same year, Benjamin V. Cohen, a
State Department postwar planner, pointed out that a major need of the

postwar U.S. economy was "how to create purchasing power outside of our country which would be converted into domestic purchasing power through exportation. In practical terms, this matter comes down to the problem of devising appropriate institutions to perform after the war the function that Lend-Lease is now performing."[15]

The projected "appropriate institutions," whose details were worked out largely during the last two years of the war, turned out to be the International Monetary Fund (IMF) and the International Bank for Reconstruction and Development (or the World Bank). In fact, as early as July 1941 the War and Peace Studies groups of the Council on Foreign Relations had recommended that international means of payments and "appropriate" financial institutions were needed for the purpose of "stabilizing currencies and facilitating programs of capital investment for constructive undertakings in backward and underdeveloped regions."[16] While the general ideas of establishing the IMF and the World Bank were initially developed by the council experts in the second half of 1941 and the early part of 1942, it remained for the Treasury Department experts, especially Harry Dexter White, to work out the technical details of these institutions during the next two years. The official announcement of the formation of these institutions was made during the historical gathering of world capitalist leaders at Bretton Woods, New Hampshire, in 1944, which formally ushered in what came to be known as the Bretton Woods monetary system of international trade, investment, and development.

The core mission of these institutions (and of the Bretton Woods system in general) was to revive and spread the capitalist system worldwide. While the IMF was designed to provide international means of payments and facilitate international trade, the World Bank was assigned the task of providing credit and/or capital for the rebuilding of the war-ravaged economies and the development of less-developed countries in general. To further facilitate reconstruction and development of capitalism on a global scale, two additional plans were soon devised: the Marshall Plan for the reconstruction of war-torn Europe and the Point Four program for the development of the less-developed world. Most of the financial facilities extended to less-developed countries through the World Bank were either in the form of aid or long-term, low-interest credit designed for infrastructural development projects. In other words, most of the bank's initial lending to less-developed countries was "concessionnal" lending geared to development programs. A major reason for those favorable credit conditions was the fact that at that time many of the less-developed countries seemed to be at the crossroads between the "socialist camp" headed by the Soviet Union and the "capitalist camp" headed by the United States. As noted, while at the time the planned economies of the Soviet type enjoyed stability and respectable growth rates, the market economies of the West, having hatched the two devastating imperialist world wars and the Great Depression, seemed in disarray. As a result, a number of third world countries had eschewed the Western model of capitalist development and opted instead for the Soviet model of "noncapitalist" development. In a vigorous effort to woo away the "crossroads" countries from joining the "Soviet camp," the United States tended to be quite generous with the aid, trade, and credit it extended to those countries.

U.S. planners of the Pax Americana[17] world of the postwar period were keenly aware that the old, "classic" imperialism of the European type was not an appropriate framework for shaping the postwar world. To this end, they officially decided at a meeting in May 1942 that while the United States "had to exercise the strength needed to assure 'security,' it needed at the same time to 'avoid conventional forms of imperialism.' The way to do this . . . was to make the exercise of that power international in character through a United Nations body." Thus began the systematic planning of the United Nations. In January 1943, Secretary of State Cordell Hull initiated the "secret steering committee" of what was later called the Informal Agenda Group; the group eventually came to be called the United Nations. The Agenda Group met and discussed regularly the various aspects and details of the projected United Nations. After occasional consultation with a number of other governments such as the Soviet Union, Canada, and England, the final draft of the Charter of the United Nations was discussed with President Roosevelt on June 15, 1944. "The chief executive gave his consent and issued a statement to the American people that very afternoon." Despite certain modifications in the course of discussions with other nations, "the substance of the provisions finally written into the Charter in many cases reflected conclusions reached at much earlier stages by the United States Government."[18]

*   *   *

A fundamental property of capitalism is that it develops in a cyclical pattern: periods of economic expansion are followed by those of contraction, and vice versa. During periods of expansion and prosperity, champions of laissez-faire economic doctrine tirelessly flaunt the blessings of the "invisible hand" of the market mechanism for such prosperous economic times. Accordingly, and just as tirelessly, they warn governments against any intervention in economic affairs. But when long expansive cycles turn into long depressive cycles such as the Great Depression, which threaten to make the market system vulnerable to social turmoil and challenges from *below*, business and government leaders, including the usually anti-intervention elites, dispel all pretensions of deferring the management of the economy to Adam Smith's "invisible hand" and rush to the rescue of the system with all kinds of reform and restructuring measures. These include not only domestic measures of legal, economic, political, and institutional restructuring but also foreign policies designed to facilitate or capture new markets and investment opportunities abroad. The fate of the capitalist system is integrally intertwined with its ability to weather the challenges posed by such "menacing" long periods of crises—crises that, if not resolved or tempered by reforms, could lead to revolutions.

Thus, for example, in the face of the Great Depression of 1929–1937 (which precipitated widespread popular discontent and working-class unrest, and therefore threatened the established order) government and business leaders, setting aside their conflicts and disagreements, urgently mobilized around the administration of President Roosevelt and embarked on the massive New Deal reform and restructuring programs that brought about the eventual recovery from the depression. In response to the onerous economic conditions of the depression, large numbers of the discontented frequently took to the streets in the early 1930s. Their contempt for the status quo and desire for change swelled the ranks of socialist, communist, and other opposition parties and groups. Left activists gained certain influence among labor ranks, and workers movement for unionization—illegal in many industries until 1935—spread rapidly. Labor and other grassroots support for third party candidates in the 1932 presidential election resulted in unprecedented number of votes for those candidates—the socialist and communist presidential candidates together won slightly more than one million votes. Third party votes were even more impressive in congressional and local elections, resulting in their winning a number of congressional seats and many local elections. Business and government leaders clearly understood the gravity of the situation and the need for action. The need for reform to fend off revolution became evident, as the pressure form "below" created consensus and coalitions at the "top." Massive government intervention in response to the depression, followed by further intervention in response to war-time economic conditions, count among the most intensive instances of government restructuring efforts to rescue the market mechanism.

But the plans that the U.S. "imperial brain trust," the Council on Foreign Relations in collaboration with the state bureaucracy, devised for the postwar world went way beyond the restructuring schemes on a national level; they amounted to a comprehensive restructuring, or rescue mission, of capitalism on a global level. The U.S. capitalist elite did not fail to envision as early as 1940 that, without a diligent and effective "custodian," the postwar capitalist world would be in disarray. Government-sponsored reforms in response to the Great Depression, coupled with government-regulated national economies of war period, had effectively supplanted the invisible hand of the market mechanism in all the core capitalist countries. The market fared even worse in the less-developed world. Anticolonial and/or anti-imperial national liberation struggles often developed into anticapitalist revolutions. And many of the newly emerging less-developed nations opted for a "noncapitalist" or "socialist-oriented" path of development, which often placed them squarely on the side of the then popular Soviet Union. Not surprisingly, these circumstances frightened the big business-government leaders of the United States. And they set out to tackle the challenges thus facing the world capitalist system.

While military forces fought in the battle fields during the war, the imperial brain trust, working largely through the Council on Foreign Relations and the government, worked behind closed doors to prepare for the postwar world—a world of unhindered expansion of market mechanism headed by the United States. They worked to not only contain the spread of socialist or noncapitalist developments in many parts of the less-developed world, but also to roll back or curtail the extensive involvement of governments in the economic life of the core capitalist countries as a result of war and the depression. In short, they worked to reestablish the market mechanism worldwide. This involved a massive social, economic, political, and governmental restructuring on a global scale. The elaborate international political and institutional frameworks such as the United Nation, the IMF, the World Bank, the Marshall Plan, the Point Four program—backed by the firmly positioned U.S. military forces in various parts of the world, including the institution of the NATO military alliance in Europe—were designed to serve this truly historic mission.

Today, most writers on socioeconomic and political issues, including many on the Left, shy away from using terms such as "imperialism" and "class." Yet, the brief discussion presented in this chapter clearly shows how the keenly class-conscious ruling elite of the United States, cleverly defining their class interests in terms of national interests, methodically crafted the imperial designs of the postwar world after their own image. U.S. architects of the postwar world portrayed their global designs as not only serving the "national interests" of the United States but also those of all other countries and peoples. By planning to restore the war-ravaged capitalist system worldwide, they strived—and largely succeeded—to avert a possible relapse of major world economies into another depression, with all the unpredictable social and political consequences. And by reestablishing international trade and economic interdependence through the Bretton Woods international monetary system, and related multilateral institutions such as the IMF and the World Bank, they aimed at fending off future wars of economic nationalism, thereby fostering what some observers called Pax Americana: international peace and cooperation according to their vision of the new world order. They also reinforced and further spread U.S. military power to various parts of the world in order to safeguard and keep open global markets and resources to U.S. capital.

U.S. architects of the postwar world did not make any bones about the fact that the success of their plans for the new world order was premised on the United States' exercise of world domination. Neither did they deny the fact that those plans contained elements of an imperial power projection. But they argued that they were shaping a progressive, benevolent, or benign imperialism. President Roosevelt certainly seems to have seen nothing sinister in the plan: "Roosevelt appears to have believed that the ruthless imperialism of the older colonial powers might be replaced by a liberal and benevolent penetration that would be of advantage to both the natives and American commerce," points out historian Richard Hofstadter.[19]

Whatever the plans and intentions of the U.S. architects of the postwar world (and I take their designs and deliberations at their face value, as speculation about intentions may not be very productive for analytical purposes), actual postwar policies of the United States turned out to be not as benign as its architects portrayed (or hoped). Drastic deviations of the actual postwar foreign policies of the United States from the theoretical designs of the architects of "benign" imperialism obviously beg an explanation. But first let's have a brief discussion of the theory of benign imperialism.

The Theory and Praxis of "Benign" Imperialism

Depending on the status or degree of their economic competitiveness in global markets, leading capitalist countries always tend to alternate military muscle with economic power as the thrust of their foreign policy: when they are not seriously challenged by economic rivals, they tend to promote free trade and economic liberalism while downplaying military might; on the other hand, when their global market position is threatened by competition from other countries, they would not hesitate to flex their military muscle and resort to economic protectionism. Thus, for example, as long as Great Britain faced economic competition from the Dutch and other European countries, it used its colonial military power, along with mercantilist policies of import restriction and export promotion, in order to bring about industrialization and economic development. But once (by virtue of more than two centuries of colonialism and mercantilism) it achieved economic superiority in world markets by the late eighteenth century, it began promoting economic liberalism as desired economic gains could now be achieved by virtue of free trade without military operations. And while some of the now redundant military-administrative apparatus of the colonial days was eliminated in order to cut costs, sufficient military force was nonetheless kept in the background to insure enforcement of the newly adopted policy of free trade. While proponents of the new policy called it laissez-faire or economic liberalism (also called benign or benevolent imperialism), critics called it "free trade imperialism,"[20] because economic advantages were now extracted from the weak or noncompetitive trading partners by virtue of market superiority.

Thus, the use of the word "benign" to characterize the U.S. imperial power that emerged from World War II was not altogether new; the idea had been used nearly 150 years earlier by the British champions of economic liberalism in their ideological battle against proponents of mercantilism and colonialism. Britain's policy of advocating free trade and letting the military power play second fiddle to economic power, however, lasted only as long as its economic position in world markets remained unrivaled. Once that superior economic position was threatened in the late nineteenth and early twentieth centuries by the United States, Germany, and other European economic rivals, colonial and militaristic policies were revived accordingly.

The controversy over benign versus military imperialism has recurred a number of times since it originally surfaced in England in the late eighteenth century. A most notable instance of that controversy took place among the leading socialists and social democratic theorists of imperialism in conjunction with World War I. V. I. Lenin, the leading figure of the Bolshevik Revolution in Russia, argued (in his famous book, *Imperialism: The Highest Stage of Capitalism*) that the war was essentially an imperialist war over global markets and resources. More generally, Lenin maintained that wars under capitalism were often reflections of fierce market competition by military means, and that, therefore, the only way to end imperialist wars was to overthrow the capitalist system that produced them. Accordingly, he called on the workers/farmers/soldiers of the world to unite against their class enemy, the war-mongering imperialists, instead of fighting each other on behalf of world capitalist rivals. The strategy worked in Russia, culminating in the overthrow of the czarist rule and the establishment of what came to be known as the Soviet Union. But the social democratic and other bureaucratic-working class leaders in Europe and the United States did not go along. Instead, they opted for collaboration with their ruling powers and set out to mobilize the worker and farmer masses to fight the imperialist war.[21]

Karl Kautsky, a leading intellectual figure in the German Social Democracy, disagreed. He argued, by contrast, that after the war major interests of the world capitalist class could come to an understanding—similar to various firms in a cartel—of dividing world markets and resources in a peaceful fashion. Calling such a projected arrangement "ultra-imperialism" Kautsky postulated more generally that, because war creates uncertainty and disruption in world markets, capitalism is therefore inherently averse to war: "There is no economic necessity for continuing the arms race after the World War, even from the standpoint of the capitalist class itself, with the exception of certain armaments interests. On the contrary, the capitalist economy is seriously threatened precisely by the contradictions between its states. Every far-sighted capitalist today must call on his fellows: capitalists of all countries, unite!"[22]

Prima facie, Kautsky's argument sounds quite reasonable. But the argument is premised on a number of implicit assumptions and conditions that tend to weaken its apparently strong plausibility. One such assumption is that international capitalist rivals who wage wars against each other must somehow be misguided or, as he puts, must not be sufficiently "far-sighted" to call for "capitalists of all countries, unite!" The powerful economic interests that embark on devastating wars in pursuit of the lion's share of world markets and resources would certainly dismiss such *advice* as theoretical naiveté, or intellectual hubris. It is true that capital, as "self-expanding value" (Karl Marx's term), grows better if not hampered by war and uncertainty. Such expansion, however, does not take place in isolation from other capitals, or in a world of unlimited resources—hence, the possibility and, sometimes, the reality of conflict and war. It is true that, as Nick Beams points out, "far-sighted bourgeois politicians will, at certain times, seek to represent the interests of 'capital-as-a-whole,' even against certain sections of the capitalist class. But these efforts are limited by the fact that 'capital-as-a-whole' exists in the form of many capitals that are in conflict with each other."[23]

A second implicit assumption in the theory of "benign" or "ultra-imperialism" is that the conflicting interests between or among competing industries or business entities can always be resolved and reconciled peacefully. While it is true that competing economic interests within or between countries often try to resolve their conflicts peacefully, they do not always succeed. And when the contending interests fail to settle their claims peacefully, violent means of settling accounts will follow inevitably. Thus, it seems that the theory of benign or ultra-imperialism is based on an implicit theory or idealism of *ultra-humans*, humans perhaps living on another planet under a mode of production where material interests do not collide—that is, an ideal or mythical (utopian) world.

In general, conflicting capitalist and/or imperialist interests are more amenable to peaceful resolution when economic times are good, when there is a relative abundance of economic surplus and resources that can, more or less, satisfy all the competing forces and interests—and this usually means long cycles of economic expansion. Accordingly, the theory of benign imperialism has a higher likelihood to be realized during such periods of economic expansion. But capitalism develops in cycles. And when a long cycle of expansion turns into a long cycle of contraction, competing interests over the shrinking economic pie are less likely to resolve their conflicting claims peacefully. War and the end of benign imperialism would follow accordingly.

Thus, benign or ultra-imperialism and "classical" or European-type military imperialism recur alternately after the cyclical pattern of long waves of economic expansion and contraction.[24] Here is how Lenin explained this alternating pattern in response to Kautsky's theory of ultra-imperialism: "Alliances embracing all the imperialist powers are inevitably nothing more than a 'truce' in periods between wars. Peaceful alliances prepare the ground for wars, and in their turn grow out of wars; the one conditions the other, producing alternating forms of peaceful and non-peaceful struggle on one and the same basis of imperialist connections and relations within world economic and world politics."[25]

The fact that there have not been any large-scale wars among major world powers since World War II has led some observers to conclude that, therefore, the Kautskian theory of ultra-imperialism has withstood the test of reality better than the Leninist theory of imperialism.[26] Such sweeping judgments, however, might prove premature as they seem to overlook a number of important intervening factors that might have delayed or rendered dormant violent confrontations between world capitalist powers but not eliminated such potential clashes altogether. For one thing, the bipolar Cold War world of East–West rivalry played a crucial role in overshadowing potential conflicts within the capitalist world. For another, the war-ravaged economies of Europe and Japan effectively meant no competition for the U.S. transnational capital in the immediate postwar period. This meant that for the most part of Cold War years, the United States could afford to play a custodial role in guiding and/or managing the capitalist world. When Western Europe and the Far East needed help to rise from the ashes of war, the United States provided that help. But when they recovered and began to challenge U.S. capital in international markets, the United States coerced them to accept international trade and investment rules that were favorable to its own interests. The "golden" economy of the immediate postwar period (1948–1968) allowed or enabled the United States to play the role of benign imperialism toward its potential economic rivals in Europe and Japan. Indeed, the United States played a crucial role in the rebuilding and industrialization of Japan and Western Europe. While it is true that self-interest and the East–West rivalry of the time were crucial factors in that reconstruction strategy, the fact remains that the United States did nurture the war-ravaged economies of Western Europe and Japan largely by virtue of its golden economy of the immediate postwar period. As long as that economic boom continued, and as long as the rising economic powers such as Japan and Germany had not sufficiently grown to threaten U.S. global markets, the U.S. policy of benign imperialism vis-à-vis those potential rivals continued.

But as the long 1970s U.S. economic contraction replaced the previous long cycle of expansion, it also signaled the end of the nearly frictionless relations between the United States and other advanced capitalist countries that had prevailed since the end of World War II. The ensuing fierce economic competition drastically weakened the "benign" aspects of

U.S. imperialism while, by the same token, it strengthened the militaristic and/or unilateralist aspects of it. It is true that the resulting competition in international markets has not so far erupted in wars, but that has not been because the "far-sighted" world capitalists a la Kautsky have always reached mutually beneficial trade agreements freely and voluntarily. Instead, it has largely been due to the fact that at every crucial juncture of the clash of international economic interests since the early 1970s (e.g., as in the cases of steel, textiles, and automobile industries), the United States has unilaterally and/or imperially dictated self-serving terms of trade to its trading partners.

The end of the Cold War and the rise of newly emerging capitalist powers in China, India, Russia, Europe, and elsewhere, ushering in new challenges to the long unrivaled transnational U.S. capital, also point to newly evolving rivalries and likely confrontations in world markets. The evolving new economic powers in global markets seem to have already contributed to the recently heightened militaristic muscle flexing in the United States in anticipation of such potential confrontations. An examination of the economic and geopolitical developments that have contributed to the decline of the "benign" aspect of U.S. imperialism and the rise of its aggressive militaristic tendencies will be offered next.

Decline of "Benign Imperialism" and the Rise of Military Imperialism: Domestic–Foreign Interactions

In the face of the Great Depression, World War II, and the ensuing paralysis of international economics, the U.S. ruling elite, working largely through the Council on Foreign Relations and the Roosevelt administration, played a critical role in shaping the postwar framework for a relatively stable capitalist world under the leadership of the United States. Whether one agrees or disagrees with President Roosevelt's labeling of the U.S. designs of that framework as "benign imperialism," there is no gainsaying the fact that those designs proved very effective in restoring and expanding the war-ravaged capitalist world. That framework and the resulting success of world capitalism lasted for nearly three decades.

Not surprisingly, when the long expansion of the "golden" economy of the immediate postwar period turned into the long contraction of the 1970s, the intellectual heirs of the architects of that framework moved quickly (once again, largely through the institutional umbrella of the Council on Foreign Relations) to duplicate their crisis-management successes of the immediate postwar years. As they now faced drastically changed domestic and external circumstances, their efforts to duplicate, or to modify and build upon, their model of the immediate postwar architecture ran into serious resistance.

For one thing, the abundant economic resources of the booming U.S. economy of the immediate postwar period had by now significantly dwindled. For another, the market economies that the United States had so assiduously helped build in Japan and Western Europe (vis-à-vis the centrally planned economies of the Soviet Bloc countries) had by now developed into fierce U.S. competitors in global markets. In addition, U.S. economic architects now faced a new domestic challenge: the challenge posed by the military-industrial complex. Prior to World War II, that is, for over 150 years, the U.S. armed forces were viewed (and used) largely as a means for economic and geopolitical gains. This meant that at the end of each conflict the enlarged war-time armed forces were demobilized and reduced to their prewar size. But the prolonged military buildup that started in the late 1940s and early 1950s gradually evolved from a means for economic and geopolitical gains into an end in itself—the giant military establishment that came to be known as the military-industrial complex. By the 1970s, the complex had grown large and powerful enough that when the tight financial resources of that decade placed the idea of curtailing military spending on the national agenda, powerful beneficiaries of military spending resisted vehemently and, as shown below, succeeded in putting an end to such suggestions.

The combined effects of these new circumstances—tight economic resources, fierce economic competition from Japan and Germany, and the rise of the military-industrial complex as a relatively new and powerful force in U.S. politics—effectively undermined both the so-called postwar domestic "governing consensus" and the hitherto relatively "benign" U.S. policies vis-à-vis Japan and other industrialized countries.

When the Bretton Woods conference made the U.S. dollar as good as gold in 1944, that is, convertible into gold on demand, the U.S. gold reserves amounted to more than $25 billion. At the same time, U.S. dollars abroad, the so-called Eurodollars, were less than $5 billion. By 1970, while Eurodollars had climbed to $70 billion, U.S. gold holdings had dwindled to less than $10 billion. While the astronomical rise in Eurodollars was largely due to extravagant U.S. expenditures overseas (both military and nonmilitary), the decline in its gold reserves was mostly precipitated by its trade deficit and balance-of-payments problems in the late

1960s and early 1970s. The huge disproportionality between the U.S. gold reserves and its overseas dollars, on the one hand, and its balance-of-payments problems, on the other, together with rampant inflation and the waning U.S. competitiveness in world markets, created a crisis of confidence in the United States in 1970–1971. As this prompted an increasing demand for gold in exchange for Eurodollars, President Nixon severed the link between the dollar and gold (August 15, 1971), thereby effectively ending the Bretton Woods monetary system.

Did President Nixon have a choice? Not really, because by then it no longer made sense to say the dollar was convertible to gold, as potential dollar claims against the U.S. gold reserves were seven times larger than could be honored. In the area of international trade, the president displayed a harsh economic nationalism by slapping a 10 percent surcharge on the value of all imports into the United States. In addition, he virtually ordered Japan, Taiwan, South Korea, and Hong Kong to curb their exports of textiles to the United States. Japan and a number of European countries were also asked to allow more U.S. goods to be sold in their markets at more competitive prices.[27]

While Nixon and his economic advisors called these protectionist measures a "new economic policy," many others called them "Nixon Shocks." Nixon Shocks violated most of the international monetary and trade principles that the United States had cherished so dearly in the context of the Bretton Woods system and the General Agreement on Tariffs and Trade (GATT) since World War II.

Disagreement over Nixon's policies, and over how to respond to the declining U.S. economic competitiveness, led to a split between powerful government, business, and military leaders in the United States. Differences of opinion were especially acute over the size of military spending and its impact on the national economy.

Additional factors contributed to those disagreements. One such factor was that by this time the United States and the U.S.S.R. had agreed on the principle of détente, or relaxation of strained relations between the two countries, which had accordingly weakened the rationale for continued military buildup. Another factor was related to the fact that, at the time, the German and Japanese economies with little or no military spending were faring much better than the U.S. economy with its huge military spending. While this weakened the arguments of the military-industrial complex that military spending contributed to economic growth, it strengthened the voices that called for the curtailment of military spending.

Whereas powerful beneficiaries of military spending and proponents of economic nationalism and/or protectionism hailed Nixon's muscle flexing as reassertion of U.S. supremacy, representatives of (nonmilitary) international capital viewed them with dismay as they raised the specter of trade wars that could paralyze international trade. Partisans of the former persuasion included business interests whose operations were limited to national markets (textile, footwear, steel, and the like); defense contractors and other major industries connected to them; and the military establishment, intelligence agencies, the national security apparatus, and key committees of Congress. Advocates of the latter view—who came to be known as "Trilateralists," or more generally as multilateralists—represented the interests of civilian or nonmilitary international capital, that is, of major banks and corporations with investment, production, and sales on a global level.[28]

This unraveling of the postwar U.S. "governing consensus" marked the emergence of what might be called the new, perhaps second, *head* of the U.S. imperial power: the military-industrial complex. The propitious circumstances of the Golden Age, especially the long cycle of economic expansion, had up to the early 1970s provided favorable grounds for the relatively smooth governing consensus. The economic boom had provided for the expansion of both the proverbial guns and butter, thereby satisfying both the champions of military buildup and those of social insurance programs. Economic boom and technological superiority of the immediate postwar period had also allowed the United States to vigorously pursue international economic liberalism and self righteously preach free trade to the rest of the world. But the rise of powerful industrial competitors in Europe and Japan, combined with the stagnation of the U.S. economy in the 1970s, forced the U.S. policy makers to retrench and rethink their relatively expansive policies of the boom time, both at home and abroad.

As noted, representatives of the nonmilitary transnational capital were strongly disappointed at President Nixon's unilateral termination of the Bretton Woods international monetary system and his heavy-handed trade restrictions against Japan and the European community. Expressing that frustration, Fred Bergsten, a leading proponent of continued international economic liberalism and multilateralism, wrote that in so doing the president had "promoted a protectionist trend which raises questions about the future of the U.S. economy." Such protectionist policies, Bergsten further pointed out, "also encourage a disastrous isolationist trend which raises questions about the future of U.S. foreign policy."[29] Transnationalists also criticized what they called the stagnant forces of "economic nationalism" that tried to make up for their inability to compete in global markets by asking the government for "their share of welfare" through protection: "By and large, the major political sources of the recent resurgence of economic nationalism . . . [have been] relatively immobile domestic groups pressing the government for protection of their share of welfare in the competition with transnational competitors."[30]

Disappointed at Nixon's "new economic policy" in the face of the economic challenges of the early 1970s, representatives of the nonmilitary transnational capital set out to put forth their own plan for a "new world order"—a world order that would modify and supplant the immediate postwar architecture. Once again, as during and immediately after World War II planning, the Council on Foreign Relations took the lead. The new plan, formally called "The 1980s Project," did not mean a new philosophy; rather, it meant that, within the same transnational economic philosophy that had guided the immediate postwar U.S. economic architecture, new economic strategies were required in response to the changed global circumstances over the previous three decades. As the council's President Bayless Manning put it, "The last systematic, overall examinations of the international system . . . took place during the Second World War and in the early years of the Cold War. Since then there have been some adjustments, but no thoroughgoing attempts to re-examine the pattern as a whole." Consequently, Manning continued, "The time is ripe for an attempt to analyze the characteristics of the kind of international system that would be suited to deal with the conditions and problems of the upcoming decade. . . . The Council's 1980s Project will undertake that effort."[31] A close scrutiny of the council's "1980s Project" clearly indicates that the project represented a systematic and rigorous effort by the proponents of multilateralism to fend off the rise of economic nationalism and unilateral militarism in response to the economic challenges of the 1970s.[32]

Just as in the early 1940s the Council on Foreign Relations had selected a special committee, the War and Peace Studies Project, to spearhead its plans for the postwar world order, so too now it instituted an equally important group, the Trilateral Commission, to draw plans for the new world order. The term "Trilateral" referred to the council's apparent emphasis on the shared, trilateral (U.S.-Japan-European Community) responsibility for global economic management and security concerns. Accordingly, the commission included representatives of international capital from the three regions. Although the council was as active in the debate and the planning of the 1970s as it was in those of the early 1940s, it now kept a relatively low profile and, instead, deferred the center stage to the commission. Formal establishment of the Commission was announced in 1973 on the initiative of the council chairman David Rockefeller:

> Rockefeller proposed setting up such a body in the spring of 1972 and provided the initial financial support until foundation funding could be obtained. Initial meetings of Trilateral leaders, in July 1972 and March 1973, were held at Rockefeller's New York estate, Pocantico. The Commission brings together 180 leaders from the three main industrial capitalist regions: North America, Western Europe, and Japan. There are close ties between the Council and the Commission. The majority of U.S. commissioners are CFR [Council on Foreign Relations] members and no less than eleven Council directors sit on the Commission. Council Director Zbigniew Brzezinski is [also] the director of the Commission. . . . David Rockefeller continues to play a central role, serving on the executive committee and on a small, informal steering group which advises the officers of the Commission.[33]

Like the Council on Foreign Relations, the Trilateral Commission preambled its plans for policy change, and for a new world order, with descriptions of the changed global circumstances since World War II. These included the disintegration of the Bretton Woods international monetary system, the oil/energy crisis, the signing of détente (relaxation of strained relations) with the Soviet Union, the emergence of dozens of new nation-states from anticolonial national liberation struggles, and the economic slowdown in the United States in the face of the emergence of powerful economic competitors in Europe and Japan. The commission then advised that the changed circumstances required new, "realistic" assessments and strategies. As Michael Blumenthal, a well-known Trilateral Commission strategist and spokesperson, and the secretary of the Treasury during the Carter administration, put it, "The effort to define a new strategy must be based, first, on realism, on a willingness to think about the world as it is and not as it once was, and second, on a recognition that U.S. hegemony in economic affairs has come to an end. The triangular power bloc of the United States, Japan and the European Economic Community, and the three-currency grouping of the dollar, mark, and yen has taken its place."[34] Accordingly, the Trilateralists called for "collective management" of the world economy by major economic powers:

> The international system, which depended heavily upon U.S. leadership and sustenance, now requires a truly common management to which North America, the European Community and Japan must . . . make special contribution. For the United States this means a sense of loss of power because decisions have to be shared more than in the past; for the European Community and Japan it means a sense of burden, because new responsibilities have to be assumed and, in some sense, paid for.[35]

To be sure, this did not mean that the trilateralists were advocating genuine equality between nations, but that they perceived the interests of transnational capital to be served better by an enlistment of the cooperation of other major economic powers. Indeed, Trilateralists too, like their political rivals within the U.S. ruling circles, the unilateralist-militarist faction, advocated an international "custodial" role for the United States "for a stable world order."[36] The difference between the two factions lay in the fact that the Trilateralists emphasized market forces and economic power more than military strength, arguing that the United States owed its postwar golden years to its economic superiority, and that a restoration of economic expansion can bring about stability and prosperity both at home and abroad. (These two competing views within the U.S. ruling circles regarding the global role of the United States continue to this day, notwithstanding the fact that in recent years the unilateral militarists have decisively gained the upper hand over their largely subdued multilateralists.)

To this end, the commission planned a relatively comprehensive transnational macroeconomic policy, a policy that emphasized integration and interdependence of world economies. Accordingly, it aimed at a global, not just national, economic recovery. On a national level, the strategy urged the government to embark on an industrial policy that would eliminate or reduce corporate taxes, encourage and even subsidize research and development in the areas of "futuristic" high technology, improve human capital, and refurbish industrial infrastructure. In order to make national stimulus packages of this sort more effective, the Trilateralists further urged major industrialized countries to simultaneously embark on easy or expansive monetary and fiscal policies. Not only would such orchestrated growth policies by the industrialized countries have mutually reinforcing effects on their own economies but also on the economies of the less-developed countries. Trilateral strategists called such transnationally reinforcing growth effects "locomotive" effects, meaning that just as in the immediate postwar period the United States played a locomotive role in pulling many of the war-torn economies out of the doldrums of stagnation, so too now a similar role could be played by all industrialized countries.

Commission planners expressed considerable interest in the growth of the less-developed economies and the full integration of those economies into the world capitalist system. They made no bones about the fact that their emphasis on the growth and integration of the less-developed world was primarily out of self-interest: the need for bigger export markets for their manufactured products and stable import markets for their raw materials and/or land-based products. As a 1974 document of the commission put it, "The Trilateral countries increasingly need the developing countries as sources of raw materials, as export markets, and . . . as constructive partners in the creation of a workable world order."[37] Accordingly, commission planners were sympathetic to the less-developed countries' demands for a new international economic order (NIEO) that called for international policy measures that would stabilize their export earnings by (a) opening the markets of the industrialized countries to their exports; and (b) designing certain mechanisms that would stabilize the prices of those exports. Obviously, stable export earnings for less-developed countries would also mean stable export earnings for exporters of manufactured products, that is, for more developed countries.

Government intervention was crucial in ending the Great Depression of the 1930s, as well as in rebuilding the war-torn economies of the 1940s. Such expansive or stimulating government policies have since come to be known as demand-management or Keynesian economics, after the British economist John Maynard Keynes, who advised that during periods of severe economic stagnation governments could stimulate the economy by boosting demand even if, at times, it meant deficit spending. The Trilateral Commission's solution to the 1970s economic stagnation was essentially a Keynesian or, more specifically, neo-Keynesian solution. Neo-Keynesianism includes the original Keynesian demand-management policies plus an industrial policy based on business-government-labor collaboration in crucial areas such as infrastructure building, research and development, and human capital enhancement. Equally important, the commission's strategists aimed at expanding such an economic strategy to a global or transnational level. They argued that because transnational economies were now more integrated and interdependent, stimulus economic policies would not be very effective if they were limited to a national level. Only a coordinated or synchronized transnational policy could remedy the stagnant economies of the 1970s.

Trilateral strategists considered unhindered international trade and investment crucial to the success of their economic strategy. Only unfettered cross-border mobility of capital could serve as the proverbial conveyer belt in transmitting the inducing or locomotive growth effects from more to less-developed countries—and vice versa. This emphasis of the commission's architects on transnationalism led a number of their critics to argue that they were trying to undermine the power and authority of the nation-state in favor of extraterritorial or supranational authorities and institutions. A close examination of the commission's extensive policy documents clearly indicates, however, that it was not interested in weakening or undermining national governments. Instead, it was merely interested in utilizing the power and authority of the nation-state to further its ideals of capitalist globalization.[38]

Initially, the transnationalists scored a number of achievements. Several members of the Trilateral Commission—including William Coleman, Elliot Richardson, and William Scranton—were chosen for high positions in the Ford administration. And a number of the commission's international economic recommendations such as flexible exchange rates, elimination of gold as a monetary vehicle within the IMF, increased use of the IMF's Special Drawing Rights, and improvement in the use of short-term credit to offset balance-of-payments deficits were adopted and implemented. Most importantly, the commission played a crucial role in the election of Jimmy Carter to the presidency in 1976. The rise of Jimmy Carter, a founding member of the Trilateral Commission, to the presidency and the emergence of a number of other prominent Trilateralists in his cabinet (including Cyrus Vance, Zbigniew Brzezinsky, and Michael Blumenthal) suggested, for a time, the dawn of a new world order based on government-sponsored industrial policy in the advanced capitalist countries, collective management of the world economy by these countries, and relaxation of Cold War militarism. But the Trilateralists' *honeymoon* was cut short by powerful political rivals in the opposing faction of the U.S. ruling class. Powerful beneficiaries of war and militarism (the military-industrial complex), united with nationalist proponents of unilateralism and economic protection, moved swiftly to undermine the plans and projections of the multilateralists. Before long, they succeeded in putting an end to the plans and policies of the Trilateralists altogether.[39]

The subsequent rise of unilateralism and militarism, which both helped and was helped by the rise of Ronald Reagan to presidency, will be discussed next.

Underlying the relatively smooth "governing coalition" of the immediate postwar period were, as pointed out earlier, the abundant material resources of the "golden economy" of that period. Under those facile economic conditions, potential conflicts of interest could be minimized or contained by pouring money into various programs and by allowing government bureaucracies and departments to grow. Thus, as Alan Wolfe points out, "when Truman or Kennedy wished to provide overall direction to the national security apparatus, they could do so without cutting back on the prerogatives of specific interests. Indeed, because of expanding economic conditions, they could hold out the 'sweeteners' of an increase in prerogatives in order to win support for centralizing mechanism."[40] As the easy economic conditions provided for the demands of various interest groups, they also helped expand and entrench bureaucratic empires, especially within the military/security establishment.

But when the economic expansion turned to contraction in the 1970s, and the well-entrenched powerful interest groups began to vie for bigger slices of the now shrinking or stagnant pie of national resources, the governing coalition began to unravel. The ensuing factional fighting within the ruling circles, often expressed through influence peddling over government programs and policies, was further aggravated by the competitive challenges posed by the Japanese and European producers to U.S. manufacturers in global markets. These adverse economic circumstances threatened two powerful interests: the military-industrial complex that feared the specter of a tightening Pentagon budget, and the internationally noncompetitive manufacturers who feared their Japanese and European economic rivals. The interests of these two groups converged over aggressive militarism and economic nationalism.

The Trilateral Commission's proposed solutions (based on international economic liberalism, tension reduction with the Soviet Union, and military downsizing) to the economic challenges of the 1970s threatened these two powerful interests. A contributing factor that further aggravated the fears of the military-industrial complex was the so-called Vietnam syndrome. It must be pointed out here that the Trilateralists' ephemeral success in the mid-1970s was not altogether due to their political clout, economic influence, or smart strategizing. Perhaps more importantly, they were aided by the general or popular revulsion at the time against militarism following the Vietnam fiasco. Indeed, the timing of their strategy to streamline the military apparatus and to steer U.S. foreign policy toward multilateralism, international cooperation, and peaceful coexistence with the Soviet Union was not altogether fortuitous; it had a lot to do with that antimilitarist social environment of the time. The bitter experience of the Vietnam War had generated a strong aversion against war and militarism, a social sentiment that came to be known as the "Vietnam syndrome." In the mid-1970s, for example, 72 percent of the respondents to a Harris public opinion survey felt that the government was spending too much on defense. Policy makers were forced to react, and military expenditures as a percentage of the GNP fell to pre-1950 levels. "Many prematurely concluded," points out James Cypher, "that the United States had left militarism permanently behind and that other ways would be found to forge a national consensus behind U.S. foreign policy."[41]

But the deeply entrenched vested interests in the gigantic state apparatus, especially in the military/security establishment, were not easily amenable to reorganization or structural and strategic overhauls. "Bureaucratically powerful cold warriors," points out Alan Wolfe, "were operating unchecked, leading not only to duplication but to contradictory policies all over the globe. . . . One of the main concerns of the Trilateral Commission was to reorganize the making of the foreign policy so that some sense of order and consistency could be brought to the U.S. global stance."[42] The specter of such an overhaul frightened the military-industrial complex.

Unsurprisingly, the powerful interests that had felt threatened by the Trilateralists' strategies—and by the Vietnam syndrome—fought back. In the debate over military spending, proponents of increased militarization have almost always outmaneuvered those of restraining military expansion. These proponents have proven quite resourceful in generating the necessary rationale for increased military spending. Their strategies and tactics to increase the Pentagon budget are not limited to the notoriously well-known lobbying of politicians. They also includes some more subtle methods such as occasionally commissioning a "disinterested civilian group of experts" to study issues of "national security," or "strategic directions," or "military capabilities" of the United States. Often the findings of such studies turn out to be predetermined. During the Cold War era, such findings invariably indicated that "our national interests were threatened by communism." Since then, it has been the "threat of rogue states," of "global terrorism," or of "militant Islam" that needs to be guarded against.

Policy recommendations of such studies are also often unmistakable: additional increases of the Pentagon budget and further expansion of the military-industrial complex.

Thus, for example, in 1950 the Korean War and the "communist threat" were manipulated by the proponents of military buildup to overrule those who called for limits on military spending. Representatives of the military-industrial complex, disproportionately ensconced in the State and Defense departments, succeeded in having President Truman embark on his well-known overhaul of the U.S. foreign policy that drastically increased the United States' commitments abroad, along with the concomitantly drastic remilitarization following the ephemeral demobilization at the end of World War II.

Likewise, in the face of the relative slowdown in military spending in the mid-1970s, powerful beneficiaries of war and militarism, once again, raised the specter of "Soviet threat." A false alarm was sounded that the Soviet Union was "outspending the United States on armaments and would soon surpass the U.S. in overall military power." Frightened by the antiwar social environment of the 1970s, as well as by the Trilateralists' proposals of transnationalism and tension reduction with the Soviet Union, these influential beneficiaries of military spending set out to "challenge the Ford and Carter administrations' drift toward multipolarity and compromise in world affairs." Organizing around opposition to tension-reducing talks with the Soviet Union, they reconstituted the brazenly militaristic Committee on the Present Danger (CPD), which had been instrumental to President Truman's militarization policies of the early 1950s. In his study of the role of CPD as a major brain trust of the military-industrial complex, and how it succeeded in moving away both presidents Ford and Carter from tension-reduction negotiations with the Soviet Union and in the direction of distrust and confrontation, James Cypher writes the following:

> Although the history of CPD is too complex to recount here, the group did succeed in driving then President Ford into a reassessment of the National Intelligence Estimate (NIE). The NIE is normally conducted by the Foreign Intelligence Advisory Board which draws on CIA data to determine the level and direction of Soviet arms outlays. . . . The CPD charged that the NIE estimate of Soviet arms outlays was too low and that there should be an "independent" analysis. Ford eventually concurred and a seven-member panel comprised of four CPD members (Nitz, Foy Kohler, William Van Cleave, and

Richard Pipes) generated the now famous Team B report. Since the CPD's announced objective was to convince policy-makers that "the principal threat to our nation . . . is the Soviet drive to dominance based upon an unparalleled military buildup," it is hardly surprising that the Team B report "discovered" a sizable error in previous CIA estimates of Soviet outlays: the USSR was said to be spending 11–13 percent of its GNP, not 8 percent, on arms. Multiplying this "error factor" times 10 (for the 10-year period 1970–80), Reagan's advisors, as already noted, came up with the figure of $300 billion as the margin by which the Soviets had outspent the United States.[43]

Two important points need to be highlighted here. The first point is that, years later, the CIA and the U.S. government in general acknowledged that the Team B report on Soviet military spending was grossly exaggerated in order to justify continued military buildup in the United States. The second point pertains to the similarity between CPD's tactics of inventing external "threats to national security" in order to justify increased military spending and jingoistic posturing, on the one hand, and the current administration of President George W. Bush's employment of similar tactics for similar objectives, on the other. Just as CPD questioned and overrode the CIA and NIE estimates of the Soviet military capabilities in the 1970s, so too today under the Bush administration dubious ad hoc intelligence think tanks (set up largely in the Pentagon or in the office of Vice President Cheney) overruled the official CIA assessments of Iraq's armaments or military capabilities under Saddam Hussein, and paved the way for the invasion of that country and drastic increases in military spending.

But let us continue with Cypher's account of how partisans of unilateralism and militarism, mobilizing around the CPD, succeeded in undermining the Trilateralists' plans and, by the same token, heightening both the tensions between the United States and the Soviet Union and the Pentagon budget in the late 1970s and early 1980s:

> In 1976, with the Team B report and the combined power of its 140 prestigious members, the CPD attempted to sway President-elect Carter to stack his military-policy appointments toward the CPD's recommendations. Failing in that endeavor, the CPD set out to divert the Carter Administration from its détente/global-interdependence/human-rights course. In this they were successful. By late 1977 or early 1978 President Carter had moved from his campaign pledge to reduce military spending every year to increasing it. Furthermore, in late 1977 or early 1978 Carter issued a classified document known as Presidential Decision 18 (PD-18) [that] . . . outlined the concept of

need for a Rapid Deployment Force. . . . PD-18 followed quite closely upon a meeting President Carter had with seven members of the CPD, a group referred to as the CPD "power structure" by the CPD's director. Pressured by the CPD . . . Carter began a sustained buildup in military expenditures in July of 1979. Thus long before the Soviet invasion of Afghanistan, Carter had moved considerably over to the CPD's position. By December 1979 . . . Carter revealed comprehensive long-term plans for a major military buildup to the influential Business Council at the White House.[44]

Evidence thus clearly indicates that partisans of nationalism and champions of militarism successfully highjacked President Carter's initially Trilateralist agenda soon after he arrived in the White House. His militaristic political opponents outmaneuvered and coerced him to abandon most of his campaign pledges. He was neither able to reduce the trade disputes within the trilateral U.S.-Japan-EU regions, nor the geopolitical tensions of the Cold War atmosphere. Indeed, in the second half of his presidency, Carter moved to revive the ephemerally relaxed Cold War tensions of the early to late 1970s and, instead, embark on a confrontational course with the Soviet Union. But no matter how far he strayed from his originally Trilateralist positions and policies, he could not dispel the Cold Warriors' and conservative nationalists' distrust or dislike of him. As James Cypher puts it, "Although Carter had moved from elected dove to self-proclaimed Cold Warrior in late 1978, his actions were not sufficient to satisfy the CPD," the powerful think tank that advocated a policy of renewed Cold War and militarism.[45] It remained for Ronald Reagan's pugnacious style and flamboyant rhetoric to fight the "evil empire" (as he called the Soviet Union) and expand the military structure to please such powerful militaristic interest groups.

Beginning with Ronald Reagan's presidency, the United States pursued a twin policy of aggressive international diplomacy and expanding military spending. President Reagan declared that raising military spending was part of his policy of "rearming America." As usual, the policy of "rearming America" was presaged by sounding the alarms of the "Soviet threat" and by highly exaggerating Soviet military expenditures. Thus, citing the now discredited report by the aforementioned "Team B" of the Committee on the Present Danger, President Reagan announced on February 18, 1981, that the Soviet Union "had outspent the United States on arms by $300 billion since 1970."[46] A massive military buildup, comparable to that brought about in the early 1950s, was deemed "necessary" to achieve parity with the Soviets. Thus followed President Reagan's drastic shift of the taxpayers' money away from the nonmilitary public spending in favor of military spending.

Most of the fantastic increase in the Pentagon budget under President Reagan took place during his early years in the White House, when he embarked on an anticommunist crusade and called the Soviet Union an "evil empire"—a policy that came to be known as the Second Cold War.[47] As a result, military spending during his first term in office rose from 5 percent of GNP to nearly 7 percent of GNP (or slightly over one-third of the federal budget).[48] The military-industrial complex was, of course, ecstatic over the election of their champion to the presidency and the resulting hike in the Pentagon budget. But when the complex suspected a "softening" of President Reagan toward the Soviet Union during his second term in office, they moved to fend off a possible slowdown in military spending. Thus, when it became apparent in the second half of the1980s that the Soviet Union was unraveling, and the Cold War coming to an end, powerful beneficiaries of war and militarism began to redefine and/or redirect the role of the U.S. military from its traditional mission of "Soviet containment" to an even broader "responsibility of global militarism," that is, to maintaining "stability" in all areas of conflict in the world.

Once again, the power of a "disinterested, nonpartisan" study group of "national security experts" was invoked to justify the newly projected expansion of the U.S. military's "responsibilities" beyond the conventional "communist threat" of the Cold War era. To this end, a panel of influential experts such as Fred Ikle, Henry Kissinger, Zbigniew Brzezinsky, Albert Wohlstetter, and Samuel Huntington was charged with studying the strategic direction/redirection of the U.S. military doctrine in the face of the waning of the Cold War hostilities. In its 1988 report, the study noted that conflicts in the third world have had "an adverse cumulative effect on U.S. access to critical regions, on American credibility among allies and friends, and on American self-confidence. If this cumulative effect cannot be checked or reversed in future," the study noted, "it will gradually undermine America's ability to defend its interests in the most vital regions, such as the Persian Gulf, the Mediterranean and the Western Pacific."[49]

To respond to "turbulences in the most vital regions" of the world, the study called for a "discriminate deterrence"—a military strategy that would contain and quell regional and/or local conflicts in the third world with lightning speed and sweeping effectiveness before they "get out of hand." Following the strategy of a discriminate deterrence, other supplementary terms such as "low-intensity" and "mid-intensity" wars began to creep into the lexicon of the Pentagon. "Low- or mid-intensity" does not refer to the level of fire power or the degree of violence and destruction; it refers to geographic or spatial scale, for example, local or regional, compared to an all-out war on a broader or global range.[50]

This marked the beginning of the unilateral militarists' strategy of justifying increased military spending in the post–Cold War world: search and discovery of new "threats to our national security" in place of the "communist threat" of the Cold War era. The newly discovered (and sometimes manufactured) sources of "threat" have included "rogue states," "axis of evil," decontextualized "global terrorism," and "militant Islam." I shall discuss these developments in some detail in the next chapter.

CHAPTER 4

Inventing "Threats to Our National Interests"

It is always a simple matter to drag the people along, whether it is a democracy, or a fascist dictatorship, or a parliament, or a communist dictatorship. Voice or no voice, the people can always be brought to the bidding of their leaders. That is easy. All you have to tell them is that they are being attacked and denounce the peacemakers for lack of patriotism and exposing the country to danger. It works the same in any country.

—Hermann Goering (Nuremberg Trials)

"External threats" and "national interests" have almost always been used as two blades of a metaphorical pair of scissors to cut through any opposition to war and militarism. In his well-known *Imperialism and Social Classes*, the late economic historian Joseph Schumpeter described the hoary pretext of "threatened national interests" for war and militarism in the following words:

There was no corner of the known world where some interest was not alleged to be in danger or under actual attack. If the interests were not Roman, they were those of Rome's allies; and if Rome had no allies, then allies would be invented. When it was utterly impossible to contrive such an interest—why, then it was the national honor that had been insulted. The fight was always invested with an aura of legality. Rome was always being attacked by evil-minded neighbors, always fighting for a breathing-space. The whole world was pervaded by a host of enemies, and it was manifestly Rome's duty to guard against their indubitably aggressive designs.

In a similar fashion, the U.S. military-industrial complex has proven quite resourceful in frequently inventing new "external threats to our national interests," or "the interests of our allies," in order to stifle opposition to its militaristic plans that are often designed to justify its colossal apparatus and its lion's share of national resources. During the Cold War years, the "threat of communism" served this purpose. Since then new substitutes for the threat of communism have been discovered in order to rationalize continued expansion of military spending. These have included "rogue states, global terrorism, axis of evil, militant Islam," and, more recently, "enemies of democracy." Scrutiny of the claims of such threats to the national security or interests of the United States is the focus of this chapter. Due to its far-reaching importance, "threat of militant Islam" and/or "the clash of civilizations" will be discussed in the next chapter.

Communist Threat and Remilitarization after World War II

At the end of World War II hostilities in 1944, the Unites States embarked on a major demobilization of the war-time military structure. Many of the war-time personnel in or connected to the armed force were sent home. The huge and numerous factories churning out military products during the war were either shut down or drastically downsized, and many people were laid off. The demobilization was altogether in tune with the U.S. tradition of over 150 years of not maintaining large standing armies during times of peace. But the demobilization did not last long. With the onset of the Cold War and the U.S. leap into the Korean War in the late 1940s and early 1950s, remilitarization began anew. What is more, the new remilitarization turned out to be on a permanent basis, which effectively reversed the long tradition of antimilitarism. In constant (2002) dollars, military spending rose from $150 billion in 1950 (the last year of the ephemeral postwar demobilization) to $500 billion in 1953.[1]

To rationalize the institutionalization of the large and growing military apparatus that started in 1950, the American people were told that permanent war mobilization was necessitated by the "threat" of communism. "The Pentagon line," according to Colonel William H. Neblett, national president of the Reserve Officers Association, "was that we were living in a state of undeclared emergency, that war with Russia was just around the corner."[2] President Truman played a big part in heightening the "red scare" and expanding the military structure. "Republican senator Arthur

Vandenberg told Truman that he could have his militarized economy only if he first 'scared the hell out of the American people' that the Russians were coming. Truman obliged. The perpetual war began."[3] But how real was the "threat of communism"?

There is strong evidence that the U.S.–U.S.S.R. hostilities of the Cold War years were provoked not so much by the alleged Soviet plans to attack the Unites States, or its allies, but by the fact that U.S. guardians of world capitalism simply could not tolerate the presence of a planned economy anywhere in the world—a market fundamentalism or fanaticism that continues to this day. These self-appointed custodians or prophets of the worldwide market mechanism were (and continue to be) intolerant not only of the centrally planned, Soviet-type economies but, in fact, of any "undue" government intervention in the economic affairs of any country in the world. "Regimented economies," declared President Harry Truman in a speech at Baylor University (1947), were the enemy of free enterprise, and "unless we act, and act decisively," those regimented economies would become "the pattern of the next century." To fend off that danger, Truman urged that "the whole world should adopt the American system." The system of free enterprise, he went on, "could survive in America only if it becomes a world system."[4]

This was an honest acknowledgment of what in effect amounts to a sacred mission that has guided the foreign policy of the United States ever since it emerged as a world power. Although the mission of globalizing the American system has always been carried out in the name of spreading democracy, the essence of that mission is not very different from what Lord Cecil Rhodes, who conquered much of Africa for British imperialism, suggested long time ago: the simplest way to achieve peace was for England to convert and add the rest of the world to its colonies.

There is convincing evidence that not only Joseph Stalin and his successors in the Soviet Union had no plans to wage war against the United States or its allies but that, in fact, they played a restraining role to contain independent revolutionary movements worldwide.[5] "It is often forgotten," points out Sidney Lens, "that for a few years after the war, he [Stalin] assumed an exceedingly moderate posture. . . . His nation had lost 25 million people in the war, was desperately in need of aid for rebuilding, and continued for a long time to nurture hopes of coexistence. Far from being revolutionary, Stalin in those years put the damper on revolution wherever he could."[6] To accommodate the United States and other Western powers in the hope of peaceful coexistence, Stalin often advised, and sometimes ordered, the pro-Moscow communist/leftist parties in Europe and elsewhere in the world to refrain from revolutionary policies that might jeopardize the hoped-for chances of coexistence. The Soviet leader "scoffed at communism in Germany," writes historian Fleming, "urged the Italian Reds to make peace with the monarchy, did his best to induce Mao Tsetung to come to terms with the Kuomintang and angrily demanded of Tito that he back the monarchy, thus fulfilling his (Stalin's) bargain with Churchill."[7]

Stalin's collaborationist policy toward Western powers in the early years after the war followed from his doctrine of the "possibility of building National Socialism," that is, "socialism in one country." According to that doctrine, "socialism can be built on the basis of a national state if only there is no intervention," explained Leon Trotsky in a critical analysis of the policy. "From this there can and must follow . . . a collaborationist policy toward the foreign bourgeoisie with the object of averting intervention, as this will guarantee the construction of socialism [in the Soviet Union]." The task of pro-Moscow communist/leftist parties in other countries therefore assumes, Trotsky further pointed out, "an auxiliary character; their mission is to protect the U.S.S.R. from intervention and not fight for the conquest of power."[8] Thus, for example,

> [t]he communists dissuaded their followers in North Africa from taking the path of revolution . . . leaving the field to non-Communist nationalists like Ahmed Ben Bella. Stalin ordered Soviet troops out of Azerbaijan—north-west Iran—thereby liquidating the communist regime under Jafar Pishevari. He failed to lift a finger while British forces put down an EAM revolt in Greece, a circumstance for which he won lavish praise from no less a personage than Winston Churchill. Stalin, wrote Churchill, "adhered strictly and faithfully to our agreement of October, and during all the long weeks of fighting the communists in the streets of Athens not one word of reproach came from Pravda or Izvestia."[9]

A number of leading political figures and statesmen in the United State also acknowledged Stalin's live-and-let-live policy in the early years following the war. Here is a sample: "It was perfectly clear to anyone with even a rudimentary knowledge of the Russia of that day [i.e., of the early Cold War period] that the Soviet leaders had no intention of attempting to advance their cause by launching military attacks with their own armed forces across frontiers" (George Kennan, May 1965). The Soviet government "does not contemplate the use of war as an instrument of its national policy. I do not know any responsible official, military or civilian, in this government, who believes that the Soviet government now plans conquest by open military aggression" (John Foster Dulles, March 1949). The Russians "would not move this summer—in fact, at any time" (James Forrestal, June 10, 1946). "In my view the Russians do not want war" (General Walter Bedell Smith, advisor to the War Council, August 3, 1948). "Our government has kept us in a perpetual state of fear—kept us in a continuous stampede of patriotic fervor—with the cry of a grave national emergency. . . . Yet, in retrospect, these disasters seem never to have happened, seem never to have been real" (General Douglas MacArthur, mid-1957).[10]

Evidence thus clearly suggests that the U.S. policy makers built the gigantic military-industrial complex not out of any genuine fear of Soviet military attack but out of other motives. Top among those motives, as pointed out earlier, was to establish a U.S.-led world capitalist order in which unhindered market forces would flourish, a world no part of which would be excluded from the free flow of trade and investment. William Appleman Williams, documenting U.S. policy makers' statements at the end of the war, shows how those policy makers believed that the United States' objective must be to seek "world power as a trustee for civilization." He also quotes business and government leaders referring to the U.S. role as "missionaries of capitalism and democracy." More revealing, however, was Undersecretary of State Dean Acheson's testimony before a congressional committee in 1944: "It is a problem of markets. . . . We have got to see what the country produces is used and is sold under financial arrangements which make its production possible." Under a different economic system, Acheson conceded, "you could use the entire production of the country in the United States," but under our system of market mechanism, the government "must look to foreign markets." If it didn't, he continued, "it seems clear that we are in for a very bad time . . . having the most far-reaching consequences upon our economic and social system."[11]

Evidence clearly indicates, therefore, that the Soviet "threat" that the U.S. policy makers frequently invoked as the apparent rationale for the postwar military buildup was not a threat of invasion or military attack, but a threat of "regimented economies," as President Truman had put it. What concerned the U.S. ruling elite was not the danger of a Soviet military attack; instead, the "danger," as they saw it, stemmed from the fact that "regimented economies" had restricted global mobility of U.S. capital—it had narrowed the global "elbow room" or "living space" of the

United States, as Winfield W. Riefler of the Council on Foreign Relations had put it.

The planned economy of the Soviet Union loomed especially menacing to world capitalism because (a) it remained unscathed by the Great Depression of the 1930s and, therefore, appeared recession-proof by virtue of planning; and (b) it had weathered the harrowing circumstances of war years better than the more advanced market economies of Europe. As these observations made the leaders of world capitalism nervous, they also prompted them to resolve that "regimented" economies simply could not coexist with "free" economies. Winston Churchill had earlier expressed the fears of the leaders of world capitalism of "regimented economies" in a very succinct and clear fashion. In a letter to Lloyd George, explaining why he promoted the military attacks of 14 foreign armies on Soviet soil from 1918 to 1920, Churchill wrote that the example of the Russian revolution could accelerate revolutions elsewhere and destroy England's colonial empire: "We may well be within measurable distance of universal collapse and anarchy throughout Europe and Asia." If the empire was to be saved, he continued, "the baby [Bolshevism/communism] must be strangled in its crib."[12] While these words were intended to justify the 14-army attack on the Soviet Union, they seem to equally explain what really lay at the heart of the Cold War conflict—what provoked it, and what sustained it. Perhaps more tellingly, they also explain why today the mighty U.S. power is so eager to strangulate the small island country of Cuba.

The End of the Cold War, Demands for "Peace Dividends," and the "Threat of Rogue States"

> So long as the Soviet Union existed, this policy could be presented as "fighting communism," but that increasingly transparent excuse disappeared entirely with the fall of the Soviet Union a decade ago—and, remarkably enough, the disappearance of the Evil Empire affected US "defense" spending not a whit—because of course it was never the real issue. The USSR was a bete noir, useful to cover US hegemony.
>
> —C. G. Estabrook

The demise of the Soviet Union and the end of the Cold War appeared to usher in a somewhat peaceful or, at least, less competitive world. Accordingly, it removed a powerful rationale for the United States to maintain the gigantic military-industrial complex of the Cold War era. By the same token, it also promised what at the time came to be called "peace dividends"—a reference to the benefits that, it was hoped, many would enjoy in the United States as a result of reorienting part of the Pentagon's budget toward civilian and/or social needs. Proponents of reducing the Pentagon budget of the Cold War era included broad social layers who hoped to benefit from the diversion of part of the military budget into more socially gainful domestic expenditures. They also included a section of the ruling elite who viewed the huge military spending as a drain on the economy and who, therefore, hoped to divert part of the national resources away from military expenditures toward deficit reduction, infra-structural building, and economic revitalization.

But while the majority of the U.S. citizens celebrated the prospects of what appeared to be imminent "peace dividends," the powerful vested inter-ests in the expansion of the Pentagon budget felt threatened, as they were (and continue to be) more likely to benefit from war than peace dividends. Not surprisingly, the influential interests vested in the military-industrial complex moved swiftly to safeguard their interests in the face of the "threat of peace." To this effect, once again, they invoked "national interests" and "external threats." The American people were told that instead of the "Soviet threat" of the Cold War era "external threat" now came from the "rogue states" of the lesser-developed world. Successful substitution of the "threat of rogue states" for the "Soviet threat" of the Cold War era removed the greatest threat of all to the military-industrial complex—the "threat of peace"!

There are some interesting parallels between the debate over military spending at the end of the Cold War, the debate at the end of World War II, and the debate in the mid-1970s. All three debates were prompted by either an end to a war or a reduction in international (U.S.–U.S.S.R.) ten-sions that promised military downsizing and, therefore, "peace dividends." And in all three instances, beneficiaries of war dividends overruled those who called for limits on military spending by resorting to the long-established "golden" tactic of militarism: "external threats to national interests/ security." In the late 1940s and early 1950s, the Korean War and the "com-munist threat" were manipulated by the proponents of military buildup to outmaneuver those who called for downsizing the military structure. In the mid- to late 1970s, as tension-reduction negotiations (détente) with the Soviet Union, in conjunction with budgetary constraints, threatened continued expansion of the Pentagon budget, partisans of militarism, mobi-lizing around the Committee on the Present Danger, managed once again to revive the specter of the "Soviet threat" and fend off efforts to curtail military spending. Similarly, in the face of the demise of the Soviet Union and the end of the Cold War, creative beneficiaries of war dividends managed, once more, to invent "new threats to our national interests"—international drug trafficking, rogue states, global terrorism, militant Islam, and now enemies of democracy—and stifle the voices that called for "peace dividends."

As noted, those who welcomed the prospects of peace dividends in the wake of the Cold War hostilities included a faction of the ruling elite who viewed the huge Pentagon budget as a drain on the national economy. They also viewed U.S. military adventures abroad as inimical to U.S. exports and investment markets. This view reflected the interests of civilian, or nonmilitary, transnational capital, that is, major banks and corporations with investment, production, and sales on a global scale. Proponents of this view were largely remnants and co-thinkers of the "Trilateralists" who, in the face of the 1970s economic and budgetary challenges, designed a joint multilateral framework for the management of world economic affairs in collaboration with Japan and Western European countries. As discussed in the previous chapter, Trilateralists hailed the mid-1970s tension-reducing negotiations with the Soviet Union, and called for limits on military spending.

Although the Trilateralists' ideas of joint global economic management, along with their plan of curtailing the Pentagon budget, were defeated by the powerful Cold Warrior forces of the 1975–1985 decade, those ideas began to resurface when the Cold War came to an end. Thus, William Hyland, editor of *Foreign Affairs*, organ of the Council on Foreign Relations, which was instrumental in shaping both the immediate post–World War II capitalist world and the Trilateralist strategy in the mid-1970s, argued that

[t]he Cold War was a broadly conceived struggle that gave primacy to geopolitics and military preparedness. At the outset, the United States was the most powerful nation in the world. Few questioned that it could afford the Truman Doctrine, the Marshall Plan, the rearmament of NATO, the strategic arms race, the interventions in Korea and Vietnam, or more recently, the build up of armaments in the early 1980s. For the next decade, however, ideological and military issues are likely to recede, economic factors will predominate and other issues (i.e., the environment, terrorism, drug trafficking) will grow in importance.[13]

Theodore Sorenson, also a prominent multilateralist thinker, likewise pointed out the following: "The touchstone for our national security concept—the containment of Soviet military and ideological power—is gone. The primary threat cited over forty years in justification for most of our military budget, bases and overseas assistance is gone."[14] Arguing along these lines, Robert McNamara, secretary of Defense from 1961 to 1968 and president of the World Bank for the 1968–1981 period, suggested a reduction in military spending from 6 percent of gross national product to 3 percent.[15]

But what a faction of the political elite and broad strata of the public celebrated as the end of the Cold War and the start of the benefits of peace dividends, the military-industrial complex viewed with anxiety. In the face of heightened expectations for peace dividends, the military establishment resorted, once again, to that age-old ploy of militarism: "external threats to our national interests"—as always camouflaging special interests behind national interests. But partisans of war and militarism now began to redefine both the "external threats" and "national interests" in accordance with the post–Cold War circumstances. These partisans now defined the U.S. national interests in such broad terms that they required the "stability" of almost all corners of the world, their markets and resources. Accordingly, they required worldwide U.S. military "responsibilities," or as James Cypher put it, "global militarism."[16] Champions of militarism also began to redefine the post–Cold War "sources of threat" in the broader framework of the new multipolar world, which goes way beyond the traditional "Soviet threat" of the bipolar world of the Cold War era. The "new sources of threat" are said to originate largely in the "unpredictable" and "unreliable" regional powers of the so-called Third World. "Instead of the Soviet Union, the 'menace' of China, Fidel Castro, drug lords . . . and more recently, terrorism, weapons of mass destruction, and the 'axis of evil'—Iran, Iraq, and North Korea—would have to do as new enemies."[17]

Most of the reassessment of the post–Cold War world came from top military brass or civilian proponents of militarism. For example, General Carl Vuno, chief of staff of the U.S. Army, told a House Committee in May 1989, "Much more complex [than any peril posed by the Soviet Union] is the threat situation developing in the rest of the world. Periods of change present a fertile environment for increased instability and increased danger. In this increasingly multipolar world, we face the potential of multiple threats from countries and factors which are becoming more sophisticated militarily and more aggressive politically."[18] General

A. M. Gray, commandant of the Marine Corps, similarly argued,

> The international security environment is in the midst of changing from a bipolar balance to a multipolar one with polycentric dimensions. The restructuring of the international environment has the potential to create regional power vacuums that could result in instability and conflict. We cannot permit these voids to develop either through disinterest, benign neglect, or lack of capability. If we are to maintain our position as a world leader and protect our interests, we must be capable of and willing to protect our global interests. This requires that we maintain our capability to respond to likely regions of conflict.[19]

General Gray further argued that poverty and inequality can serve as breeding grounds for social upheavals in various parts of the less-developed world that could "jeopardize" vital U.S. interests abroad, thus "increasing our requirements of forces capable of responding unilaterally":

> The Underdeveloped World's growing dissatisfaction over the gap between rich and poor nations will create a fertile breeding ground for insurgencies. These insurgencies have the potential to jeopardize regional stability and our access to vital economic and military resources. This situation will become more critical as our nation and allies, as well as potential adversaries, become more and more dependent on these strategic resources. If we are to have stability in these regions, maintain access to their resources, protect our citizens abroad, defend our vital installations and deter conflict, we must maintain within our active force structure a credible military power projection capability with flexibility to respond to conflicts across the spectrum of violence throughout the globe.[20]

General Colin Powell, chairman of the Joint Chiefs of Staff at the time, likewise argued before a Senate Committee that despite the collapse of the Soviet Union the United States needed to continue its military buildup because of numerous other obligations: "the going war in El Salvador, the coup attempt in the Philippines, restoration of democracy in Panama . . . [our] worldwide commercial and security interests which requires a strong navy." He further argued: "With all these challenges and opportunities confronting our nation, it is impossible for me to believe that demobilizing or hollowing out the American military is a feasible course of action for the future. The true 'peace dividend' is peace itself. . . . Peace comes about through the maintenance of strength."[21]

Policy prescriptions of these self-fulfilling prophecies were unmistakable: having thus portrayed the post–Cold War world as a place fraught with "multiple sources of threats to U.S. national interest," powerful beneficiaries of the Pentagon budget succeeded in maintaining military spending at essentially the Cold War levels. (Since the arrival of George W. Bush in the White House the Pentagon budget has been raised beyond the Cold War levels.) Proponents of continued militarism "moved with remarkable speed to ensure that the collapse [of the Soviet Union] would not affect the Pentagon's budget or our 'strategic position' on the globe we had garrisoned in the name of anti-communism."[22] Shortly after the Berlin Wall went down, Dick Cheney, secretary of Defense at the time, recommended increased Pentagon spending. Commenting on Cheney's budget in January 1990, Michael R. Gordon, military correspondent of the *New York Times*, reported that "in Cheney's view, which is shared by President [George H. W.] Bush, the United States will continue to need a large Navy to deal with brushfire conflicts and threats to American interests in places like Latin America and Asia."[23]

Early in 1990, the White House unveiled a new National Security Strategy before the Congress that focused on "unpredictable turbulent spots in the Third World" as new sources of attention for the U.S. military power in the post–Cold War era: "In the new era, we foresee that our military power will remain an essential underpinning of the global balance . . . that the more likely demands for the use of our military forces may not involve the Soviet Union and may be in the Third World, where new capabilities and approaches may be required." To respond to "turbulences in the most vital regions," the new situation called for a strategy of "discriminate deterrence"—a military strategy that "would contain and quell regional or local conflicts in the Third World with lightening speed and sweeping effectiveness before they get out of hand." In the post–Cold War world of "multiple sources of threats" the United States would also need to be prepared to fight "low-intensity" and "mid-intensity" wars. "Low-intensity" or "mid-intensity" does not refer to the level of firepower and violence employed but to its scale compared to an all-out war on a global or broad geographic range.[24]

The post–Cold War agenda of U.S. militarism was elaborate and long-term. Instead of declaring the end of the Cold War a victory and demobilizing the military structure that had been premised upon it, unilateral militarists used it for propaganda purposes, for U.S. triumphalism, and for the inauguration of a new, aggressive, and imperial role for the United States. Despite the overwhelming evidence that the Soviet Union had begun unraveling in the late 1960s and early 1970s, long before Ronald Reagan became president, its eventual collapse was attributed to President Reagan's aggressive foreign policy. Intended political dividends of endlessly celebrating "Reagan's victory over the Soviet Union" went beyond the infusion of heavy doses of gratuitous and hollow pride and patriotism into the American people. More importantly, it was used to convey the militaristic message that aggressiveness pays off, that the United States was no longer one of the two superpowers trying to contain the other superpower, but that it was now an unrivaled imperial power that could go beyond the defensive posturing of the Cold War era and embark, instead, on a unilateral and aggressive foreign policy characteristic of imperial powers.

Accordingly, the militarist forces within the ruling elite began to view the role of the United Nations and other Cold War international institutions as passé. Most of those multilateral institutions were created in the immediate post–World War II years for the reconstruction of the war-ravaged world and restoration of international trade and development. As discussed in chapter 3 of this study, they were part of President Roosevelt's "benign imperialism" that gave primacy to economic superiority and market efficiency as sources of international power—military power was still considered important, but as a safeguarding measure to keep global markets and resources open to U.S. capital. Partisans of unilateralism and/or militarism within the U.S. ruling circles have always been hostile to such multilateralist foreign policies that relied on international consultation and dialogue. But as long as the Soviet Union existed as a balancing power, these partisans had little choice but to (grudgingly) work within the framework of multilateral institutions such as the United Nations. The demise of the Soviet Union, however, removed that "restraining" framework from the militarists' path of aggression and unilateralism. Soon after the collapse of the Berlin Wall, they began treating the United Nations as obsolete. International disputes could now be settled, they seem to believe, by the new all-powerful and unrivaled world arbitrator: the military might of the United States. "Rather than continuing to serve as first among equals in the postwar international system, the United States would now act as a law unto itself, creating new rules of international engagement without agreement by other nations."[25] In his well-known *The Sorrows of Empire*, Chalmers Johnson describes this change in the thinking of the military establishment, and the resulting changes in the U.S. foreign policy:

> From 1989 to 2002, there was a revolution in America's relations with the rest of the world. At the beginning of that period, the conduct of foreign policy was

still largely a civilian operation, carried out by men and women steeped in diplomacy, accustomed to defending American actions in terms of international laws, and based on long-standing alliances with other democratic nations. There had always been a military component to the traditional conduct of foreign policy, and men from a military background often played prominent roles as civilian statesmen. . . . But, in general, a balance was maintained in favor of constitutional restraints on the armed forces and their use. By 2002, all of this had changed. The United States no longer had a "foreign policy." Instead, it had a military empire.[26]

Many people believe that the overtly unilateralist and/or militaristic U.S. foreign policy of the past several years started with the arrival of the Bush-Cheney team in the White House. Evidence suggests, however, that broad outlines of the aggressive foreign policy were formulated and projected soon after the fall of the Berlin Wall—although mainly by the same members of the Bush-Cheney team. Indeed, as demonstrated in the previous chapter, the militarists' agenda of aggressive unilateral foreign policy goes even further back to the mid- to late 1970s when the militarist forces of the ruling elite, spearheaded by the Committee on the Present Danger, effectively challenged and defeated the multilateralist forces, led by the Trilateral Commission, and ultimately succeeded in sending Ronald Reagan to the White House as their champion of militarism and aggressive foreign policy. Not surprisingly, the military establishment was euphoric during the first term of Reagan presidency as he effectively elevated the ephemerally relaxed tensions with the Soviet Union to such new heights that came to be called the Second Cold War—thereby also drastically increasing military spending. But as realpolitiks "softened" President Reagan during his second term in office, militarists began to search for a new champion and wait for another opportunity. That opportunity arrived with the arrival of George W. Bush in the White House.

Publicly available documents indicate that the designs and projections of the militarist planners for the post–Cold War world, crafted largely in the late 1980s and early 1990s, were quite ambitious. But these planners were also well aware that their elaborate strategic or intellectual blueprints for the new world order would not be very effective unless they managed to keep the American people on constant alert that "threats to our national security/ interests" are on the march everywhere. It was to their advantage to create the impression that the post–Cold War world was fraught with multiple sources of dangers that threatened the interests of the United States and/or its allies. To this end, they assiduously sought to invent—or to create by deliberate provocation, if necessary—such sources of danger. The ensuing pretexts for relentless Pentagon appropriations and for military adventures abroad have included charges and accusations of supporting, harboring, or condoning terrorism; possessing, or in the process of producing, or having plans and intentions to produce weapons of mass destruction; engaging in drug trafficking, or collaborating with drug traffickers; obstructing democracy and/or free enterprise; and the like.

The drastically increased number of U.S. military operations in various "trouble spots" of the world in the post–Cold War era is a reflection of this aggressive policy. The Federation of American Scientists has recorded a list of U.S. foreign military engagements that shows that in the first decade after the collapse of the Berlin Wall (1989–1999) the United States engaged in 134 such operations, the majority of which are altogether unknown to the American public. The following list is a sample: Operation Eagle Eye (Kosovo), Operation Determined Effort (Bosnia-Herzegovina), Operation Quick Lift (Croatia), Operation Nomad Vigil (Albania), Operation Nomad Endeavor (Taszar, Hungary), Operation Sharp Guard (Adriatic Sea), Operation Desert Thunder (Iraq), Operation Seva Verde (Columbia), Operation Constant Vigil (Bolivia), Operation Fundamental Response (Venezuela), Operation Infinite Reach (Sudan and Afghanistan), Operation Noble Response (Kenya), Operation Safe Border (Peru and Ecuador), Operation United Shield (Somalia), Operation Safe Haven/Safe Passage (Cuba), Operation Sea Signal (Haiti), Operation Provide Transition (Angola), Operation Safe Harbor (Haiti), Operation Desert Storm (Southwest Asia), and many more.[27] As noted, profiteers of war and militarism have managed to launch these capricious military adventures often under false premises and cooked-up pretexts.

Many of these military operations took place during the Clinton administration. President Clinton was known to be a champion of neoliberalism and multilateralism, seeking to advance U.S. interests through unhindered international trade and investment in the context of multilateral economic institutions such as the World Trade Organization, International Monetary Fund, and the World Bank. To insure the success of the policy of global neoliberalism (sometimes called the "imperialism of free trade"), military force was not ruled out but only as the guarantor of the last resort, and in the context of the multilateral, NATO framework. The Clinton administration also managed to slow down the pace of the growth of the Pentagon spending. Nonetheless, as this record of U.S. military operations in the 1990s shows, he did have his own (indeed, large) share of military adventures abroad. This shows that, contrary to popular perceptions, the rise of U.S. militarism did not start with the arrival of George W. Bush in the White House—although he has embraced it quite enthusiastically and has, consequently, elevated it to new heights. It also shows that although on philosophical or political grounds a president might not favor or embrace certain projects of militarism, in practice that president is more likely to has to go along with such projects than being able to resist or to stop them—if not enthusiastically, then grudgingly he would have to go along. Presidents might slightly modify military plans, or offer different justifications for those plans, but they cannot drastically change or put a stop on them. As Howard Swint, Democratic candidate for Congress in West Virginia, put it, "The seat of power for formulating foreign policy and defense strategy is not in the White House but rather in the Pentagon. While a civilian Commander-in-Chief may tweak policy in four year increments, it's obvious that military careerists together with major defense contractors effectively control the Congressional budget process and drive defense appropriations."

Beneficiaries of war dividends sometimes find "external enemies and threats" by definition, "by deciding unilaterally what actions around the world constitute terrorism," or by arbitrarily classifying certain countries as "supporters of terrorism," as Bill Christison, retired CIA advisor, put it.[28] They also create international frictions and provoke military entanglements in ways that can best be characterized as bullying, or godfathering. Such war-mongering provocations include labeling certain countries with slanderous and humiliating titles such as "axis of evil" or "rogue states," imposing economic and other sanctions against "unfriendly" countries, promoting armed insurgencies and other destabilizing forces against such "unfriendly" countries, and so on. Tactics of this sort seem to be part of a cynical strategy of perpetuating the vicious cycle of terrorism and war: provoking anger and violence, thereby justifying war and destruction, which will trigger further acts of terror and violence. Of course, the nefarious driving force behind this self-fulfilling strategy of war and terrorism is to maintain the high dividends of the business of war. Gore Vidal has satirically characterized this wicked need of the beneficiaries of war and militarism to constantly come up with new threats and enemies as an "enemy of the month club: each month we are confronted by a new horrendous enemy at whom we must strike before he destroys us."[29]

* * *

U.S. foreign policy makers have always harbored expansionist or imperialistic ambitions, even when they shunned large standing armies and militarism.

Prior to the rise of militarism, however, foreign policy, including decisions on war and military operations, was made largely by civilian authorities. Furthermore, decisions on war and military engagements were largely prompted by economic, territorial, ideological, or geopolitical pursuits. By contrast, in the post–Cold War era, it has often been the militarists and/or beneficiaries of war dividends who have been calling the shots, so to speak. Moreover, the rationales and objectives of military adventures that have been instigated since the collapse of the Berlin Wall have become increasingly fuzzy, confused, and shifting. With the exception of lucrative dividends for the stockholders (and or stakeholders) of war industries, even the economic consequences of these military adventures have been dubious.

The main reason for these pre- and post–Cold War foreign policy differences is that the post–Cold War military engagements seem to have been prompted primarily by a frantic search on the part of the beneficiaries of war and militarism to protect their lion's share of national treasury in the absence of the "threat of communism" of the Cold War era. A small war here, a small war there, a "low-intensity" war in region "x," and a "mid-intensity" war in region "y"—cynically scripted as "controlled wars"—are strategies that would keep military appropriations flowing into the coffers of the military-industrial complex without causing a major or worldwide conflict that could cripple world markets.

These developments also seem to signify a gradual degeneration of a superpower into military or parasitic imperialism: degeneration from a time when military power was used as a means for economic, territorial, ideological, or geopolitical gains to a time when military establishment becomes an end in itself, a parasitic empire in its own right. When a military establishment thus evolves into a military empire, its military adventures abroad (usually prompted not by a desire to expand the empire's wealth beyond the existing levels, but by a desire to appropriate the lion's share of the existing wealth and treasure for the military establishment) tend to resemble bullying or godfathering. This explains, for example, why the Bush administration's stated "reasons" for invading Iraq have been so woefully muddled, shifting, and purely bogus.

9/11 Attacks and the "War on Terrorism"—Opportunity for Increased Militarism

The threat of "terrorism," some of it real, most of it invented, is the new Red Scare. The parallels are striking. In America in the 1950s, the Red

Scare was used to justify the growth of war industries, the suspension of democratic rights and the silencing of dissenters. That is happening now.

—John Pilger

Against this backdrop—the collapse of the Soviet Union, the "threat of peace dividends" to the interests of the military-industrial complex, and the consequent need of the beneficiaries of war dividends for substitutes for the "communist threat" of the Cold War era—the Bush administration's approach to the heinous attacks of 9/11 as an opportunity for war and aggression should not have come as a surprise to anyone familiar with the vicious needs of militarism. The monstrous attacks were treated not as crimes—which would have required criminal prosecution through coordinated international intelligence-gathering operations, law enforcement actions, and public diplomacy efforts—but as "war on America." Once it was thus established that the United States was "at war," military buildup and imperialist aggression followed accordingly. The successful substitution of the threat of terrorism for the Soviet threat of the Cold War era removed the greatest danger of all to the interests of the military-industrial complex—the "threat of peace"! As Chalmers Johnson put it in his *The Sorrows of Empire*, the 9/11 tragedy "served as manna from heaven to an administration determined to ramp up military budgets."[30]

Many Americans will probably cringe at the thought that their government used the monstrous 9/11 crimes as a pretext to embark on the path of war and militarism. Sadly, however, it is true. There is overwhelming evidence that top officials in the Bush administration viewed the tragedy as an opportunity for war, callously calculating that the traumatized U.S. public would now support significant military interventions abroad. There is also irrefutable evidence that the militarist partisans within and around the administration, who were at the time firmly in control of U.S. foreign policy, had long before the 9/11 attacks contemplated strategies of "regime change" in Iraq and a number of other countries in the Middle East. These partisans had already labeled "unfriendly" governments such as those ruling in Iran, Iraq, Syria, Libya, North Korea, and Cuba as rogues, terrorists, or supporters of terrorism. Before the 9/11 attacks, however, such demonizing labels were apparently not enough to convince the American people to support unilateral wars of preemption. The 9/11 tragedy served as the militarists' coveted pretext for such wars—hence, the invasion of Iraq.

Partisans of war and militarism can no longer dismiss this indictment as false or speculative; it has been amply corroborated by both official and unofficial evidence. For example, Nicholas Lemann of the *New Yorker* magazine wrote in an April 2002 issue that Condoleezza Rice told him that, in the wake of the 9/11 attacks, she had called together the senior staff of the National Security Council and asked them "how do you capitalize on these opportunities" to fundamentally change American doctrine. "I really think," Rice continued, "this period is analogous to 1945 to 1947 in that the events so clearly demonstrated that there is a big global threat that has started shifting the tectonic plates in international politics. And it's important to try to seize on that and position American interests and institutions and all that before they harden again." Another top official was even more blunt: "Inside government, the reason September 11 appears to have been 'a transformative moment' . . . is not so much that it revealed the existence of a threat of which officials had previously been unaware [but] that it drastically reduced the American public's usual resistance to American military involvement overseas, at least for a while."[31]

The view that the Bush administration's response to the 9/11 attacks was prompted more by dubious considerations or evil calculations than by a genuine effort to reduce or eradicate terrorism is reinforced by the fact that the administration embarked on the path of war almost immediately after the attacks. A number of recently published books and reports, some of them by government "insiders," make it clear that even as the American people, and indeed the entire world, were still in shock of witnessing the unimaginable and traumatic collapse of the World Trade Center, top U.S. officials were planning war.[32] For example, the Associated Press White House correspondent Ron Fournier wrote in a September 5, 2002 article that barely 12 hours after the terrible strikes, moments after his nationally televised address, President Bush and his national security team decided on war: the president told his national security team, "Get the troops ready. . . . This is a time for self defense. . . . This is our time."[33]

Indeed, evidence shows that the Bush administration began searching for ways to change Saddam Hussein's regime soon after arriving in the White House—long before the 9/11 attacks. For example, Pulitzer Prize-winning journalist Ron Suskind's book, *The Price of Loyalty: George W. Bush, the White House and the Education of Paul O'Neill*, reveals that the civilian militarist team of the Bush administration (the so-called chicken hawks headed by Vice President Dick Cheney, Defence Secretary Donald Rumsfeld, Deputy Defence Secretary Paul Wolfowitz, and National Security Advisor Condoleezza Rice) was determined to oust Saddam

Hussein from "day one." Suskind reports that at the first National Security Council meeting, ten days after President Bush's inauguration in January 2001, "regime change" in Iraq was "topic A" on the president's agenda. On January 10, 2004, Paul O'Neill, President Bush's treasury secretary until December 2002, told *Time Magazine*, "From the start, we were building the case against Hussein and looking at how we could take him out and change Iraq into a new country. . . . It was all about finding a way to do it. That was the tone of it. . . . The president saying, 'Fine. Go find me a way to do this.' "[34] O'Neill's and Suskind's claims have since been bolstered by a number of other accounts, including those by Richard Clarke, the Bush administration's national coordinator for counterterrorism, in his *Against All Enemies: Inside America's War on Terror*; by Michael Scheuer, retired senior CIA official's *Imperial Hubris: Why the West is Losing the War on Terror*; and by Bob Woodward of *The Washington Post* in his *Plan of Attack*.

Cynical manipulation of the 9/11 attacks for purposes of war and militarism makes it clear why those atrocious attacks were labeled as "war on America" instead of criminal acts of mass murder, or crimes against humanity. Only by so labeling, the War Party of neoconservatives could carry out their own, real wars. Calling things by their right name often involves more than just semantics; implications, solutions and consequences can be vastly different. It is not unreasonable to imagine that if, for example, the horrific assaults of 9/11 were logically called criminal acts, and the fight against them were accordingly conducted through an all-out criminal prosecution on an international scale—involving law enforcement actions, coordinated international intelligence-gathering operations, and public diplomacy efforts—the world political scene, especially in the Middle East and the United States, would have looked much different now. Not only could much of the death and destruction have been avoided, but also the fight against terrorism would have been more effective; at least, it would not have generated the escalating vicious circle of war and terrorism that the Bush administration's policy has generated.

The global outpouring of sympathy for the victims of the 9/11 attacks provided the United States with a unique opportunity to capitalize on all that goodwill to rally genuine international support for a coordinated and effective strategy of finding the planners and abettors of the attacks and prosecuting them through mechanisms of international law. Instead, the administration squandered that opportunity by declaring the 9/11 atrocities as "acts of war against America," or "against freedom and democracy," by employing a poisonous narrative of "war between good and evil," and by dividing the world into two irreconcilable forces and civilizations: "us and them." The result has been an incredible amount of unnecessary and preventable death and destruction, further sullying of the image of the United States as global bully, and a dramatic increase in terrorism. "From 1993 through the 9/11 assaults of 2001, there were five major al-Qaeda attacks worldwide; in the two years since then there have been seventeen such bombings, including the Istanbul suicide assaults on the British consulate and an HSBC Bank."[35]

That the Bush administration's politically expedient policies of war and militarism—prompted primarily by powerful special interests that are vested in military expansion and the business of war—should have played into the hands of Bin Laden and his co-thinkers should not be surprising. As Michael Scheuer points out in his *Imperial Hubris: Why the West is Losing the War on Terror*, "an avaricious, premeditated, unprovoked war against a foe [Saddam Hussein] who posed no immediate threat but whose defeat did offer economic advantage" was bound to create more resentment, and therefore more followers for Bin Laden who, in essence, personifies a movement and a mood that was precipitated by exactly such imperial transgressions. The administration's professed "war on terrorism" has thus turned out to be, in effect, war *for* terrorism. The resulting "action-reaction" vicious circle has been expanded by the unfortunate fact that the Bush administration does not seem to be interested in an understanding of what produces terrorism; it seems to be content with its own self-serving explanation that terrorist acts are prompted by "hatred of our freedom." Nor does it seem to be interested in considering any alternatives to war in the fight against terrorism. The problem with this approach is that, points out Ronald I. Spiers, retired U.S. ambassador, "terrorism is a tool—a weapon—not an actor. Like war, terrorism is the use of violence by groups or individuals to advance a political objective. . . . It is a weapon used by the weak against the strong, the colonial subject against the imperial power, the occupied against the occupier, and the dispossessed and disenfranchised against the oppressor." The ambassador further points out,

> But how do you win a "war" against a tool that, like war itself, is a method of carrying on politics by other means? A "war on terrorism" is a war without an end in sight, without an exit strategy, with enemies specified not by their aims but by their tactics. Relying principally on military means is like trying to eliminate

a cloud of mosquitoes with a machine gun. "Terrorism" by its nature can't and won't be eradicated or abolished as long as there are grievances that the aggrieved believe cannot be resolved nonviolently. . . . We have not as a nation defined our objective in the specific terms that might make it winnable. Until we do, we risk the diversions that come from being in a struggle against an abstraction.[36]

What is especially remarkable is that, based on historical accounts and precedents, most of the disastrous consequences of the Bush administration's war on terrorism were predicted not only by the Left and liberals but also by many traditional conservatives, moderate Republicans (also called Rockefeller Republicans), and libertarians. For example, in a policy study for the (libertarian) Cato Institute two days after the 9/11 attacks, Charles V. Peña wrote, "But how exactly will increased defense spending on tanks, airplanes, and ships remedy the situation? The answer is that it won't . . . a larger military would not have prevented that devastating tragedy. And it won't prevent future terrorist actions."[37] Right. But the Bush administration seems to have had its own agenda; and the "war on terrorism" seems to have been a charade to advance that agenda. Besides, as Ambassador Spiers points out, "A war makes the role of commander in chief more dramatic. Our commander in chief seems smitten with the so-called 'war' on terrorism. . . . The president has found this 'war' useful as an all-purpose justification for almost anything he wants or doesn't want to do; fuzziness serves the administration politically. It brings to mind Big Brother's vague and never-ending war in Orwell's '1984.' A war on terrorism is a permanent engagement against an always-available tool."[38]

In a similar vein, Brent Scowcroft, who served as the national security advisor to both presidents Ford and Bush Sr., and a number of his co-thinkers in the ranks of moderate Republicans repeatedly warned President Bush Jr. against the dangers of invading Iraq. For instance, in a August 15, 2002 *Wall Street Journal* op-ed piece, titled "Don't Attack Saddam," Scowcroft wrote, "Our nation is presently engaged in a debate about whether to launch a war against Iraq. . . . It is beyond dispute that Saddam Hussein is a menace. . . . That said, we need to think through this issue very carefully. . . . Our pre-eminent security priority—underscored repeatedly by the president—is the war on terrorism. An attack on Iraq at this time would seriously jeopardize, if not destroy, the global counterterrorist campaign we have undertaken." Scowcroft added, "The United

States could certainly defeat the Iraqi military and destroy Saddam's regime. But it would not be a cakewalk. On the contrary, it undoubtedly would be very expensive—with serious consequences for the U.S. and global economy—and could as well be bloody."

* * *

Led by the United States, military spending on a global level has risen by 18 percent since 2001. According to a U.S. congressional study, terrorism has risen by 35 percent since then. From the fact that the increase in military spending has coincided with an increase in terrorism, Brandon J. Snider concludes, "With every dollar, the U.S., which accounts for 47 percent of the spending, manufactures new terrorists, which will, in turn, lead to demands for increased defense spending."[39] This positive correlation between military spending, war, and terrorism is not fortuitous. In his classic book on war and militarism, *The Military-Industrial Complex*, the late Sidney Lens explained this relationship in these words, "The mere availability of planes and weapons is a temptation to use them. It may be a temptation which is acceded to in a minority of instances, but it is enough to make the preparation for war an independent factor in creating it. . . . Being prepared thus becomes a pressure, a temptation, for being at war. The merry-go-round never stops."[40] This is an essential dynamic of militarism. As discussed in the second chapter of this study, under precapitalist formations, all the military establishment needed to justify and maintain its apparatus and privileges was the specter of war or the environment of fear—not necessarily the actual, shooting war. Under capitalism, where production of military hardware is subject to market imperatives, actual wars are needed in order to generate "sufficient" demand for war-dependent industries and their profitability requirements. Perhaps more than anything else, it is this combination of private ownership of the means of warfare and market imperatives of profitability that drives the war today. It is also this business imperative of war that, more than any other factor, underlies the U.S. militarists' constant search for enemies, or new "threats to our national security"—communism, rogue states, axis of evil, global terrorism, militant Islam, et cetera. Furthermore, it is this market-driven force behind the war that underlies, at least partly, the Bush administration's fuzzy and shifting "reasons" for invading Iraq, and the consequent death, destruction, and turbulence in today's world. Despite its apparent complexity, reducing international acts of terrorism and fostering global peace and stability would not be very difficult in the absence of this perverse dynamics of the business of war. As Brandon J. Snider points out, "Nations like Britain and the U.S. don't really have to do anything to fight terrorism; they only have to stop doing things that provoke terrorist responses: keep out of the affairs of other nations."[41]

CHAPTER 5

Militant Islam, Terrorism, and "Clash of Civilizations"

To say that an effective cure of a disease requires a sound diagnosis is to state the obvious. Yet, in the face of the 9/11 plague, and of the scourge of terrorism in general, the Bush administration has utterly failed to shed any light on some of the submerged factors that might have provoked such heinous attacks. Not only has the administration not shed any light on the political issues behind terrorism, but it has, in fact, created more heat and confusion by attributing it to simplistic and politically expedient factors such as "hatred of our freedom," or "good versus evil," or the "Islamic incompatibility with the modern world." The administration further compounded the confusion by shifting the focus of the narrative on terrorism from the perpetrators of the 9/11 atrocities to the U.S.-defined "global terrorism" in general, and to Saddam Hussein and Iraq in particular.

Media analysis and political punditry have likewise been dominated by the dubious theory of "the clash of civilizations" that has been proposed by Samuel Huntington and his co-thinkers since the early 1990s.[1] War debriefings, administration spokespersons, news reporters, editorials, and talk shows harp on the theme—some directly, like Fox News, others in subtle ways—that the roots of conflicts in the Muslim world must be sought in Islam itself. In discussing the sociopolitical turbulence in the Middle East, these manufacturers of public opinion are quick to ask, "What in Islam has led to these convulsions?" But they rarely bother to ask, "What is it in the recent developments in the Middle East that has led political opposition to take a distinctly religious form?"

Instead of calling the 9/11 attacks mass murder criminal acts, the administration does not seem to have been able to resist the politically expedient temptation of calling them acts of "war on America, on our way of life, or on our civilization." Accordingly, instead of responding to those criminal acts through coordinated international investigative police and/or intelligence work, as many suggested both at home and abroad, the trigger-happy administration launched its own wars on Afghanistan and Iraq that have claimed many more innocent lives than those claimed by the 9/11 atrocities, thereby drastically increasing acts of terror and violence.

The Bush administration's drive to war is a logical policy prescription based on its own diagnosis of terrorism as being driven by a "hatred of our way of life," as President Bush and his militarist advisors have repeatedly stated. This is essentially a popularized version of the theory of "the clash of civilizations," which implies that Islam is inherently incompatible with modernization and Western values. The theory, initially expounded by Samuel Huntington in the early 1990s, sets out to identify "new sources" of international conflicts in the post–Cold War world. During the Cold War years, major international conflicts were explained by the "threat of communism" and the rivalry between the two competing world systems. In the post–Cold War era, however, argue Huntington and his co-thinkers, the sources of international rivalries and collisions have shifted to competing and incompatible civilizations, which have their primary roots in religion and/or culture. Thus, in his initial written work on the subject, Huntington envisioned a future where the "great divisions among humankind and the dominating source of conflict will be cultural."[2]

An obvious weakness of this theory is that it views culture as static and immutable—immune to social, economic, and historical changes. More importantly, it ignores (or denies) the role of economic, territorial, and geopolitical factors in international conflicts. It is on the basis of these dubious assumptions that Huntington can argue that international conflicts erupt not because of imperialistic pursuits of economic, territorial, or geopolitical advantages but because of non-Western civilizations' reactions to Western power and values. To fend off such "threats to its civilization," Huntington concludes that the West needs to further reinforce its power.[3]

Huntington's theory of "the clash of civilizations" is essentially a subtle version of Richard Perle's strategy of "de-contextualization." Perle, a leading neoconservative militarist (and a prominent advisor of the Likud Party, the hard-line Zionist party of Prime Minister Arial Sharon of Israel) coined the term "de-contextualization" as a way to explain both the desperate acts of terrorism in general and the violent tactics of the Palestinian resistance to occupation in particular. He argued that in order to blunt the widespread global criticism of the Israeli treatment of Palestinians, their resistance to occupation must be decontextualized; that is, we must stop trying to understand the territorial, geopolitical, and historical reasons that some groups turn to terrorism. Instead, he suggested, the reasons for the violent reactions of such groups must be sought in the arenas of culture and/or religion—in the Islamic way of thinking. Like the "clash of civilizations" theory, decontextualization strategy has been part of a well-orchestrated effort to divert attention from the root causes of terrorism and attribute it to "pathological problems of the Muslim mind."[4]

Neoconservative militarists in and around the Bush administration, and beneficiaries of war dividends in general, have found—indeed, also promoted—this sinister strategy of obfuscation quite useful for the purposes of justifying their military adventures in the Middle East and elsewhere in the Muslim world. As discussed in the previous chapter, ever since the collapse of the Berlin Wall beneficiaries of war and militarism have been searching for substitutes for the "communist threat" of the Cold War era in order to maintain and justify their lion's share of national resources, or tax dollars. The view that Western civilization is threatened by militant Islam has provided these beneficiaries with a "perfect" substitute for the communist threat of the Cold War era. The view has gained additional strength as a result of the 9/11 terrorist attacks. President Bush's explanation that those atrocious attacks were prompted by a "hatred of our way of life" can be better understood in this context.

Although short sightedly self-serving, this "explanation" of terrorism and the concomitant justification of war and militarism harbor an element of dangerously misleading plausibility: once the public is convinced that the "hostile and irredeemable Islam or Islamists are out in force to drown our civilization," preemptive war would be hailed as the logical response. The danger is further compounded because this explanation of terrorism possesses the power of self-fulfilling prophecy, the power to make what is theorized appear real.

Not only do such explanations tend to sow the seeds of hatred and ignorance, and are bound to poison international relations, but they also fail the test of history. The history of the relationship between the modern Western world and the Muslim world shows that, contrary to popular perceptions in the West, from the time of their initial contacts with the capitalist West more than two centuries ago until almost the final third of the twentieth century, the Muslim people were quite receptive to the economic and political models of the modern world. Many people in the Muslim world, including the majority of their political leaders, were eager to transform and restructure the socioeconomic and political structures of their societies after the model of the capitalist West. The majority of political leaders, as well as a significant number of Islamic experts and intellectuals, viewed the rise of the modern West and its spread into their lands as inevitable historical developments that challenged them to chart their own programs of reform and development.

In light of this background, this question arises: what changed all of that earlier receptive and respectful attitude toward the West to the current attitude of disrespect and hatred?

I hope to demonstrate in this chapter that the answer to this question rests more with the policies of the Western powers in the region than the alleged rigidity of Islam, or "the clash of civilizations." I hope to show that it was only after more than a century and a half of imperialistic pursuits and a series of humiliating policies in the region that the popular masses of the Muslim world turned to religion and the conservative religious leaders as sources of defiance, mobilization, and self-respect. In other words, for many Muslims the recent turn to religion often represents not so much a rejection of Western values and achievements as it is a way to resist or defy the oppressive policies and alliances of Western powers in the Muslim world.

Early Responses to the Challenges of the Modern World

Not only did the early modernizers of the Muslim world embrace Western technology, but they also welcomed its civil and state institutions, its representational system of government, and its tradition of legal and constitutional rights. For example, the Iranian intellectuals Mulkum Khan (1833–1908) and Agha Khan Kermani (1853–1996) urged Iranians to acquire a Western education and replace the Shariah (the religious legal code) with a modern secular legal code. Secular political leaders of this persuasion joined forces with the more liberal religious leaders in the Constitution Revolution of 1906, and forced the Qajar dynasty to set up a modern constitution, to limit the powers of the monarchy and give Iranians parliamentary representation.[5]

Even some of the Ottoman sultans (kings) pursued Western models of industrialization and modernization on their own. For example, Sultan

Mahmud II "inaugurated the *Tanzimat* (Regulation) in 1826, which abolished the Janissaries [the fanatical elite corps of troops organized in the fourteenth century], modernized the army and introduced some of the new technology." In 1839 Sultan Abdulhamid "issued the Gulhane decree, which made his rule dependent upon a contractual relationship with his subjects, and looked forward to major reform of the empire's institutions."[6]

More dramatic, however, were the modernizing and/or secularizing programs of Egypt's renowned modernizers Muhammad Ali (1769–1849) and his grandson Ismail Pasha (1803–1895). They were so taken by the impressive achievements of the West that they embarked on breakneck modernizing programs that were tantamount to trying to hothouse the Western world's achievements of centuries into decades: "To secularize the country, Muhammad Ali simply confiscated much religiously endowed property and systematically marginalized the *Ulema* [religious leaders], divesting them of any shred of power."[7] In the face of dire conditions of underdevelopment and humiliating but unstoppable foreign domination, those national leaders viewed modernization not only as the way out of underdevelopment but also out of the yoke of foreign domination.

Not only the secular intellectuals, the political elite, and government leaders but also many Islamic leaders and scholars, known as "Islamic modernizers," viewed modernization as the way of the future. But whereas the reform programs and policies of the political/national leaders often included secularization, at least implicitly, Islamic modernizers were eclectic: while seeking to adopt the sources of the strength of the West, including constitutionalism and government by representation, they wanted to preserve their cultural and national identities as well as Islamic principles and values as the moral foundation of the society. These Islamic modernizers included Jamal al-Din al-Afghani (1838–1897), Muhammad Abduh (1849–1905), Qasim Amin (1863–1908), and Shaikh Muhammad Hussain Naini in Egypt and Iran; and Sayyid Ahmad Khan (1817–1898) and Muhammad Iqbal (1875–1938) in India.

To be sure, there was resistance to change. But, by and large, nationalist modernizers in many Muslim countries did manage to pursue vigorous agendas of social, economic, and political reform. John Esposito, one of the leading experts of Islamic studies in the United States, describes the early attitude of the political and economic policy makers of the Muslim world toward the modern world of the West:

> Both the indigenous elites, who guided government development programs in newly emerging Muslim states, and their foreign patrons and advisers were

Western-oriented and Western-educated. All proceeded from a premise that equated modernization with Westernization. The clear goal and presupposition of development was that every day and in every way things should become more modern (i.e., Western and secular), from cities, buildings, bureaucracies, companies, and schools to politics and culture. While some warned of the need to be selective, the desired direction and pace of change were unmistakable. Even those Muslims who spoke of selective change did so within a context which called for the separation of religion from public life. Western analysts and Muslim experts alike tended to regard a Western-based process of modernization as necessary and inevitable and believed equally that religion was a major hindrance to political and social change in the Muslim world.[8]

Karen Armstrong, author of a number of books on religious fundamentalism, likewise points out,

> About a hundred years ago, almost every leading Muslim intellectual was in love with the West, which at that time meant Europe. America was still an unknown quantity. Politicians and journalists in India, Egypt, and Iran wanted their countries to be just like Britain or France; philosophers, poets, and even some of the *ulama* (religious scholars) tried to find ways of reforming Islam according to the democratic model of the West. They called for a nation-state, for representational government, for the disestablishment of religion, and for constitutional rights. Some even claimed that the Europeans were better Muslims than their own fellow countrymen since the Koran teaches that the resources of a society must be shared as fairly as possible, and in the European nations there was beginning to be a more equitable sharing of wealth.[9]

Armstrong then asks, "So what happened in the intervening years to transform all of that admiration and respect into the hatred that incited the acts of terror that we witnessed on September 11?"

While profound questions of this type could contribute significantly to a national discussion concerning some of the more submerged factors contributing to heinous crimes such as the 9/11 attacks, the administration of President Bush, in conjunction with major media outlets, have so far effectively kept such questions out of the national debate.

It is necessary to acknowledge, once again, that the Muslim world's earlier openness to the modern world was far from even or uniform: along with advocates of change and adaptation there existed forces of resistance and rejection. Focusing primarily on such instances of rejection, proponents of the theory of "the clash of civilizations" can certainly cite, as they frequently do, many such incidents of resistance in support of their arguments that horrific acts like those committed on 9/11 are due to inherent incompatibility of the Muslim world with Western values.[10] But such selective references to historical developments in order to support a predetermined view do not carry us very far to the way of setting historical records straight. A number of issues need to be pointed out in this context. To begin with, change almost always generates resistance. Resistance to change is, therefore, not limited to Muslims or the Muslim world. In fact, the Christian church's nearly 400-year resistance to capitalist transformation in Europe was even more traumatic than that of the Muslim world. The resulting travail of transition created more social turbulence than has been observed in the context of the Muslim world. Whereas the Church of the Middle Ages anathemized the very idea of gain, the pursuit of gain and the accumulation of property are considered noble pursuits in Islam. Opponents of transition to capitalism in Europe not only tried (and almost hanged) Robert Keane for having made a 6 percent profit on his investment and "prohibited merchants from carrying unsightly bundles" of their merchandise, but also "fought for the privilege of carrying on in its fathers' footsteps."[11] As Karen Armstrong points out, during the nearly 400 years of transition, the Western people often "experienced . . . bloody revolutions, reigns of terror, genocide, violent wars of religion, the despoliation of the countryside, vast social upheavals, exploitation in the factories, spiritual malaise and profound anomie in the new megacities."[12]

Second, Muslim societies, like less-developed societies elsewhere, are expected, or compelled by the imperatives of the world market, to traverse the nearly 400-year journey of the West in a much shorter period of time. Furthermore, the travails of transition in the case of these belatedly developing countries (vis-à-vis the case of early developers of the West) are often complicated by foreign interventions and imperial pressures from outside. External pressure has included not only direct colonial and/or imperial military force, but also pressure exerted from the more subtle market forces and agents such as the International Monetary Fund and World Trade Organization.

Despite its turbulence, the painful process of transition to capitalism in the West was largely an internal process; no foreign force or interference could be blamed for the travails of transition. And the pains of transitions were thus gradually and grudgingly accepted as historical inevitabilities. Not so in the case of belatedly developing countries. Here, the pains of change and transition are sometimes perceived not as historical necessities but as products of foreign designs or imperialist schemes. Accordingly, the agony of change is often blamed (especially by the conservative proponents of the status quo) on external forces or powers: colonialism, imperialism, and neoliberalism.

Actual foreign intervention, realizing and reinforcing such perceptions, has thus had a retarding impact on the process of reform in the Muslim world. For intervention from outside often plays into the hands of the conservative, obscurantist elements who are quite adept at portraying their innate opposition to change as a struggle against foreign domination, thereby reinforcing resistance to reform, especially religious reform. Today, for example, U.S. intervention in the internal affairs of countries such as Egypt, Pakistan, Iran, Saudi Arabia, Kuwait, Iraq, and Turkey, far from facilitating the process of reform or helping the forces of change in these countries, is actually hurting such forces as it plays into the hands of their conservative opponents and strengthens the forces of resistance.

Third, contrary to the rising political influence of "radical Islamists" in recent years, radical Islamic circles of the earlier periods did not sway much power over the direction of national economies and policies. Their opposition to Western values and influences was often in the form of passive "rejection or elusion."[13] They simply refused to cooperate or deal with the colonial powers and their institutions (such as modern European school systems) spreading in their midst: "They did not attempt to assume direct political control but used their position to preserve tradition as best as they could under the rapidly changing conditions of the time." And while they "remained an important factor in influencing public opinion . . . , they basically used their position to encourage obedience to those in power."[14]

To the extent that conservative Islamic figures or groups actively opposed policies of change, such obscurantist challenges were almost always defeated, coerced, or co-opted by the modernizing, reforming, or revolutionary secular nationalist leaders. Thus, in all the major social movements of the first two-thirds of the twentieth century (i.e., in the anticolonial/anti-imperial national liberation movements as well as in the subsequent radical reform movements of a "noncapitalist" or "socialist-oriented" character of the 1950s and 1960s) national leadership lay with secular nationalists. This is not to deny that, at times, religious nationalism played an important role in the anticolonial/anti-imperial struggles, but that because Islamic leaders lacked national development or nation-building plans, political leadership on a national level often fell into the hands of secular nationalists who offered such plans.

Those plans were fashioned either after the U.S. model of economic development, as in the case of the shahs of Iran and the king of Jordan, or after the Soviet model of "noncapitalist development," as in the cases of Nasser's Egypt, for example. While it is now relatively easier to see, in hindsight, the shortcomings and the failures of those development programs, such programs did at the time hold promises of lifting the respective societies out of dependence, poverty, and underdevelopment. Thus it was not simply a lack of an "Islamic alternative" that gave the leading role of national development to secular nationalism. Perhaps more important were the hopes and aspirations nurtured by those national development projects.

As long as the hopes and aspirations that were thus enlivened remained animated, the appeals of vague promises of an "Islamic alternative" were not strong enough to challenge the rule of the secular nationalist leaders and their development programs—and that meant, approximately, the first two-thirds of the twentieth century. But as those hopes turned sour, such promises began to sound appealing. By the late 1960s and early 1970s, all the propitious factors and circumstances that had until then nurtured those dreams of economic progress, democratic rights, and political sovereignty seemed unreal and disappointing.

The secular national governments that had emerged in a number of Muslim countries from the process of national liberation struggles turned out to be headed largely by the allies and collaborators of the colonial/imperial powers they had formally replaced—that is, the landed aristocracy and the big commercial interests, known as "comprador bourgeoisie." As such, they were more willing to continue the inherited pattern of socioeconomic structures than to carry out land and other reform programs that would change such structures in favor of the masses who had fought for independence.

Likewise, it soon became clear that revolutionary nationalist leaders who replaced the comprador bourgeoisie in countries such as Egypt, Algeria, and the Sudan, and who had initially embarked on extensive reform programs in the name of socialism or noncapitalist development, had done so primarily out of self-interest or political and economic expediency. Once firmly in power, they began to enrich themselves by virtue of their positions at the commanding heights of national economy. And once they had thus accumulated sufficient capital in the shadow of state capitalism, they began to modify or reverse their original radical course and revert back to the many of the social and economic policies of the regimes they had replaced.[15]

It was, therefore, only after the plans and programs of secular nationalist leaders (whether of a pro-U.S. capitalist type or of a pro-Soviet "noncapitalist" model) had failed to bear the fruits promised that the disappointed masses of the Muslim world found the radical message of Islam, giving voice to their pent up grievances, attractive. As Hrair Dekmejian puts it: "The recent quest for a return to the Islamic ethos appears to be a natural response to the successive pathological experiences which have buffeted Islamic societies in contemporary times."[16] Or, as John Voll points out, "The failure of existing institutions and regimes to cope with the challenges of the late twentieth century experiences is accepted by most as an important dimension of the [Islamic] resurgence."[17]

Sociohistorical Contours of Islam

A number of sociohistorical comparisons between the industrialized West and the Muslim world, as well as between Islam and other major religions, might help dispel some of the demonizing myths that have been attributed to Islam in the West.

Islam Is Not Monolithic

The view that Islam is a rigid, monolithic, and intrinsically violent religion fails to explain the multitude of interpretations and practices of Islam, both across time and space. It fails to take into account the fact that, for example, both the essence and interpretations of Islam, like those of other major religions, are not independent of the actual social needs and circumstances; and that, as such, its message is as much reactive to real social, political, and economic needs as it is divine and proactive. The view of Islam as an intrinsically violent, antiprogressive religion is not only dangerous but also incapable of explaining the flexibility and maneuverability of Islam, like all religious traditions, to be both rigid and pragmatic, revolutionary and quietist, combatant and pacifist—depending on the social circumstance.

A cursory look at the ruling powers and state policies in the contemporary Muslim world defies perceptions of a monolithic Islamic threat. While most of the ruling authorities in the Muslim world invoke "Islamic principles" to legitimize and strengthen their power, interpretations and implementations of those principles vary significantly from one Muslim country to the next. Such differences can readily be observed in all the major aspects of both polity and policy: the forms of government, domestic policies and programs, as well as international relations and foreign policy. Kings, military rulers, presidents, and clergy all have used Islam to implement their often markedly diverse social and economic programs and to solidify their power.

Diverse, and sometimes diametrically opposed, Islamic interpretations of social, economic, and political issues exist, often side-by-side, both within and between Muslim countries and communities. Not only have the incumbent authorities in recent years tried to utilize Islamic symbolism to advance their objectives and enhance their power, but, perhaps more importantly, the opposition forces and movements have also invoked Islam to attract popular support for their agendas. Such contentious interpretations of Islam can clearly be observed in today's national debates raging in most Muslim countries, including Iran, Iraq, Pakistan, Egypt, Afghanistan, Saudi Arabia, Kuwait, Indonesia, Turkey, Algeria, and Jordan.

Divergent views of the role of Islam in governance and policy is also reflected in the diverse foreign policies and international relations pursued by various Muslim countries. Foreign policy imperatives of Muslim countries, like those of other countries, are determined largely by special interests, specific circumstances, national interests, or geopolitical considerations—not by a pan-Islamic or united nations of Islamic countries. Accordingly, international relations among Muslim countries are no less prone to frictions and conflicts than relations among non-Muslim countries, or among Muslim and non-Muslim countries. Diversity of foreign policy objectives is also reflected in the markedly different relations of Muslim states and Western powers, especially the United States. For example, while ruling powers in Egypt, Saudi Arabia, Kuwait, Jordan, and Pakistan have been among the closest allies of the United States, those in Iran and Libya have been among its severest critics.[18]

These observations—which view the recent revival of political Islam as a response to specific socioeconomic issues, policies, and interests— strongly refute the claim that the revival stems from "a mood and a movement far transcending the level of issues and policies and the governments that pursue them."[19] As John Esposito points out, the claim that attributes the resurgence to the "inherently confrontational nature of Islam" and/or a historical continuity of "the clash of civilizations" tends to "downplay or overlook specific political and socioeconomic causes for Muslim behavior, to see Muslim actions as an irrational reaction rather than a response to specific policies and actions." In this way, continues Esposito, "The primacy of competing political interests, policies, and issues is dismissed or eclipsed by the vision of an age-old rivalry between 'them' and 'us.' "[20]

The Rise of Fundamentalism is Not Limited to Islam

The establishment media and political pundits in the West, especially in the United States, tend to paint the resurgent Islam of recent years with the proverbial broad brush of *Islamic fundamentalism*, maintaining that the resurgence is simply due to the inherently rigid, static, retrogressive, and antimodern foundation of Islam. This represents a distorted, obfuscating interpretation. Despite the fact that the term *Islamic fundamentalism* is readily used to characterize all types of Islamic movements and political activism, "it tells us everything and yet, at the same time, nothing," points out John Esposito.[21] Perhaps the best way to appreciate the facile use of fundamentalism and its inadequacy is to consider the following:

> This term has been applied to the governments of Libya, Saudi Arabia, Pakistan and Iran. Yet what does that really tell us about these states other than the fact that their rulers have appealed to Islam to legitimate their rule or policies? Muammar Qaddafi has claimed the right to interpret Islam, questioned the authenticity of traditions of the Prophet Muhammad, silenced the religious establishment as well as the Muslim Brotherhood, and advocated a populist state of masses. The rulers of Saudi Arabia, by contrast, have aligned themselves with the *ulama* (clergy), preached a more literalist and rigorous brand of Islam, and used religion to legitimate a conservative monarchy.[22]

By focusing almost exclusively on the violent behavior of the frustrated and embattled Muslims, the corporate media and the political pundits of the establishment in the United States tend to create the impression that the rise of religious fundamentalism is a purely Islamic phenomenon. Such depictions are false. The rise of religious fundamentalism is universal—and this universality is not fortuitous. It is because fundamentalism arises largely in response to modernity and secularism, which tend to weaken and threaten religious principles and traditions. Fundamentalism has recently been on the rise not only in Islam but also in Judaism, in Christianity, in Hinduism, in Buddhism, in Sikhism, and even in Confucianism.[23] As John Voll points out,

> By the early 1990s, violent militancy was clearly manifest among Hindu fundamentalists, Buddhists in Sri Lanka, Jewish fundamentalists in Israel, and

others elsewhere. As a result, analyses that interpret the militancy of Islamic fundamentalism as being somehow directly caused by distinctive Islamic doctrines and traditions are increasingly out of touch with the realities of the global religious resurgence of the late twentieth century. The globalization of the resurgence reflects the new realities of what can be seen as a post-secular era.[24]

Furthermore, as Karen Armstrong points out, "Of the three monolithic religions, Islam was in fact the last to develop a fundamentalist strain, when modern culture began to take root in the Muslim world in the late 1960s and 1970s. By this date, fundamentalism was quite established among Christians and Jews, who had had a longer exposure to modern experience."[25] A number of factors tend to make Islamic fundamentalism more visible or dramatic while, at the same time, they tend to mask or downplay Christian or Jewish fundamentalism.

One such factor pertains to the mode of expression or form of manifestation. While Islamic fundamentalism is usually expressed in traditional, direct, personal, or, let us say, "precapitalist" forms of expression, Christian and Jewish fundamentalisms are often masked by modern forms of lobbying or the less-visible methods of market subtleties. For example, the subtle, sophisticated, and institutionalized mode of operation tends to camouflage the fact that the influence of powerful fundamentalist forces over the policies of the administrations of both President Bush and Prime Minister Sharon is not less than the influence of the fundamentalist forces over the state policies of a number of Muslim countries. Religious fundamentalism has in recent years been spreading in both the United States and Israel like wild fires.

In fact, George W. Bush owes his presidency largely to fundamentalist Christian voters, to a coalition of evangelical Christians, Christian "Rapturists," fundamentalist partisans of the biblically "Promised Land" in Palestine, and the relatively more religious voters from the rural areas of the Deep South. The president makes no bones about the fact that he is genuinely committed to their faith-based ideals and their agenda of infusing the society with "moral values." As Eric Margolis of *The Toronto Sun* puts it, "These groups tend to share a loathing of Europe, the UN, the Pope, Muslims in general, Arabs in particular, intellectuals, anything international, and believe themselves God's chosen people. Some born-again Christians see Bush as a kind of messiah. . . . The 41 percent of Americans calling themselves born-again Christians are being whipped into a pro-Bush frenzy by many of their preachers. So much for separation of church and state." Christian Rapturists, one of the fastest growing religious groups, "believe once Greater Israel is created and all Jews converted to Christianity, they will be instantly transported to heaven while the world will be destroyed and all non-believers slowly burned alive. . . . Their unofficial bible, the Left Behind series of books, has sold nearly 60 million copies. They are Bush's most ardent supporters." The president himself has occasionally pointed out that "he communicates with God regularly," and that he is on a "divine mission" to spread God's message and carry out His will. At home, this means returning prayers to public schools, amending the Constitution to include definition of marriage, posting the Ten Commandments in public buildings, overturning Roe v. Wade, and banning the "sacrilegious" stem cell research. Abroad, it means spreading "liberty" by any means necessary, including "changing regimes" by military force.[26]

The rise of religious fundamentalism is even more dramatic in Israel than in the United States. Zealously religious groups in and out of the state apparatus have grown so powerful and moved so far to extreme social and political positions that they make the notoriously hard-line Ariel Sharon look moderate. This is most clearly reflected in the context of the Jewish settlements in the occupied territories. Most observers of the Palestinian-Israeli conflict agree that Ariel Sharon's strategy of dismantling a handful of settlements in the Gaza Strip is essentially a ploy designed to save and consolidate all other settlements. But even this halfhearted, minimalist idea is not acceptable to the mostly fanatical settlers. As the settlers see it, points out Uri Avnery, "even the idea of removing one single settlement is a *casus belli* [cause for war]. It attacks everything that is holy to them. . . . The most eminent rabbis of the 'Religious Zionist movement' have declared that the evacuation of a settlement is a sin against God and have called upon the soldiers to refuse orders. Hundreds of rabbis, including the rabbis of the settlements and the rabbis of the religious units in the army have joined the call." Here is how Avnery summarizes some of the fundamentalist views of the expanding religious forces in Israel:

> They challenge not only the policy of the government, but Israeli democracy as such. They declare openly that their aim is to overthrow the State of Law and put in its place the State of the Halakha. . . . When the resolutions of the Knesset contradict the Halakha (Jewish religious law), the Halakha has priority. After all, the Knesset is just a gang of corrupt politicians. And what value have the secular laws, copied from the Goyim (Gentiles), compared to the word of God, blessed be his name?

The religious-rightist rebels are powerfully motivated. Many of them believe in the Kabbala . . . which says that today's secular Jews are really Amalekites who succeeded in infiltrating the People of Israel at the time of the exodus from Egypt. God Himself has commanded, as everyone knows, the eradication of Amalek from the face of the earth.[27]

A second factor that tends to magnify Islamic fundamentalism while minimizing or disguising Jewish and Christian fundamentalism seems to be related to the propaganda effects of the corporate media[28] of the West, especially of the United States. These include not only radio, television, and newspapers but also journals, books, movies, art, and so on. Analysis of the sociopolitical, economic, and historical reasons for the anti-Islamic biases of the mass media of the West is beyond the purview of our discussion here. Whatever the reasons, the facts of biases and prejudices are undeniable. For example, while the establishment media eagerly portray every angry reaction to foreign aggression by every child anywhere in the Muslim world as a manifestation of Islamic extremism, it rarely points out the fact that powerful fundamentalist Christian and Jewish forces support the more destructive military operations or geopolitical polices that trigger such violent reactions in the first place. Another example: When Muslims, as individuals or groups, rebel against the invasion or occupation of their lands and property, the corporate media tend to brand them as Jihadists, or "holy warriors," implying (and sometimes explicitly stating) that such rebellious actions are prompted not in reaction to occupation but by an inherent Islamic hatred of strangers or infidels. By contrast, often no mention is made of the fact that the occupying external forces are not very dissimilar to the crusaders of an earlier age; instead, the occupying powers are portrayed as liberators and democracy builders.

A third factor that makes the rise of fundamentalism in the Muslim world more dramatic is the oppressive foreign intervention. Proponents of the theory of "the clash of civilizations" attribute negative reactions in the Muslim world to the suffocating policies of the imperial powers almost exclusively to Muslims' fear of modernization. Yet, such essentially political reactions are prompted mainly by the predatory imperial policies and the unwelcome, onerous, and constant symbols of foreign presence in their lands, their markets, and their daily lives. That presence is imposed in a variety of ways: sometimes via direct military occupation, sometimes through military bases and advisors, sometimes through financial gurus of transnational corporations, sometimes through economic embargoes, and sometimes through aggressive commercialism and shabby cultural products such as violent video games or pornographic movies.

More importantly, people in many Muslim countries feel imperial pressure through the vicarious authority of the dictatorial regimes that rule their countries by virtue of the support of foreign powers. Since such unpopular, client regimes do not tolerate dissent or countenance alternative views, opposition views are often expressed in "illegal," violent ways. Western imperial policies in the Muslim world are, therefore, directly responsible for Muslims' resort to religion and the rise of fundamentalism because those policies prop up loyal but dictatorial rulers who suppress economic and democratic rights of their people in order to safeguard their nefarious interests, along with those of their foreign patrons.

Atrocities are Committed in the Name of Most Religions—Not Just Islam

The concept that Islam is a notably confrontational and belligerent religion stems from either intellectual dishonesty or historical ignorance or both. It fails to consider the fact that many of the angry and humiliated people in the Muslim world resort to religion as a source of self-assertion and a force of inspiration in the face of foreign aggression. It focuses on the angry and sometimes violent responses of the Muslim people to foreign aggression as evidence of "terroristic Muslim behavior," but it fails to acknowledge the fact that such responses are often reactions to certain imperialistic actions, or as Chalmers Johnson puts it, "blowbacks" from earlier foreign aggressions or imperial policies.[29] It also fails to acknowledge the fact that Muslim people are not making any claims on other people's territory, or resources, or markets. All they want is to be respected, to be left alone, and to be allowed to decide for themselves. Is this too much to ask?

More importantly, this prejudiced characterization of Islam and/or Muslims fails to consider the fact that the atrocities committed in the name of Christianity far surpass those committed in the name of Islam. The brutal wars of the Crusades, fought in the name of Christianity, continued sporadically over hundreds of years. Written in blood and terror, they were often prompted by a desire to usurp the wealth and treasures of other nations through looting and spoils of war in order to ease the domestic economic and political difficulties of the papacy and major princes of Europe.

But the atrocities committed in the name of Christianity did not cease with the end of the Middle Ages and the Crusades. Transition to capitalism and the dawn of the modern era brought forth its own share of aggression and horrific wars that were also often fought in the name of Christianity and civilization. These included the Holy Inquisition, the expulsion of the Jews from Spain, the Reformation, the Counter-St. Bartholomew Massacre, Cromwell's slaughter in Ireland, the enslavement and widespread extermination of native peoples in Africa and the Americas, the Eighty Years' War in Holland, the expulsion of the Huguenots from France, the pogroms, the burning of witches, and many other horrific events right down to the Holocaust itself, which was largely the work of people who considered themselves, as did the slave drivers of America's South, to be Christians.[30]

Aside from the wars motivated by or waged in the name of religion, far more blood and conflicts can be detected in European and American history than that of the Muslim world. Here is a sample, as collected by John Chuckman: the Hundred Years' War, the War of the Spanish Succession, the Seven Years' War, the slave trade, the Vendée, the Napoleonic Wars, the Trail of Tears, the Opium War, African slavery in the American South, the American Civil War, the Franco-Prussian War, the massacre in the Belgian Congo, the Crimean War, lynchings, the Mexican War, the Spanish-American War, World War I, the Spanish Civil War, World War II, the Korean War, the Vietnam War—and now President Bush's wars of preemption and regime change. As Chuckman puts it, "How anyone with this heritage can describe Islam as notably bloodthirsty plainly tells us that immense ignorance of history is at work here."[31]

Today many observers detect similarities between the Bush administration's war policies in the Muslim world and those that drove the Crusades; or, more importantly, between the insidious theories of "the clash of civilizations" and those that underpinned the Crusades. While the historical context, the tactics, and the means of warfare are vastly different, the drive to war, both then and now, seems to be fueled primarily by economic interests. Then, economic resources included precious metals, articles of art, and other treasures that were coveted by the popes and princes of Europe. Now, they include war-induced or war-related profits for big corporations, especially military industries, and related contractors.

Not surprisingly, many people in the Muslim world—as well as in the rest of the world, including the United States—are deeply concerned about the gravity of the implications of the theory of "the clash of civilizations," and the concomitant policy of preemptive wars. Sadly, the Bush administration's policy in the Muslim world and its rhetoric of "war on terrorism" (often couched in missionary, biblical terms such as "axis of evil, good versus evil, day of reckoning, evildoers," and the like) tend to reinforce such fears.

Historical evidence indicate that, contrary to popular perceptions in the West, far more tolerance can be detected in the history of Muslims than that shown by the history of Christians—bloody characters like Tamerlane notwithstanding. For example, Muslims, starting with the Prophet Mohammed himself, do not reject Christianity or Judaism. As Georgie Anne Geyer points out, "The Prophet Mohammed was so tolerant for his age (the seventh century) that he saw the Muslim Allah as existing existentially as the same god of the Jews and the Christians, upon whose religions he syncretistically based Islam."[32] Accordingly, Muslims view the historical place and the mission of the Prophet Mohammed in line and in accordance with the traditions of the major Judeo-Christian prophets (Noah, Abraham, Moses, and Jesus) who preceded him.

The expansion of the Islamic Empire to Europe (eighth century) was hardly brutal, or predatory, or restrictive and oppressive. On the contrary, it ushered in a period of tremendous growth in trade, in arts and sciences, and in culture. The Muslim kings of Spain, known as Moorish kings, tended to follow the same tolerant attitude toward religion that the classical Romans had done. The Romans allowed any religion to flourish, often officially adopting the gods of a conquered people, so long as the religion represented no political threat to Rome's authority. By and large, the Moorish rulers continued to adhere to this tradition of broadmindedness: "A remarkably tolerant society flourished under the Moors in Spain for hundreds of years. Jews, Christians, and Muslims were tolerated, and the talented served the state in many high capacities regardless of religion. Learning advanced, trade flourished."[33]

Recent Return of Religion is Universal

Not only the rise of religious fundamentalism but also the turn to religion in general is a universal development of recent years that goes beyond Islam or the Muslim world. As noted earlier, the recent appeal of religion in the Muslim world has been precipitated largely by a series of disappointments and frustrations over a long period of time, including the inability of the prevailing political and social structures to deliver economic security and political freedom, as well as the oppressive and humiliating interventions from outside. While it is important that policy failures be "properly" identified in the discussions of the generation and accumulation of such frustrations, it is equally important to point out the *systemic* flaws—the shortcomings of the capitalist system—that affect both policy and the socioeconomic environment. Capitalism, especially in the context of the belatedly developing economies, has often been incapable of delivering economic justice and democratic rule. Frustrations with the woes and vagaries of a market economy—especially with the imperatives of globalization of markets—coupled with popular desire for independence from foreign intervention, have provided fertile ground for Islamic resurgence in the last few decades. The rise of political Islam represents, therefore, as much a response to the systemic vices of market mechanism as it does to specific policies—the two are, of course, often inseparable. Without this crucial link, the link between social circumstances and social movements, Islamic resurgence (or any other social protest, for that matter) can hardly be explained satisfactorily.

Viewed in this light, it is not difficult to see that the resurgence represents essentially a new phase, or another form of struggle, in the long social struggles against capitalist injustices and/or imperialist aggressions. Anticapitalist, anti-imperialist struggles have, of course, not been limited to the Muslim world. Nor have such struggles in the Muslim world always taken a religious form. Throughout the nineteenth century and for most of the twentieth century those struggles were led primarily by secular forces. They included secular national liberation movements; radical Left, workers' and peasants' challenges; a whole host of guerilla warfare and "communist" insurgencies, especially in the 1940s, 1950s, and 1960s; as well as socialist, social democratic, and radical nationalist challenges. Global capitalist forces have proven, so far, to be more tenacious than those challenges. The success of world capitalism to defeat, co-opt, exhaust, or neutralize most of those earlier challenges has given birth to new configurations of social forces and new challenges, including the recent return to religion as a mobilizing force.

Formerly "socialist" countries of the "Eastern Bloc" are now pursuing capitalist development. Accordingly, the turn to religion in these countries is no less dramatic than in the Muslim world. As the end of the era of guaranteed employment and economic security—minimal as they were—has led to insecurity and vulnerability for the majority of the people in the former "Soviet Bloc" countries, the appeal and the turn to religion has grown accordingly. Even in the core capitalist countries, especially in the United States, there has been a considerable religious resurgence in recent years. Here too the turn to religion is related to social and economic policies, practices, and circumstances: a shift away from social democracy and welfare state programs to unbridled market forces of neoliberalism.

Likewise, many of the less-developed countries that pursued "noncapitalist" or "socialist-oriented" paths of development in the 1940s, 1950s, and 1960s, and accordingly, eschewed foreign capital and Western patterns of development, are now compelled by market imperatives to follow the neoliberal guidelines of developments and compete with each other to attract international capital. As the neoliberal offensive has dissipated and/or weakened the traditional sources of challenge (Left, labor, and secular radical nationalist forces and organizations) to market pressures, many of the people who resist that offensive are increasingly turning to religion as a source of self-assertion and a force of mobilization. The "return of religion" is, therefore, not limited to the Muslim world; it signifies a global phenomenon. As John Voll puts it, "While the diverse experiences of Muslims in [recent years] cannot simply be equated with religious developments in other traditions, it is also a mistake to view the Islamic developments as isolated phenomena." Voll further points out,

> Although it is interpreted in many different ways, most people now see the Islamic resurgence . . . as part of a global context. This resurgence has distinctive characteristics but it takes place on a world context in which there is also the rise of activist assertions of faith in Christian, Jewish, Hindu, Buddhist, and other major world traditions of religion. The resurgence in each of these cases is better understood when seen in the context of the "worldwide eruption of religious and quasi-religious concerns and themes." The Islamic resurgence in this context can be seen as a dynamic response to the modern historic transformations. It is not a rare and pathological response but rather an effectively articulated response in tune with some of the major global developments of the end of the twentieth century.[34]

Another characteristic of the recent turn to religion—in addition to being a worldwide trend—is that it is no longer limited to militant groups on the fringes of society; it has become a trend that is embraced by almost all social layers and classes. Whereas the poor and working classes are increasingly resorting to religion as a response to joblessness and other economic pressures of market forces, the ruling classes are also increasingly (and more vigorously) adopting religious symbols, terminology, and pretexts to legitimize their rule and justify their policies. Even the educated middle class and urban professionals, who ever since the days of Enlightenment believed that religious people tended to be "uneducated, rural, poor, and conservative," have in recent years turned to religion.[35]

Adoption of religion by the mainstream of society, or "normalization of the religious resurgence," as John Voll calls it, has far-reaching consequences for the Muslim world. Although violent protestations by extremist elements will certainly continue, the widespread use of religion as a mobilizing force of social protest will have a moderating and, ultimately, reforming impact on Islam. While out of official power structure and in opposition, Islamic (or any other) political groups speak and behave quite radically. Once in power, or part of the legal and/or institutionalized channels of political activism, they tend to become pragmatic and play by the rules of nonviolent politics and governance. Experiences of the Islamic parties in Jordan, Turkey, Iran, Bangladesh, and Algeria serve as examples of such a shift in political policy: from violent protests when they were banned or repressed, to nonviolent political activity as they were allowed to participate legally in the political process.

Whatever Happened to the Once-Popular United States in the Muslim World?

Prior to World War II, England and other European powers dominated world politics and markets, not the United States. In its drive to penetrate into those markets in competition with European powers, the United States, often citing its own war of independence from the British Empire, frequently expressed sympathy with the national liberation struggles of the peoples of the colonial and other less-developed regions. Unsurprisingly, this made the United States—not just the country, its people, and its values but also its foreign policy and its statesmen—quite popular in the less-developed world, especially the Muslim world, as it portrayed the prospect of an unconditional ally in a rising world power.

Thus, for example, when the late Egyptian leader Jamal Abdel Nasser faced the European opposition to his state-guided economic development program, he turned to the United States for help. Nasser's appeal for U.S. support had been prompted by the United States' veiled expressions of understanding of Egypt's aspirations to chart an independent national policy. Nasser perceived those sympathetic gestures as signs of genuine friendship and cooperation. But when the United States revealed its conditions for the promised cooperation, the Egyptian leader was deeply disappointed.

One major condition required Egypt to enter into the then U.S.-sponsored military alliance in the region, the Baghdad Pact. This was one of the early military alliances that the United States established in the region, not only to counter the Soviet influence but also to supplant its enfeebled allies, Britain and France. As a savvy statesman, Nasser understood the "necessity" of such alliances and was, in fact, willing to join the proposed military pact. But the United States expected more. In addition, the United States wanted to "shape" Egypt's economic policies. As Mahmood Hussein put it, "the United States claimed the right to control the Egyptian state's economic policies."[36]

Disillusioned—indeed, with his back against the wall—Nasser turned to the Soviet Union to temper the pressure thus exercised against Egypt. Nasser's turn to the Soviet Union was, therefore, precipitated more by expediency—or, more precisely, by default—than by ideological affinity.

Like Egypt's Nasser, Iran's liberal nationalist Prime Minister Mohammed Mossadeq also initially harbored illusions of unconditional friendship with the United States. This was because, in the dispute between Iran and England over the control of Iranian oil, the United States had originally conveyed signs of neutrality, even sympathy, with Iran's grievances against England. Prior to the 1953 nationalization, Iran's oil was essentially controlled by Britain. As promised during his election campaign, Mossadeq took steps to nationalize the country's oil industry soon after being popularly elected to premiership in 1951. As England resisted giving up its control of Iran's oil industry, a severe crisis ensued between the two countries. "Mossadeq had thought that the United States might warn London not to interfere, and for a while Truman and Acheson maintained the pretense of neutrality by advising both sides to remain tranquil."[37] It soon became clear, however, that while trying to weaken the British Empire, the United States was pursuing its own imperialistic agenda. And when Mossadeq resisted compliance with that agenda, he was fatally punished for "insubordination": his democratically elected government was soon overthrown by the notorious 1953 coup, which was orchestrated by the CIA and British intelligence. The coup also brought the Shah—who had fled to Rome—back to power, aboard a U.S. military plane with the CIA chief at his side.

It is now common knowledge that, since the 1953 violent overthrow of Mossadeq's government in Iran, the United States has helped or orchestrated similar coups against duly elected governments in a number of other countries. In each case, the United States replaced such legitimate governments with "friendly" dictatorial regimes of its own choice. A sample of such handpicked regimes includes those of General Pinochet in Chile, the Somoza family in Nicaragua, Duvalier in Haiti, and Ferdinand Marcos in the Philippines. The list of U.S. interventions and adventures abroad is quite long. In his latest best-seller, *Perpetual War for Perpetual Peace: How We Got to Be So Hated*, Gore Vidal lists some 200 such interventions since World War II.[38] Most of today's regimes in the Muslim world (such as those ruling in Pakistan, Egypt, Saudi Arabia, Jordan, Kuwait, and a number of smaller kingdoms in the Persian Gulf area) are able to maintain their dictatorial rule not because their people want them to stay in power but because they are useful to some powerful interests in the United States.

It is not surprising, then, that many people in these countries are increasingly asking: Why can't we elect our own governments? Why can't we have independent political parties? Why can't we breathe, so to speak? Why are our governments so corrupt? Why are our people, especially Palestinians, treated like this? Why are we ruled by regimes we don't like and don't want, but cannot change? And why can't we change them?

Well, the majority of these countries' citizens would answer, "because certain powerful interests in the United States need them and want them in power." To the overwhelming majority of these citizens, the Bush administration's claim of wanting to spread democracy in the Middle East rings woefully hollow; it is perceived as platitudes generated by the neoconservative and/or Likud partisans who have dominated the administration and plunged the region into chaos. "It's an excuse to avoid facing the truth, which is that our problem in the Middle East is our one-sided support for the terrible mistreatment of the Palestinians by the Israelis. That's it. It's not the conditions in the Arab world. It's not the Islamic fundamentalists. It's our own policy, stupid."[39]

Nor is it surprising that many people in the Muslim world, especially the frustrated youth, are flocking into the ranks of militant anti-U.S. forces and employing religion as a weapon of mobilization and defiance. It is also no accident that desperate violent reactions are usually directed at the symbols of U.S. power—not at those of the Japanese, for example. Correlation between U.S. foreign policy and such reactions was unambiguously acknowledged by the members of the U.S. Defense Science Board, who wrote in a 1997 report to the undersecretary of Defense for acquisition and science, "Historical data shows a strong correlation between

U.S. involvement in international situations and an increase in terrorist attacks against the United States."[40]

Calling such tragic and often destructive reactions to U.S. international involvements "blowbacks from imperialistic U.S. foreign policies," Chalmers Johnson in his illuminating book, *Blowback*, lists many instances of U.S. interventions in the domestic affairs of other countries, as well as some of the violent responses to such interventions:

> What the daily press reports as the malign acts of "terrorists" or "drug lords" or "rogue states" or "illegal arms merchants" often turn out to be blowbacks from earlier American operations. . . . For example, in Nicaragua in the 1980s, the U.S. government organized a massive campaign against the socialist-oriented Sandinista government. American agents then looked the other way when the Contras, the military insurgents they had trained, made deals to sell cocaine in American cities in order to buy arms and supplies. If drug blowback is hard to trace to its source, bomb attacks, whether on U.S. embassies in Africa, the World Trade Center in New York, or an apartment complex in Saudi Arabia that housed U.S. servicemen, are another matter.[41]

The point here is, of course, not to condone or justify, in any way, the destructive or terrorizing reactions to U.S. foreign interventions— legitimate grievances do not justify illegitimate responses. Nor is it meant to disrespect the innocent victims of such atrocious reactions, or to disparage the pain and agony of the loss of the loved ones. The point is, rather, to place such reactions in a context, and to suggest an explanation. As Gore Vidal puts it, "It is a law of physics . . . that in nature there is no action without reaction. The same appears to be true in human nature—that is, history."[42] The "actions" Vidal refers to here are U.S. military or covert operations abroad, which are sometimes called state or wholesale terrorism. "Reactions," on the other hand, refer to desperate individual, or group, terrorism, which are also called retail terrorism.

Summary

Close scrutiny of the Muslim world's early responses to the challenges of the modern West reveals that, despite significant resistance, the overall policy was moving in the direction of reform and adaptation. That policy of adaptation and openness continued from the time of the Muslim world's initial contacts with the modern world in the late eighteenth and the early nineteenth centuries until approximately the last third of the twentieth century. During that period, the majority of the political elite and/or national leaders viewed the rise of the modern West, and its spread into their territories, as an inevitable historical development that challenged them to chart their own programs of reform and development. Not only did the political elite, the intellectuals, and government leaders view modernization as the way of the future, but so did many Islamic leaders and scholars, known as "Islamic modernizers."

It is true that obscurantist conservative forces, both religious and otherwise, have always defied reform and resisted change. It is also true that, at times, religious nationalism played an important role in the anticolonial/ anti-imperial struggles. But because Islamic leaders often lacked clear programs or plans for the reconstruction and development of their societies, political leadership on a national level often fell into the hands of secular nationalists who offered such nation-building plans. After World War II, those plans were fashioned either after the U.S. model of market mechanism, as in the cases of the shahs of Iran and the kings of Jordan, or after the Soviet model of "noncapitalist development" and/or Arab "socialism," as in the cases of Nasser's Egypt and Qaddafi's Libya. Both models nurtured dreams of economic progress and political/national sovereignty. Accordingly, secular nationalist leaders who promoted such models, and promised economic well-being and social progress, enjoyed broader popular support than the conservative religious leaders who lacked plans of economic development and national reconstruction.

As long as the hopes and aspirations that were thus generated remained alive, promises of an "Islamic alternative" remained ineffectual in their challenge of the plans of the secular nationalist leaders. But as those hopes gradually and painfully turned into despair and hopelessness, such promises began to sound appealing. By the late 1960s and early 1970s, most of the national governments' hopeful and auspicious plans that had hitherto nurtured dreams of economic progress, democratic rights, and political sovereignty turned out to be hollow and disappointing. Frustrated, many Muslims turned to religion and sought solace in the promise of an "Islamic alternative."

Equally disappointing were the policies of the United States in the Muslim world. Before supplanting the European imperial powers in the region, the United States promised policies of neutrality and evenhandedness in the Muslim world. Once it firmly replaced its European rivals, however, the United States set out to pursue policies that have not been less imperialistic than the policies of its European predecessors. U.S.

imperial policies in the region have, therefore, strongly contributed to the nurturing of the Islamic revival of the recent decades.

These historical observations refute the claim that Islam and/or the Muslim world are inherently incompatible with modernization, and that, therefore, the rise of an Islamic militancy in the last few decades, and the violent reactions such as the 9/11 attacks, are essentially manifestations of "the clash of civilizations." The claim that attributes the Islamic resurgence to the "inherently confrontational nature of Islam" tends to downplay, or overlook, specific socioeconomic factors and geopolitical policies that underlie the rage and reactions of the majority of the Muslim people.

CHAPTER 6

Behind the Invasion of Iraq

There are only two things we should fight for. One is the defense of our homes and the other is the Bill of Rights. War for any other reason is simply a racket.

—General Smedley D. Butler

It is no longer a secret that the plans to recast the geopolitical map of the Middle East, starting with the invasion of Iraq, were drawn up long before the criminal attacks of 9/11 on the World Trade Center and the Pentagon—indeed, long before George W. Bush had arrived in the White House. There is strong evidence that the Bush administration was dedicated to regime change in the region "from the start," points out Paul O'Neill, President Bush's treasury secretary until December 2002: "We were building the case against Hussein and looking at how we could take him out and change Iraq into a new country. . . . It was all about finding a way to do it. That was the tone of it. . . . The President saying, 'Fine. Go find me a way to do this.' "[1] Barely 12 hours after the 9/11 attacks President Bush and his neoconservative advisors of civilian militarists openly declared war when the president told his team, "Get the troops ready. . . . This is a time for self defense. . . . This is our time."[2]

O'Neill's story has since been bolstered by a number of other compelling accounts, including those by Richard Clarke, the Bush administration's national coordinator for counterterrorism, in his *Against All Enemies: Inside America's War on Terror*, by the senior CIA analyst Michael Scheuer's *Imperial Hubris: Why the West Is Losing the War on Terror*, by Bob Woodward of *The Washington Post* in his *The Plan of Attack*, and by James

Bamford in his *A Pretext for War: 9/11, Iraq, and the Abuse of America's Intelligence Agencies.*

Not surprisingly, the partisans of war and militarism in and around the Bush administration viewed the 9/11 attacks as an opportunity to set in motion the war juggernaut they had been busy manufacturing ever since the collapse of the Berlin Wall in 1989. Instead of calling those heinous attacks as crimes against humanity—that required an all-out fight to hunt down the criminal perpetrators through coordinated international intelligence and security forces—the trigger-happy civilian militarists expediently called them "war on America." This, in turn, justified their own "avaricious, premeditated, unprovoked war against a foe who posed no immediate threat [to the United States] but whose defeat did offer economic advantage," as the senior CIA analyst Michael Scheuer put it. And while the bombs were still roaring in Afghanistan, they eyed Iraq as the next target. Once the stage was thus set for war, necessary justifications followed accordingly, including lies, deceptions, and fabrications of intelligence about weapons of mass destruction, about the role of Iraq in the 9/11 attacks, and about "Saddam Hussein's threat to the United States."

The question is why? What are the driving forces behind the administration's tendency to war and militarism in general and the invasion of Iraq in particular? And why are Americans allowed to die not only because of horrendous lies but, even more appallingly, after those lies have been effectively exposed?

Official explanations such as weapons of mass destruction, Saddam's threat to the United States, or his connection to Al-Qaedeh, can now easily be dispensed with as flimsy, harebrained pretexts for the invasion of Iraq. Critics have, instead, pointed to a number of other factors behind the drive to war. Those factors are divided into two categories in this chapter: secondary or minor factors and primary or major ones. Included among secondary reasons for the war are the role of domestic politics, the influence of the so-called neoconservative ideologues, and the role of oil. Primary or major factors include the military-industrial complex and the militant Zionist proponents of "greater Israel." I will call the unofficial, unspoken, de facto alliance between these two major forces, precipitated by a convergence of their respective interests on war and political convulsion in the Middle East, the military-industrial-Likud alliance. After briefly discussing the secondary factors, I will then discuss in some detail the crucial role of this alliance in the march to war.

Minor or Secondary Reasons for the War

The Role of Domestic Politics

One popular theory of the Bush administration's decision to invade Iraq emphasizes the role of domestic politics in the drive to war. Top among domestic considerations that might have influenced the push to war is said to be George W. Bush's political need to bolster his widely disputed legitimacy as president, to maintain his 9/11-induced strong status as commander in chief, and to shore up his chances of reelection as "war president." Other domestic factors that might have contributed to the drive to war include the need to divert attention away from the administration's huge tax relief to the wealthy, from the Department of Justice's curtailment of civil liberties, from corporate scandals and the looting of workers' pension funds by the corrupt and highly paid corporate leaders, and from the dubious business records of both the president and vice president before coming to the White House—especially their ties to the scandalous offshore business operations designed to dodge taxes, the so-called offshore tax-havens.[3]

While such considerations might have played important roles in the administration's push to war, initial ideas and designs of "regime change" in Iraq, as well as the institutional and political infrastructure for mobilization and preparation for war, came from the military-industrial-Likud alliance and their elaborate network of surrogate think tanks for war and militarism in the Middle East. As was shown in chapter 4 of this study, the military-industrial complex had since the demise of the Soviet Union been searching for substitutes for the "communist threat" of the Cold War era and systematically planning "small, controllable, low- and mid-intensity" local or regional wars in order to fend off demands for military downsizing and "peace dividends." Domestic politics, undoubtedly, played a significant, but largely facilitating, role in the implementation of that long-planned agenda of war and militarism.

Surely there was a convergence of interests between President Bush's desire for reelection on "national security" grounds and the Pentagon's desire to instigate war and convulsion abroad in order to assure continued expansion of military spending. But it was not so much a case of a strong president using the military establishment for personal political gains as it was the powerful military establishment that manipulated the unseasoned president for its grandiose, long-term designs: to keep the nation in perpetual war or in the grip of constant fear in order to ensure its lion's share of national treasure. (The role of the president, and how he was manipulated by the military-industrial-Likud alliance into the invasion of Iraq, is discussed later in this chapter under the subheading "Defining the President's Mission.") This distinction is important as it might help a better understanding of the sociohistorical role of militarism and/or military imperialism, which is much grander and more powerful than the power or authority of a president, even a wise and worldly one. This is not to deny the importance of political personas or the role of individuals in sociopolitical developments but to underline the sources and limitations of political personas, and to indicate that the role of militarism as an aspect or stage of imperialism, which may be called military or parasitic imperialism, looms larger than the role of individual politicians, including presidents.

For example, most of the Bush administration's plans of war and militarism were drawn up in the early 1990s in response to the collapse of the Berlin Wall in order to fend off demands for cuts in military spending. The plans were crafted during the administration of President Bush Sr., although largely by the very same militaristic figures (Dick Cheney, Paul Wolfowitz, and Lewis "Scooter" Libby, among others) who held key positions in the military establishment and who returned to power again when George Bush Jr. ascended to presidency. After a number of revisions, those plans were published in 1992 as an important document titled Defense Planning Guidance also called "America's Defense Strategy for the 1990s," which bore Dick Cheney's name as the defense secretary of the time. The document was basically neglected by President Clinton, only to be dusted off and put into effect a decade later as its authors returned to power as part of the Bush Jr. team. Although the new administration replaced Cheney's name with Rumsfeld's in May 2002, it retained the document's title as in 1992, Defense Planning Guidance. As shown later in this chapter, the document served as the cornerstone of President Bush's foreign policy, especially his strategy of "preemptive strike" and/or "regime change."

The Role of the Cabal of Neoconservatives

Another popular view regarding the forces behind the Bush administration's tendency to war focuses on the dominant role of the neoconservative militarists in and around the administration. The neoconservative ideologues often claim that their aggressive foreign policy is inspired primarily by democratic ideals and a desire to spread democracy and freedom worldwide—a claim that is far too readily accepted as genuine by corporate media and foreign policy circles. This is obviously little more than a masquerade designed to mislead the public and fend off criticism of their unilateral military adventures. The neoconservatives' earlier policies of vehement opposition to the anti–Vietnam War faction of the Democratic Party, and later to President Jimmy Carter's human rights policies, as well as their selective condemnation of human rights abuses by allies and enemies, make a mockery of their democratic pretenses.

Some critics attribute the near-missionary policies and politics of the cabal of neoconservatives in justifying and mobilizing for war to their dedication to the Likud agenda of Prime Minister Ariel Sharon of Israel, that is, to the goal of effecting geopolitical changes in the Middle East in ways that will eliminate opposition to the designs of hard-line Zionists for the future of Israel. Due to its importance, this issue is examined in some detail later in this chapter. Other critics attribute the militaristic role of neoconservatives to pure ideology: that the small but influential cabal of starry eyed ideologues, bent on spreading the U.S. economic and political system, along with American power and influence, managed to single handedly drive the country to war through lies and false pretexts. Some of these critics compare the "ideologically driven" neoconservative militarists to the idealistic Jacobinic forces of more than two centuries ago in Europe, the eighteenth-century French revolutionaries whose intention to remake Europe in revolutionary France's image launched the Napoleonic Wars. Proponents of this thesis further argue that the neoconservatives' domination of the Bush administration's foreign policy amounted to a political coup d'etat.[4]

While this argument may not be altogether false, it is woefully deficient. By placing an inordinately high emphasis on pure or abstract ideology, and on political personas or the role of individuals, the argument tends to lose sight of the bigger, but largely submerged, picture: the powerful military-industrial-Likud interests—the real architects of war and militarism—that lie behind the façade of neoconservative figures in and around the Bush administration. There is clear evidence, some of which is shown later in this chapter, that the leading neoconservative figures have been longtime political activists who have worked through think tanks set up to serve either as the armaments lobby or the Likud lobby or both—going back to the 1990s, 1980s, and, in some cases, 1970s. These corporate-backed militarist think tanks include the American Enterprise Institute, Project for the New American Century, Center for Security

Policy, Middle East Media Research Institute, Washington Institute for Near East Policy, Middle East Forum, National Institute for Public Policy, and Jewish Institute for National Security Affairs. There is also evidence that the major components of the Bush administration's foreign policy, including the war on Iraq, were designed long before George W. Bush arrived in the White House—largely at the drawing boards of these think tanks, often in collaboration, directly or indirectly, with the Pentagon and the arms lobby. (Elaboration and substantiation of this point are provided later in this chapter, in the section subtitled "The Demise of the Soviet Union, the Convergence of Interests on War, and the Unholy Alliance.")

Take the Center for Security Policy (CSP), for example. It "boasts that no fewer than 22 former advisory board members are close associates in the Bush administration. . . . A sixth of the center's revenue comes directly from defense corporations." The center's alumni in key posts in the Bush administration include its former chair of the board, Douglas Feith, who now serves as undersecretary of Defense for policy, Pentagon Comptroller Dov Zakheim, former Defense Policy Board Chair Richard Perle, and longtime friend and financial supporter Defense Secretary Donald Rumsfeld. In its 1998 annual report, the center "listed virtually every weapons-maker that had supported it from its founding, from Lockheed, Martin Marietta, Northrop, Grumman, and Boeing, to the later 'merged' incarnations of same—Lockheed Martin, Northrop Grumman, and so forth."[5]

Likewise, the American Enterprise Institute (AEI), an influential Washington think tank and a major lobbying force for the military-industrial-Likud alliance, can boast of being the metaphorical alma mater of a number of powerful members of the Bush administration. For example, Vice President Dick Cheney and his wife Lynne Cheney, State Department arms control official John Bolton, and former chair of the Defense Policy Board Richard Perle all have had long-standing ties with the institute. The institute played a key role in promoting Ahmed Chalabi's group of Iraqi exiles, the Iraqi National Congress (INC), as a major Iraqi opposition force "that would be welcomed by the Iraqi people as an alternative to the regime of Saddam Hussein" once the Untied States overthrew that regime. "From 1998 on, when there was U.S. government money openly available to support the Iraqi opposition to Saddam Hussein due to the AEI-backed Iraqi Liberation Act, Chalabi's INC grabbed the bulk of the funding." In return, the INC, working closely with the AEI, played an important role in the justification of the invasion of Iraq. It served, for example, as a major source of (largely fabricated) intelligence for the civilian militarists of the Pentagon whenever they found the intelligence gathered by the CIA and the State Department at odds with their plans of invading Iraq.[6]

Another example of the interlocking network of neoconservative forces in the Bush administration and the militaristic think tanks that are dedicated to the advancement of the military-industrial-Likud agenda is reflected in the affiliation of a number of influential members of the administration with the Jewish Institute for National Security Affair (JINSA). JINSA "is on record in its support of the Israeli occupation of the West Bank and against the Oslo Accord. . . . In its fervent support for the hard-line, pro-settlement, anti-Palestinian Likud-style policies in Israel, JINSA has essentially recommended that 'regime change' in Iraq should be just the beginning of a cascade of toppling dominoes in the Middle East."[7]

JINSA has influential friends either as liaisons with or members of the Bush administration. For example, Assistant Secretary of Defense Douglas Feith is a former JINSA advisor. General Jay Garner, the initial head of the U.S. occupation authority in Iraq, is also a former JINSA advisory board member. JINSA advisor Michael Ladeen, who also unofficially advises the Bush administration on Middle Eastern issues, has occasionally talked about the coming era of "total war," indicating that the Bush administration should expand its policy of "regime change" in Iraq to other countries in the region such as Iran, Syria, and Saudi Arabia. "In keeping with its role as a cheerleader for U.S. intervention in the Middle East, JINSA chose to honor Deputy Secretary of Defense Paul Wolfowitz . . . to receive the 2002 edition of its Henry M. 'Scoop' Jackson public service award. The corporate sponsor of the affair was Northrop Grumman, a company that Wolfowitz worked for as a paid consultant prior to joining Rumsfeld's Pentagon."[8]

The fact that neoconservative militarists of the Bush administration are organically rooted in the military-industrial complex and/or the militant Zionist supporters of "greater Israel" is even more clearly reflected in their incestuous relationship with the jingoistic lobbying think tank Project for the New American Century (PNAC). Like most of its counterpart institutes within the extensive network of neoconservative think tanks, PNAC was founded by a circle of powerful political figures a number of whom later ascended to key positions in the Bush administration. As William Hartung (author of *How Much Are You Making on War, Daddy?*) describes, "In many ways, the founding of PNAC in 1997 marked the opening salvo in the formation of the Bush policy of aggressive unilateralism. The signatories of PNAC's founding statement of principles are a rogue's gallery of intransigent hard-liners, ranging from Iran-Contra re-treat Eliot Cohen, to ex-Pentagon hawks I. Lewis Libby, Paul Wolfowitz, and Donald Rumsfeld, to neo-con standbys Frank Gaffney, former Reagan drug czar William Bennett, and Norman Podhoretza, to the President's brother and partner in electoral crime, Jeb Bush." Add the signature of Vice President Dick Cheney to the list of PNAC founders "and you have the bulwarks of the neo-con network that is currently in the driver's seat of the Bush administration's war without end policies all represented in PNAC's founding document."[9]

A closer look at the professional records of the neoconservative players in the Bush administration indicates that "32 major administration appointees . . . are former executives with, consultants for, or significant shareholders of top defense contractors."[10] For example, James Roche, former Air Force secretary who took over the Army, is a former president of Northrop Grumman; his assistant secretary Nelson Gibbs is another Northrop alumnus. An undersecretary at the Air Force, Peter Teets, was chief operating officer at Lockheed while Michael Wynne, a Defence Department undersecretary, was a former senior vice president at General Dynamics. Defence Secretary Donald Rumsfeld himself is an ex-director of a General Dynamics subsidiary, and Paul Wolfowitz, deputy defence secretary, acted as a paid consultant to Northrop Grumman. Today, point out Hartung and Ciarrocca, the armaments lobby "is exerting more influence over policymaking than at any time since President Dwight D. Eisenhower first warned of the dangers of the military-industrial complex over 40 years ago."[11] (For more on the dubious business relationship between the Pentagon Brass and its prime contractors, please see chapter 7.)

This sample evidence indicates that the view that the neoconservative militarists' tendency to war and aggression is inspired by an ideological passion to spread American ideals of democracy is clearly unwarranted. Their success in orchestrating the unprovoked war against Iraq stemmed largely from the fact they were working essentially on behalf of two immensely powerful special interests—the military-industrial complex and the influential Likud lobby in the United States. Neoconservative architects of war and militarism derive their political clout and policy effectiveness from the political machine and institutional infrastructure of these powerful interests. Thus, to the extent that the neoconservatives' ascendance to the commanding heights of U.S. foreign policy is comparable to a "political coup d'etat," as some observers have suggested, it is more akin to a military coup d'etat, engineered by some highly influential special interests, than one prompted simply by a handful of starry eyed ideologues working out of a commitment to some abstract ideals of democracy.[12]

The Role of Oil

A most widely cited factor behind the Bush administration's drive to war is said to be oil. "No Blood for Oil" has been a rallying cry for most of the opponents of the war. While some of these opponents argue that the war is driven by the U.S. desire for cheap oil, others claim that it is prompted by big oil's wish for high oil prices and profits. Interestingly, most critics use both claims interchangeably without paying attention to the fact that they are diametrically opposed assertions.

Not only do the two arguments contradict each other, but each argument is also wanting and unconvincing on its own grounds; not because the United States does not wish for cheap oil, or because big oil does not desire higher oil prices, but because war is no longer the way to achieve these objectives. To the extent that some champions of war and militarism like Paul Wolfowitz occasionally insinuate that the desire to gain access to cheap oil was part of the reason for the invasion of Iraq, they seem to be disingenuously manipulating oil—as a "national interest" issue—to camouflage other nefarious interests that drive the Bush administration's war juggernaut: the military-industrial-Likud interests.

The widely shared view that the U.S. desire for cheap oil lurks behind the Bush administration's drive to war in the Middle East rests on the dubious assumption that access to cheap oil requires control of oil fields and/or oil producing countries. There are at least two problems with this argument.

First, if control of or influence over oil producing countries in the Middle East is a requirement for access to cheap oil, the United States already enjoys significant influence over some of the major oil producers in the region—Saudi Arabia, Kuwait, and a number of other smaller producers. Why, then, would the United States want to bring about war and political turmoil in the region that might undermine that long and firmly established influence?

Let us assume for a moment that the neoconservative militarists are sincere in their alleged desire to bring about democratic rule and representational government in the Middle East. Let us further assume that they succeed in realizing this purported objective. Would, then, the thus-emerging democratic governments, representing the wishes of the majority of their citizens, be as accommodating to U.S. economic and geopolitical objectives, including its oil needs, as are its currently friendly rulers in the region? Most probably not.

Second, and more importantly, access to oil, cheap or otherwise, no longer requires control of oil fields or oil producers—as was the case in times past. For more than a century, that is, from the early days of oil extraction in the United States in the 1870s until the mid-1970s, the price of oil was determined administratively, that is, by independent producers operating in different parts of the world without having to compete with each other. Beginning with the 1950s, that pattern of local, noncompetitive price determination began to gradually change in favor of regional and/or international markets. By the mid-1970s, an internationally competitive oil market emerged that effectively ended the century-old pattern of local, administrative pricing. Since then, any country or company can have as much oil as they wish if they pay the going market (or spot) price.[13] It is true that collective supply decisions of oil producing countries can, and sometimes does, affect the competitively determined market price. But a number of important issues need to be considered here.

To begin with, although such supply manipulations obviously affect or influence market-determined prices, they do not determine those prices. In other words, competitive international oil markets determine its price with or without oil producers' supply manipulations. Such supply managements, however, do cause deviations from market-determined prices. Specifically, producers' policy to sometimes curtail or limit the supply of oil, the so-called limited flow policy, is designed to raise the actual trading price above the market-determined price in order to keep high-cost U.S. producers in business while leaving low-cost Middle East producers with an above average, or "super," profit. While for low-cost producers this limited flow policy is largely a matter of making more or less profits, for high-cost U.S. producers it is a matter of survival, of being able to stay in or go out of business—an important but rarely mentioned or acknowledged fact.

A hypothetical numerical example might be helpful here. Suppose that the market-determined, or free-flow, price of oil is $30 per barrel. Further, suppose this price entails an average rate of profit of 10 percent, or $3 per barrel. The word "average" in this context refers to average conditions of production, that is, producers who produce under average conditions of production in terms of productivity and cost of production. This means that producers who produce under better-than-average conditions, that is, low-cost, high productivity producers, will make a profit higher than $3 per barrel while high-cost, low efficiency producers will end up making less than $3 per barrel. This also means that some of the high-cost producers may end up going out of business altogether. Now, if the limited flow policy raises the actual trading price to $35 per barrel, it will raise the profits of all producers accordingly, thereby also keeping in business some high-cost producers that might otherwise have gone out of business.

Second, supply manipulation (in pursuit of price manipulation) is not limited to the oil industry. In today's economic environment of giant corporations and big businesses, many of the major industries try, and often succeed (just as do oil producers) in controlling supply in order to control price. Take, for example, the automobile industry. Theoretically, automobile producers could flood the market with a huge supply of cars. But that would not be good business as it would lower prices and profits. So, they control supply, just as do oil producers, in order to manipulate price. During the past several decades, the price of automobiles, in real terms, has been going up every year, at least to the tune of inflation. During this period, the industry (and the economy in general) has enjoyed a manyfold increase in labor productivity. Increased labor productivity is supposed to translate into lower costs and, therefore, lower prices. Yet, that has not materialized in the case of this industry—as it has in the case of, for example, pocket calculators or computers. Another example of price control through supply manipulation is the case of U.S. grain producers. The so-called set aside policy that pays farmers not to cultivate part of their land in order to curtail supply and prop up price is not different—no, it is worse—than OPEC's policy of supply and/or price manipulation.

Third, OPEC's desire to sometimes limit the supply of oil in order to shore up its price is limited by a number of factors. For one thing, the share, and hence the influence, of Middle Eastern oil producers as a percentage of world oil production has steadily declined over time, from almost 40 percent when OPEC was established to about 30 percent today.[14] For another, OPEC members are not unmindful of the fact that inordinately high oil prices can hurt their own long-term interests as this might prompt oil importers to economize on oil consumption and search for alternative sources of energy, thereby limiting producers' export markets. OPEC members also know that inordinately high oil prices could precipitate economic recessions in oil importing countries that would, once again, lower demand for their oil. In addition, high oil prices tend to raise the cost of oil producers' imports of manufactured products as high energy costs are usually reflected in high production costs of those manufactured products.

Now let us consider the widely shared view that attributes the Bush administration's drive to war to the influence of big oil companies in pursuit of higher oil prices/profits. As noted, this is obviously the opposite of the "war for cheap oil" argument, as it claims that big oil tends to instigate war and political tension in the Middle East in order to cause an oil price hike and increase its profits. Like the "war for cheap oil" theory, this claim is not supported by evidence. Although the claim has an element of a prima facie reasonableness, that apparently facile credibility rests more on precedent and perception than reality. Part of the perception is due to the exaggerated notion that both President Bush and Vice President Cheney were "oil men" before coming to the White House. But the fact is that George W. Bush was never more than an unsuccessful petty oil prospector and Dick Cheney headed a company, the notorious Halliburton, that sold (and still sells) services to oil companies and the Pentagon.

The larger part of the perception, however, stems from the fact that oil companies do benefit from oil price hikes that result from war and political turbulence in the Middle East. Such benefits are, however, largely incidental. Surely, American oil companies would welcome the spoils of the war (in the form of oil price hikes) in Iraq or anywhere else in the world. From the largely incidental oil price hikes that follow war and political convulsion, some observers automatically conclude that, therefore, big oil must have been behind the war.[15] But there is no evidence that, at least in the case of the current invasion of Iraq, oil companies pushed for or supported the war.

On the contrary, there is strong evidence that, in fact, oil companies did not welcome the war because they prefer stability and predictability to periodic oil spikes that follow war and political convulsion: "Looking back over the last 20 years, there is plenty of evidence showing the industry's push for stability and cooperation with Middle Eastern countries and leaders, and the U.S. government's drive for hegemony works against the oil industry."[16] As Thierry Desmarest, chairman and chief executive officer of France's giant oil company, TotalFinaElf, put it, "A few months of cash generation is not a big deal. Stable, not volatile, prices and a $25 price (per barrel) would be convenient for everyone."[17]

It is true that for a long time, from the beginning of Middle Eastern oil exploration and discovery in the early twentieth century until the mid-1970s, colonial and/or imperial powers controlled oil either directly or through control of oil producing countries—at times, even by military force. But that pattern of imperialist exploitation of global markets and resources has changed now. Most of the current theories of imperialism and hegemony that continue invoking that old pattern of big oil behavior/exploitation tend to suffer from an ahistorical perspective. Today, as discussed earlier, even physically occupying and controlling another country's oil fields will not necessarily be beneficial to oil interests. Not only will military adventures place the operations of current energy projects at jeopardy, but they will also make the future plans precarious and unpredictable. Big oil interests, of course, know this; and that's why they did not countenance the war on Iraq: "The big oil companies were not enthusiastic about the Iraqi war," says Fareed Mohamedi of PFC Energy, an energy consultancy firm based in Washington D.C. that advises petroleum firms. "Corporations like Exxon-Mobil and Chevron-Texaco want stability, and this is not what Bush is providing in Iraq and the Gulf region," adds Mohamedi.[18]

During the past few decades, major oil companies have consistently opposed U.S. policies and military threats against countries like Iran, Iraq, and Libya. They have, indeed, time and again, lobbied U.S. foreign policy makers for the establishment of peaceful relations and diplomatic rapprochement with those countries. The Iran-Libya Sanction Act of 1996 (ILSA) is a strong testament to the fact that oil companies nowadays view wars, economic sanctions, and international political tensions as harmful to their long-term business interests and, accordingly, strive for peace, not war, in international relations.

On March 15, 1995, President Clinton issued Executive Order 12957 that banned all U.S. contributions to the development of Iran's petroleum resources, a crushing blow to the oil industry, especially to the Conoco oil company that had just signed a $1 billion contract to develop fields in Iran. The deal marked a strong indication that Iran was willing to improve its relationship with the United States, only to have President Clinton effectively nullify it. Two months later, citing "an extraordinary threat to the national security, foreign policy and economy of the U.S.," President Clinton issued another order, 1259, that expanded the sanctions to become a total trade and investment embargo against Iran. Then a year later came ILSA, which extended the sanctions imposed on Iran to Libya as well.

It is no secret that the major force behind the Iran-Libya Sanction Act was the America Israel Public Affairs Committee (AIPAC), the main

Zionist lobby in Washington. The success of AIPAC in passing ILSA through both the Congress and the White House over the opposition of the major U.S. oil companies is testament to the fact that, in the context of U.S. policy in the Middle East, even the influence of the oil industry pales vis-à-vis the influence of the Zionist lobby.[19] ILSA was originally to be imposed on both U.S. and foreign companies. However, in the end it was the U.S. companies that suffered the most due to waivers that were given to European companies after pressure from the European Union. In 1996 the European Union pursued its distaste of ILSA by lodging complaints with the World Trade Organization (WTO) against the United States and through adopting "blocking legislation" that would prevent EU companies from complying with ILSA. Meanwhile, the contract that Iran had originally signed with Conoco was awarded to TotalFinaElf of France for $760 million; the deal also left the door open for the French company to sign an additional contract with Iran for $2 billion in 1997 with their partners Gazprom and Petronas.

In May of 1997 major U.S. oil companies such as Conoco, Exxon, Atlantic Richfield, and Occidental Petroleum joined other (nonmilitary) U.S. companies to create an anti-sanction coalition. Earlier that same year Conoco's Chief Executive Archie Dunham publicly took a stance against unilateral U.S. sanctions by stating that "U.S. companies, not rogue regimes, are the ones that suffer when the United States imposes economic sanctions." Texaco officials have also argued that the United States can be more effective in bringing about change in other countries by allowing U.S. companies to do business with those countries instead of imposing economic sanctions that tend to be counterproductive. Alas, Washington's perverse, misguided, and ineffectual policy of economic sanctions for political purposes—often in compliance with the wishes of some powerful special interests—continues unabated. "Even with the increased pro-trade lobbying efforts of the oil industry and groups like USAEngage, whose membership ranges from farmers and small business owners to Wall Street executives and oilmen, the lack of support from Washington and the Bush administration could not allow them [major oil companies and USAEngage] to overtake or counteract the already rolling momentum of AIPAC's influence on Middle East policy or the renewal of ISLA."[20]

Despite the fact that oil companies nowadays view war and political turmoil in the Middle East as detrimental to their long-term interests and, therefore, do not support policies that are conducive to war and militarism, and despite the fact that war is no longer the way to gain access to cheap oil, the widespread perception that every U.S. military engagement in the region, including the current invasion of Iraq, is prompted by oil considerations continues. The question is why?

This widely shared but erroneous view, as pointed out earlier, is partly due to precedence: the fact that for a long time military force was key to colonial/imperialist control and exploitation of foreign markets and resources, including oil. But the major reason for the persistence of this pervasive perception seems to stem from certain deliberate efforts that are designed to perpetuate the myth in order to camouflage some real economic and geopolitical special interests that drive the U.S. military adventures in the Middle East. There is evidence that both the military-industrial complex and militant Zionist proponents of "greater Israel" disingenuously use oil as a U.S. "national interest issue" in order to disguise their own nefarious special interests and objectives: justification of continued expansion of military spending, extension of sales markets for the products of war and war-related industries, and recasting the geopolitical map of the Middle East according to the designs of hard-line Zionism. Evidence indicates that for every dollar's worth of oil imported from the Persian Gulf region the Pentagon takes $5 out of the federal budget to "secure" the flow of that oil! This is a clear indication that the claim that the U.S. military presence in the Middle East is due to oil consideration is a fraud.[21]

Here is another example of how partisans of war and militarism use oil as a pretext to cover up the real forces behind war and militarism: in the early stages of the invasion of Iraq, when the anti-occupation resistance had not yet taken shape and the invasion seemed to be proceeding smoothly, two of the leading champions of the invasion, Secretary of Defense Donald Rumsfeld and his deputy Paul Wolfowitz, often boasting of the apparent success of the invasion at those early stages, gave frequent news conferences and press reports. During one of those press reports (at the end of an address to delegates at an Asian security summit in Singapore in early June 2003), Wolfowitz was asked why North Korea was being treated differently from Iraq, where hardly any weapons of mass destruction had been found. Wolfowitz responded, "Let's look at it simply. The most important difference between North Korea and Iraq is that economically, we just had no choice in Iraq. The country swims on a sea of oil."[22]

Many opponents of the war jumped on this statement, so to speak, as corroboration of what they had been saying or suspecting all along: the war on Iraq was prompted by oil interests. Yet, there is strong evidence—some of which presented in the preceding paragraphs—that for the last quarter century or so oil interests have not favored war and turbulence in the Middle East, including the current invasion of Iraq. As was shown above, major oil companies, along with many other nonmilitary transnational corporations, have lobbied both the Clinton and Bush administrations in support of changing the aggressive, militaristic U.S. policy toward countries like Iran, Iraq, and Libya in favor of establishing normal, nonconfrontational business and diplomatic relations. Such efforts at normalization of trade and diplomatic relations, however, have failed time and again precisely because Wolfowitz and his cohorts, working through AIPAC and other war-mongering think tanks such as the American Enterprise Institute (AEI), Project for the New American Century (PNAC), and Jewish Institute for National Security Affairs (JINSA), oppose them. These think tanks, in collaboration with a whole host of similar militaristic lobbying entities like Center for Security Affairs (CSA) and National Institute for Public Policy (NIPP), working largely as institutional façades to serve the de facto alliance of the military-industrial-Likud interests, have consistently thwarted efforts at peace and reconciliation in the Middle East—often over the objections and frustrations of major U.S. oil companies. It is a well-established fact that Wolfowitz has been a valuable champion of these jingoistic think tanks and their aggressive unilateral policies in the Middle East. In light of his professional record and political loyalties, his claim that he championed the war on Iraq because of oil considerations can be characterized only as demagogic: it contradicts his political record and defies the policies he has been advocating for the last several decades; it is designed to divert attention from the main forces behind the war, the military-industrial-Likud interests.

These powerful interests are careful not to draw attention to the fact that they are the prime instigators of war and militarism in the Middle East. Therefore, they tend to deliberately perpetuate the popular perception that oil is the driving force behind the war in the region. They do not even mind having their aggressive foreign policies labeled as imperialistic as long as imperialism implies some vague or general connotations of hegemony and domination, that is, as long as it thus camouflages the real, special interests behind the war and political turbulence in the Middle East.

Negative reactions of nonmilitary transnational capital to the Bush administration's drive to war have been expressed by most major financial publications such as *Business Week* and the *Economist*: "Washington's unilateral tendencies have also created nervousness in global financial markets on which the U.S. has become dependent. . . . It would therefore be vital for Washington to rekindle the more cooperative spirit in international economic affairs that existed in recent decades," wrote Jeffrey Garten in the March 17, 2003 issue of *Business Week*, just two days before the invasion of Iraq. Garten further pointed out, "Anyway you cut it, however, there is a disconnect between national security and economic policy. . . . Something—either foreign policy or economic policy—must give." Nearly a month earlier, a group of *Business Week* economic analysts had written an article titled, "War and the Economy: The Outlook," in which they had pointed out, "New Economy growth depends on globalization and innovation, both of which could be dampened by war and a potentially difficult aftermath. . . . The diplomatic tensions surrounding the war could spill over into trade talks, threatening the continued opening of global markets."[23]

The oil and other nonmilitary industries' aversion to war and military adventures in the Middle East stem, of course, from the logical behavior of global or transnational capital in the era of integrated world markets, which tends to be loath to war and international political convulsions. Considering the fact that both importers and exporters of oil prefer peace and stability to war and militarism, why would, then, the flow of oil be in jeopardy if the powerful beneficiaries of war and political tension in the Middle East—the military-industrial-Likud interests—stopped their aggressive policies in the region?

Partisans of war in the Middle East tend to portray U.S. military operations in the region as reactions to terrorism and political turbulence in order to "safeguard the interests of the United States and its allies." Yet, a close scrutiny of action-reaction or cause-effect relationship between U.S. military adventures and sociopolitical turbulence in the region reveals that perhaps the causality is the other way around. That is, social upheavals and political convulsions in the Middle East are more likely to be the result, not the cause, of U.S. foreign policy in the region, especially its one-sided, prejudicial Israeli–Palestinian policy. The U.S. policy of war and militarism in the region seems to resemble the behavior of a corrupt cop, or a mafia godfather, who would instigate fights and frictions in the neighborhood or community in order to, then, portray his parasitic role as necessary for the safety and security of the community and, in the process, fill out his deep pockets.

No matter how crucial oil is to the world economy, the fact remains that it is, after all, a commodity. As such, international trade in oil is as important to its importers as it is to its exporters. There is absolutely no reason that, in a world free of the influence of the powerful beneficiaries of war and militarism, the flow of oil could not be guaranteed by international trade conventions and commercial treaties.[24]

Major or Primary Factors behind the War

Whatever the contributory impact of the factors discussed above (oil, neoconservatives, and domestic politics), they do not seem to be the major driving forces behind the Bush administration's war machine. The administration's war juggernaut, rather, seems to have been driven by an alliance of two other forces: the military-industrial complex and the hard-line Zionist proponents of "greater Israel" in the "promised land." The unspoken, de facto, and largely tactical coalition of these two powerful forces might just as well be called the military-industrial-Likud alliance. Both of these forces perceive their interests better served by fomenting war and tension in the Middle East. It is this convergence of interests, real or perceived, on war and political convulsion in the region that underpins the alliance. The alliance is represented by a cabal of closely connected individuals who are firmly ensconced in the Pentagon. They also hold powerful positions within the National Security Council, the White House, the Congress and, to a lesser extent, the State Department. Not all the members of the cabal hold official positions in the government apparatus. They also work within and through various lobbying think tanks, unofficial interest groups, consulting/research institutes, and the media.

The cabal's strategies of war and militarism revolves around three basic themes: that "the human condition is defined as a choice between good and evil"; that military power and the willingness to use it are the fundamental determinants in relations between states; and that the Middle East and "global Islam" should be the primary focus in U.S. foreign policy. As Halper and Clarke point out, these strategic views of world affairs create certain political and policy tendencies: analyzing foreign policy in terms of "black-and-white, absolute moral categories"; espousing the "unipolar" power of the U.S. and disdaining conventional diplomacy, multilateral institutions, or international law; seeing international criticism as evidence of "American virtue"; and regarding the use of military power as the first, rather than last, resort in dealing with the enemy, particularly when anything less might be considered "appeasement."[25]

Some of the well-known figures of the cabal are as follows: Richard Cheney (vice president), Donald Rumsfeld (secretary of defense), Paul Wolfowitz (undersecretary of defense), Richard Perle (Defense Policy Board), Douglas Feith (Defense Department), James Woolsey (former director of Central Intelligence), David Wurmser (State Department), William Kristol (editor, the *Weekly Standard*), Michael Ladeen (the American Enterprise Institute), Elliot Abrams (National Security Council), Lewis Libby (Vice President Cheney's chief of staff), Fred Ikle (Defense Policy Board), Zalmay Khalilzad (White House), Dov Zakheim (Defense Department), Peter Rodman (Defense Department), Richard Armitage (State Department), Norman Podhoretz (*Commentary* Editor and well-known doyen of the neoconservatives), David Frum (President Bush's speechwriter), John Bolton (State Department), Frank Gaffney (director, Center for Security Policy), Joshua Muravchik (American Enterprise Institute), Martin Peretz (editor in chief, *The New Republic*), Leon Wieseltier (*The New Republic*), Steven Bryen (the Jewish Institute of National Security Affairs, JINSA), and former Representative Stephen Solarz of New York City. Other co-thinkers and collaborators who now seem to be trying to distance themselves from the neoconservatives as a result of the Iraq debacle include the former *Wall Street Journal* editorial features editor Max Boot, *Washington Post* columnist Charles Krauthammer, author of the *Clash of Civilizations* Samuel Huntington, the Brookings Institution's Kenneth Pollack, and author Robert Kaplan.

The number of the publicly known think tanks through which military-industrial-Likud alliance operates include the American Enterprise Institute (AEI), Project for the New American Century (PNAC), Middle East Media Research Institute (MEMRI), Hudson Institute, Washington Institute for Near East Policy, Middle East Forum, National Institute for Public Policy (NIPP), Jewish Institute for National Security Affairs (JINSA), and Center for Security Policy (CSP). Some of the well-known publications that support, formulate, and propagate the views of the alliance are as follows: the *Weekly Standard*, the *New Republic, National Review*, and the *Washington Times*.

Intellectual affinity, political collaboration, and policy coordination between these individuals and lobbying think tanks are well established. Even a cursory look at this list of individuals, their professional background, and the politico-institutional infrastructure through which they have been promoting their political agenda reveals one unmistakable picture: the military-industrial-Likud interests, the main forces behind the war on Iraq—and perhaps beyond, if and/or when they find another opportunity.[26]

The Role of the Military-Industrial Complex

> So long as you have a military class, it does not make any difference what
> your form of government is; if you are determined to be armed to the
> teeth, you must obey the only men who can control the great machinery
> of war. Elections are of minor importance.
>
> —Woodrow Wilson

As discussed in the first chapter of this study, the Founding Fathers of the United States, despite their expansionist tendencies, opposed the idea of maintaining large standing armies on grounds that, as George Washington put it, a large peace-time military establishment "hath ever been considered dangerous to the liberties of a country." With varying degrees, this antimilitarist tradition was maintained until the second half of the twentieth century. Thus, despite the fact that during that period of over 150 years the United States engaged in many wars, and the military force was expanded during each war, demobilization at the end of each conflict reduced the armed forces to their prewar size. In keeping with this tradition, the United States embarked on a major demobilization of the war-time military structure when World War II hostilities ended in 1944. But the demobilization did not last long. With the onset of the Cold War and the U.S. plunge into the Korean War in the late 1940s and early 1950s, remilitarization began in earnest and on a permanent basis— thereby reversing that long tradition of more than 150 years of antimilitarism. In constant (2002) dollars, military spending rose from $150 billion in 1950 (the last year of the ephemeral postwar demobilization) to $500 billion in 1953.[27]

The ensuing expansion of the military-industrial complex signified more than a quantitative growth. Perhaps more importantly, it also resulted, over time, in a qualitative change: change in the attitude, the sense of mission, and the historical outlook of the military establishment. As civilian policy makers relied on military power as the ultimate guarantor of their designs for the postwar world, the military establishment developed a heightened sense of identity—an added sense of autonomy, or existential mission, that went beyond the traditional responsibility for "national security" or for economic and geopolitical gains abroad. The military establishment gradually began to not only implement but also increasingly influence policy—to view itself not just as a means but also as an end in itself. In other words, protracted reliance on and steady expansion of the armed forces that started with the onset of the bipolar world of the Cold War era gradually gave birth to what is historically called militarism, or parasitic imperialism.

As discussed in the second chapter of this study, there is a historical pattern to this evolution of militarism out of an overextended superpower and its over-reliance on the armed forces for economic and geopolitical gains. Despite the importance of this distinction between imperialism in the *usual* sense, that is, economic and/or geopolitical imperialism, and parasitic/military imperialism, such a distinction is absent from most of the theories of imperialism in the context of the Bush administration's aggressive foreign policy, especially its invasion of Iraq. Whereas imperialism in the *usual* sense views military force as a means for economic, territorial, or geopolitical gains, under parasitic imperialism, instigation of international conflicts and military adventures abroad are often prompted not so much by a desire to expand the empire's wealth beyond the existing levels, but by a desire to appropriate the lion's share of the existing wealth and treasure for the military establishment. It is at such stages that military operations abroad, as well as gigantic military apparatuses at home, tend not to be cost-effective even from the standpoint of the empire itself. Today U.S. imperialism seems to have degenerated to this status or stage of parasitic imperialism.[28]

The first open challenge to civilian authority by the military-industrial complex came in the mid-1970s. As the long economic contraction of that decade and the resulting budgetary constraints forced spending cuts on the government, policy makers seriously considered curtailment of the Pentagon budget. As discussed in chapter 4 of this study, a faction of the ruling elite headed by the so-called Trilateralists argued that, in the face of financial challenges, coupled with the tension-reducing (détente) agreements with the Soviet Union, military spending could be significantly cut without compromising "national security or global obligations."

Faced with the prospects of downsizing, the military-industrial complex reacted swiftly. The powerful beneficiaries of the Pentagon budget rallied around Cold Warrior think tanks such as the Committee on the Present Danger and successfully quashed discussions of military curtailment. Instead, once again, by hyping up the "threat of communism," they managed to effectively sabotage the short-lived détente of the first half of the 1970s with the Soviet Union and replace it with heightened tensions between the two superpowers that came to be known as the Second Cold

War in the late 1970s and early 1980s. It was this successful political maneuvering of the champions of militarism that paved the way for the early 1980s' dramatic "rearming of America," as President Reagan put it.

Since the rationale for the large and growing military apparatus during the Cold War years was the "threat of communism," U.S. citizens celebrated the collapse of the Berlin Wall as the end of militarism and the dawn of "peace dividends"—a reference to the benefits that, it was hoped, many would enjoy in the United States as a result of a reorientation of part of the Pentagon's budget toward nonmilitary social needs. Such hopes, however, were quickly shattered. Instead of declaring the end of the Cold War a victory and demobilizing the military structure that had been premised upon it, partisans of war and militarism used it for propaganda purposes and U.S. triumphalism in order to usher in a new, aggressive, and imperial role for the United States.

To stifle the voices that demanded peace dividends, champions of militarism resorted, once again, to the oldest trick in the books of militarism, the tried-and-true pretext of "external threats to our national security/ interests." Instead of the Soviet Union, the "menace of China, rogue states, global terrorism, weapons of mass destruction, the axis of evil, and militant Islam" would have to do as new enemies—thereby justifying appropriation of bigger and bigger shares of national resources for military spending. Having thus successfully substituted "new sources of threat" for the "communist threat" of the Cold War era, powerful beneficiaries of military spending managed not only to maintain but, in fact, expand the Pentagon budget beyond the Cold War years.

The Bush administration's invasion of Iraq can be better understood against this backdrop: the unilateral militarists' post–Cold War strategies to fend off demands for "peace dividends" following the collapse of the Berlin Wall. Most of such strategies were drafted by Pentagon officials soon after the demise of the Soviet Union. In his relatively thorough study of the Pentagon's post–Cold War plans to prevent military/Pentagon downsizing, James Mann of the Center for Strategic and International Studies points out,

> The Berlin Wall came down in November 1989, effectively ending the Cold War and prompting the Pentagon to undertake a search for a new set of principles, in part to prevent Congress, then controlled by the Democrats, from slashing the defense budget. The key participants were Cheney, Wolfowitz and Colin L. Powell, then chairman of the Joint Chiefs of Staff . . . the three men

worked closely together on forestalling cutbacks. The Soviet Union's collapse added new urgency to their task. "What we were afraid of was people who would say, 'Let's bring all of the troops home, and let's abandon our position in Europe,' " recalled Wolfowitz in an interview.[29]

Mann further points out, "Some of the most important and bitterly debated aspects of the war in Iraq—including the administration's willingness to engage in preemptive military action—can be traced to discussions and documents from the early 1990s, when Pentagon officials, under then-Defense Secretary Dick Cheney and then-Undersecretary of Defense Paul D. Wolfowitz, led the way in forging a new, post–Cold War military strategy for the United States." Most of what the Pentagon team crafted in the early 1990s as the post–Cold War military strategy is unclassified and well documented. The end product of those early drafts, which were originally written by Zalmay Khalilzad, then a Wolfowitz aide and now U.S. ambassador to Iraq, and by I. Lewis "Scooter" Libby, then principal deputy undersecretary of Defense for Strategy and now Vice President Cheney's chief of staff, eventually appeared in 1992 as the now well-known Pentagon document titled Defense Planning Guidance (DPG). In January 1993, as the Bush Sr. team left the White House and Cheney's tenure as defense secretary came to an end, the document was published as a government document under Cheney's name as America's "Defense Strategy for the 1990s."[30]

Most of the Bush administration's military strategies—unilateralism, preemption, and regime change—can be clearly traced back to Cheney's "Defense Strategy for the 1990s" of a decade earlier. For example, Cheney's document projected that the United States would build up its military capabilities to such an extent that there could never be a rival. America would develop such enormous superiority in military power and technology that other countries would realize it would be self-defeating to try to compete. Although the document gave lip service to collective responses to global conflicts, it also pointed out that collective action would "not always be timely." Therefore, the document concluded, the United States had to be ready to protect its critical interests abroad "with only limited additional help, or even alone, if necessary." And while the document did not mention preemption specifically, it noted that "sometimes a measured military action can contain or preclude a crisis."

The Pentagon's "Defense Strategy for the 1990s" also spoke about maintaining and expanding America's "strategic depth"—a term coined by the then Defense Secretary Dick Cheney. "Strategic depth" had a geopolitical connotation, meaning that, in the aftermath of the collapse of the Berlin Wall, the United States must extend its global presence—in terms of military bases, listening and/or intelligence stations, and military technology—to areas previously neutral or under the influence of the Warsaw Pact.

The Clinton administration basically ignored Cheney's "Defense Strategy for the 1990s" without actually or officially disclaiming it. During the 1992 presidential election, Clinton's deputy campaign manager, George Stephanapoulos, had aptly characterized the document as an effort by the Pentagon "to find an excuse for big budgets instead of downsizing."

Ever since the emergence of classical liberalism in England in the late eighteenth century as a competing school of socioeconomic thought vis-à-vis mercantilism and colonialism, there have been two rival theories of imperialism: benign, benevolent, or free trade imperialism versus aggressive, colonial-type, or unilateral militarism. While benign or liberal imperialism usually relies on market efficiency and free trade to gain international economic advantage, heavy-handed military imperialism relies on military power to achieve global dominance. And while liberal imperialism prefers negotiations through multilateral institutions—though largely with a paternal/custodial attitude—as vehicles of international trade and diplomatic relations, colonial-type imperialism favors nationalism, unilateralism, and militarism. A clear manifestation of these two competing approaches to international relations in the United States was the 1970s debate between multilateralists, formally affiliated with the so-called Trilateral Commission, and unilateralists, associated with the Committee on the Present Danger. Whereas Trilateralists favored reducing tensions with the Soviet Union and, consequently, reducing military spending, unilateralists opted for heightening tensions with the Soviet Union and increasing military spending. (Of course, no concrete partition separates the two approaches. For example, even the most liberal-minded, free trade imperialists do not hesitate to use military force when their superior international economic position is undermined or threatened by competitors. On the other hand, military imperialists often justify their unilateral military adventures abroad by a desire to spread democracy and bring about economic liberalism.)

Clinton pursued a policy akin to multilateralism and economic liberalism, also called (in recent years/decades) neoliberalism. He sought to advance global U.S. interests through further integration of world markets, additional expansion of multilateral institutions (led by the United States), greater international free trade, and increased development of international alliances, including U.S.-led collective military actions. While representatives of civilian or nonmilitary transnational capital celebrated Clinton's policies of neoliberalism, those of the arms industry and related business spurned those policies because they were not "sufficiently" lucrative for the beneficiaries of war dividends.

Clinton's modest increases of the Pentagon budget and his multilateralist foreign policies fell short of the militarists' expectations, despite the fact he too had his own share of military operations abroad—in Somalia, Iraq, Haiti, and various provinces of the former Yugoslavia, for example. Not surprisingly, the Pentagon authors of the 1992 Defense Planning Guidance (Cheney, Wolfowitz, Lewis "Scooter" Libby, and their collaborators) vehemently criticized his "defense" policies as "inept and passive." They called on the Clinton administration to "finish the job [of overthrowing Saddam Hussein after his military forces were driven out of Kuwait] by arming Iraqi opposition forces and sending U.S. ground troops to defend a base of operation for them in the southern region of the country." In a 1996 editorial, Paul Wolfowitz, one of the authors of the 1992 Defense Planning Guidance, raised the prospect of launching a preemptive attack against Iraq: "Should we sit idly by, with our passive containment policy and our inept covert operations, and wait until a tyrant possessing large quantities of weapons of mass destruction and sophisticated delivery systems strikes out at us?"[31]

As expected, Pentagon critics of President Clinton's military and foreign policies celebrated his departure from the White House and the ascension of George W. Bush to the presidency as the opportunity they were seeking to implement their long-shelved Defense Planning Guidance, including the plan to "finish the job" of ousting Saddam Hussein. Even as the vote count was still being disputed in Florida, and the Supreme Court was deliberating George W. Bush's dubious claim to victory, Dick Cheney moved from Texas to Washington D.C. with a huge entourage and fanfare, camped out next to the White House and stacked the would-be Bush administration with other Pentagon hawks, including all of his coauthors of the 1992 Defense Planning Guidance, ready to move in. While Cheney's and his thus handpicked civilian militarists' de facto occupation of the premises of the White House may not have played as an important role in George W. Bush's rise to the White House as the Supreme Court decision, it nonetheless played a key role in influencing the outcome of that controversial election—a role that largely skipped the attention it deserved.

Thus, with the accession of George W. Bush to the presidency, all the Pentagon contributors to the early 1990s Defense Planning Guidance also returned to positions of power in the government. Cheney of course became vice president, Powell became secretary of state, Wolfowitz moved into the number two position at the Pentagon, as Donald Rumsfeld's deputy, and Lewis "Scooter" Libby, who served as Wolfowitz's deputy during Bush Sr.'s administration, became the vice president's chief of staff and national security adviser.

Although George W. Bush's administration thus arrived in the White House with plans of "regime change" in the Middle East, it could not carry out those plans without a pretext. Before 9/11, the militarists in and around the administration were without tools and excuses to drum up public and political support for the war on Iraq. The 9/11 attacks provided the needed pretext. The administration wasted no time manipulating the public's fear of further terrorist attacks to rally support for the invasion of Iraq, which had nothing to do with the attacks. It heightened people's fear by constant terror warnings while marketing the "war on terrorism" as an epic battle between "good and evil."

Soon after the heinous attacks of 9/11, the Pentagon dusted off the 1992 Defense Planning Guidance, replaced Cheney's name with Rumsfeld's, and promoted it as the Defense Planning Guidance for the "new, post-9/11 circumstance." James Mann, author of *The Rise of Vulcans: The History of Bush's War Cabinet*, describes, "The Clinton administration set aside Cheney's vision without actually repudiating it. A decade later, as the second Bush administration moved toward war with Iraq, the ideas in the 1992 document took on heightened significance. What the Pentagon officials had succeeded in doing, within months of the Soviet collapse, was to lay out the intellectual blueprint for a new world dominated—then, now and in the future—by U.S. military power."[32]

The Pentagon's post-9/11 version of Defense Planning Guidance retains—indeed, strengthens—all the major elements of the 1992 version, although at times it uses slightly modified terminology. The preemptive attacks projected in the original document are now called "unwarned attacks." The old Powell-Cheney doctrine of military "forward presence," put forth in the early 1990s in response to the demise of the Soviet Union, is now called "forwarded deterrence." And the use of overwhelming force to defeat an enemy called for in that old doctrine is now branded as "effects-based" vision. But the new version also adds a few new ideas, including the incredibly dangerous concept of "preemptive strikes" with nuclear weapons. These would be earth-penetrating nuclear weapons used for attacking "hardened and deeply buried targets" such as command-and-control bunkers, missile silos, and heavily fortified underground facilities used to build and store weapons of mass destruction. The new version also directs the military to develop cyber-, laser-, and electronic-warfare capabilities to enhance global capabilities of the U.S. military might.[33]

As the administration was preparing for the invasion of Iraq in early 2003, it also revealed the refurbished Defense Planning Guidance as the "Bush Doctrine" for the new, post-9/11 world. After Rumsfeld's signing of the document in May 2002, the Pentagon leaked it to *The Los Angeles Times* in July and the administration officially endorsed it on the occasion of President Bush's 2002 West Point speech. It is worth noting that what was once called the "Wolfowitz Doctrine" by Pentagon insiders came to be relabeled as the "Bush Doctrine." As David Armstrong points out, "Commentators parrot the administration's line, portraying the concept of preemptory strikes as a 'new' strategy aimed at combating terrorism . . . [yet] Preemption, of course, is just part of the Plan, and the Plan is hardly new. It is a warmed-over version of the strategy Cheney and his coauthors rolled out in 1992 as the answer to the end of the Cold War."[34]

That the U.S. military response to the collapse of the Berlin Wall in 1989 and its response to the collapse of the World Trade Center in 2001 were basically the same should not come as a surprise to anyone familiar with the dynamics and market imperatives of the business of war: continued increase of the Pentagon budget and/or continued expansion of sales markets for the war industry and related businesses. This also confirms the overriding argument of this book: that the pretexts or tactics for pursuing higher profits for the business of war may change (from the "threat of communism" to the "threat of rogue states, global terrorism, militant Islam, . . .") but the objective or strategy remains the same—war and militarism and, consequently, further escalation of the Pentagon budget and war dividends.

This brief review of the events that led to the invasion of Iraq in early 2003 clearly reveals that the plans for the invasion were drawn up nearly a dozen years earlier. As William Hartung and Michelle Ciarrocca of the World Policy Institute write,

> Each major element of the Bush administration's national security strategy . . . was developed and refined before the Bush administration took office, at

corporate-backed conservative think tanks like the Center for Security Policy, the National Institute for Public Policy and the Project for a New American Century. . . . Unilateralist ideologues formerly affiliated with these think tanks, along with the 32 major administration appointees who are former executives with, consultants for, or significant shareholders of top defense contractors, are driving U.S. foreign and military policy.[35]

This is a clear indication of the fact that the cabal of neoconservative militarists is more akin to the executive arm of some real, powerful special interests than a group of starry eyed ideologues committed to the goal of spreading democracy worldwide.

The Role of Militant Zionism

> Peace cannot be kept by force. It can only be achieved by understanding.
>
> —Albert Einstein

Just as the beneficiaries of war dividends, the military-industrial complex, view international peace and stability inimical to their interests, so too the militant Zionist proponents of "greater Israel" perceive peace between Israel and its Palestinian neighbors perilous to their goal of gaining control over the "promised land." The reason for this fear of peace is that, according to a number of the United Nations' resolutions, peace would mean Israel's return to its pre-1967 borders, that is, withdrawal from the West Bank and Gaza Strip. But because proponents of "greater Israel" are unwilling to withdraw from these occupied territories, they are therefore afraid of peace—hence, their continued efforts at sabotaging peace negotiations, including the heinous crime of assassinating the late Prime Minister Yitzhak Rabin for having signed the Oslo Peace Accord with the Palestinians. By the same token, these proponents view war and convulsion (or, as David Ben-Gurion, one of the key founders of the State of Israel, put it, "revolutionary atmosphere") as opportunities that are conducive to the expulsion of Palestinians, to the geographic recasting of the region, and to the expansion of Israel's territory.

This judgment is neither theoretical nor conjectural. It is based on the well-known Zionist philosophy of establishing a Jewish state in the "promised land." It is also based on the actual policies and practices of the leaders of the State of Israel ever since it was founded in 1948. According to that philosophy, conceived and formulated by the pioneers of modern Zionism in the late nineteenth century, institution of the State of Israel must be based on an overwhelmingly (if not homogeneously) Jewish population. Despite occasional public rhetoric to the contrary,

> [t]he idea of transfer [of Palestinians from their land] had accompanied the Zionist movement from its very beginnings, first appearing in Theodore Herzl's diary. In practice, the Zionists began executing a mini-transfer from the time they began purchasing the land and evacuating the Arab tenants. . . . "Disappearing" the Arabs lay at the heart of the Zionist dream, and was also a necessary condition of its existence. . . . With few exceptions, none of the Zionists disputed the desirability of forced transfer—or its morality.[36]

While almost all Zionists would say that they dream of living in Palestine, they greatly differ over what this really means. Generally speaking, two broad approaches have evolved over this issue: the moderate and the radical approaches. Moderate Zionists, who have almost always been a small minority, do not deny the right of non-Jews to live in Palestine. They favor the idea of accommodation and peaceful coexistence with the non-Jewish natives of Palestine within the framework of a democratic, federal state. Accordingly, they oppose the idea of forceful occupation of land, expulsion of indigenous people, and the establishment of a Jewish state based on an exclusively or overwhelmingly Jewish population.

Albert Einstein's continues to be the most well-known name associated with this persuasion. His name, his visits to Israel, and his letters raised a lot of money in support of establishing universities and resettling European Jews suffering under violent anti-Semitism long before the founding of Israel. But even in a cause so dear to his heart, Einstein opposed the establishment of a formal Israeli state based on an exclusively or overwhelmingly Jewish population: "My awareness of the essential nature of Judaism resists the idea of a Jewish state with borders, an army, and a measure of temporal power, no matter how modest. I am afraid of the inner damage Judaism will sustain—especially from the development of a narrow nationalism within our own ranks, against which we have already had to fight strongly, even without a Jewish state." Not only did Einstein oppose the idea of a formal Israeli state based on an exclusively or overwhelmingly Jewish population, but "he [also] always supported treating the Arabic people of Palestine with generosity and understanding."[37]

Obviously, the path advocated by Einstein and other moderate Zionists has not been the one followed by the Israeli leaders. The actual course adopted by Israel has been, instead, more in tune with the hard-line policy of "the iron wall," a phrase put forward by Ze'ev Jabotinsky in the 1920s as the appropriate posture for Zionists to adopt toward the non-Jewish population in Palestine. This maximalist policy aims at capturing the "entire Palestine," stretching from Jordan to the Mediterranean, and establishing a state there based on an exclusive or overwhelming majority of Jewish people.

Because the overwhelming majority of the inhabitants of Palestine were not Jewish but Muslim and Christian Arabs, the question that faced the planners of a Jewish state in Palestine was, therefore, how to bring about the "necessary" expulsion of Palestinians from the their land. Obviously, such expulsions could not be carried out during normal, peaceful times; war and application of force were deemed necessary for the projected expulsions. But because waging war and applying force in the name of expulsions would be politically unpalatable, instigation of diversionary or proxy wars in the region were considered necessary in order to avail the expansionist Zionist forces of the needed pretext for the projected expulsions. David Ben-Gurion explained the importance of the convulsive or "revolutionary" social circumstances to the goal of expelling Palestinians and expanding the Jewish territory in these words: "What is inconceivable in normal times is possible in revolutionary times; and if at this time the opportunity is missed and what is possible in such great hours is not carried out—a whole world is lost."[38]

The actual measures that were adopted for the creation of the Jewish state followed this strategy as squarely as a theatrical play following a script. Once the Zionist forces gained a foothold in Palestine as a result of Britain's issuance of the Balfour Declaration, they embarked on a path of territorial expansion that led to the 1948 war under whose cover they managed to expel 750,000 Palestinians (more than 80 percent of the indigenous population), and thus achieve an overwhelmingly Jewish state.[39]

But while the Jewish state that was thus created achieved the objective of "overwhelmingly Jewish population," it fell short of achieving the second major goal of Zionist planners: capturing the entire Palestine, the "land of Israel," from Jordan to the Mediterranean. It remained for another war, the 1967 war, to gain control of additional land, the West Bank and the Gaza Strip. Occupation of additional land, however, could not this time be accompanied by the expulsion of its inhabitants. Additional territory, therefore, also meant an additional dilemma, the so-called demographic problem: the non-Jewish inhabitants of the occupied territories, combined with their higher rates of population growth, posed a long-term threat to the ideal of an overwhelmingly Jewish state of Israel.

Years of wrenching debate over how to resolve this "dilemma" led (by the late 1980s) to a major fissure in the ranks of the Israeli leaders. The realist faction, headed by the Late Prime Minister Yitzhak Rabin and his co-thinkers, gradually became convinced that the goal of capturing the entire Palestine based on the overwhelmingly Jewish population was unattainable; and that the time had come for Israel to consider the "land-for-security" proposals, along with the underlying ideas of two independent, side-by-side states of Israel and Palestine. This line of thinking eventually became the basis for the 1993 Oslo Peace Accord between the Palestinians and the Israelis.

Economics played an important role in the emergence of this line of thinking. Gradual transnationalization of the Israeli capital and integration of its economy into the world economy were crucial to the willingness of a segment of the Israeli leadership, representing the interests of the transnational capital, to discuss peace with the Palestinians in the early 1990s. Ever since the establishment of the Israeli state in 1948, until the late 1980s and early 1990s, the country's economy resembled a closed, war economy; its capital and/or its business entrepreneurs were, by and large, "home-bound" and its investment abroad remained negligible. The state played a major role in the economic life of the country, coordinating private enterprise with both war requirements and welfare state commitments. This nationally guided economic mechanism worked relatively well as long as the country's economy remained relatively isolated from global market imperatives.

But the Israeli capital was bound to spread beyond its borders. The rising tide of economic globalization, greatly reinforced by the so-called supply-side economics and neoliberal policies of the 1980s and 1990s, began to gradually link some of the major Israeli corporations with the world economy by the late 1980s. Statistics on international capital flows show that since then the outflow of the Israeli capital, that is, its investment abroad, has grown from 0.2 percent to about 1 percent of the country's gross domestic product (GDP), a fivefold or 400 percent increase. Foreign investment in Israel has likewise multiplied during this period, rising form 0.5 to 2 percent, a fourfold or 300 percent increase.[40] This increased transnationalization of the Israeli capital has had momentous sociopolitical implications: the geographically blind and borderless transnational capital, preferring stability in global markets and, therefore, willing to negotiate peace with Palestinians, has torpedoed the Zionist plans of "greater Israel." In their interesting book, *The Global Political Economy of Israel*, Jonathan

Nitzan and Shimshon Bichler describe these changes as follows:

> Until recently, Israeli capitalism went well with the Zionist project. The country's ruling class, from its colonial beginnings, through its statist institutions, to its emergence as dominant capital, managed to interweave Jewish colonial ideas with capitalist praxis. . . . The social cohesion needed to sustain the war economy was cemented by religious and racial rhetoric, authoritarian welfare institutions, and frequent armed conflict against external enemies. . . . The shift toward transnationalism upset this delicate "equilibrium." With the elite increasingly focused on the Nasdaq, the high-tech business, and markets in the rest of the world, the prospects of peace dividends began to look much more attractive than dwindling war profits. Dominant capital was less and less receptive to the "garrison state," and calls for an end to the Arab-Israeli conflict mounted. Once the "peace process" started and the globalization wagon began rolling, however, the Zionist package began to unravel.[41]

Heightened integration of world markets and neoliberal policies of the 1980s and 1990s gave birth to widespread antiglobalization protest movements in many countries in the 1990s. In Israel such antiglobalization reactions have perhaps been the most intense, not only because globalization has eroded traditional employment and social safety net programs, but also because it has threatened support for the Zionist project. As a faction of the ruling elite, representing the interests of transnational capital, leaned toward negotiation and reconciliation with Arab neighbors in the 1990s, the hard-line Zionist faction, unwilling to give up an inch of the occupied territories, rebelled. The rebellious, uncompromising faction was (and continues to be) supported not only by the economically vulnerable layers of Israeli society who are afraid of globalization, but also by the beneficiaries of the arms industry and related businesses. More importantly, the radical faction continues to enjoy the backing of the zealously religious Zionist forces who have declared that the evacuation of a settlement "is a sin against God." In fact, many Israelis who oppose peace negotiations with the Palestinians, or are against any kind of compromise with Arab neighbors, have in recent years shifted their loyalties from secular to religious and ethnic political parties, such as SHAS and Yisrael Ba-aliyah.

Emboldened by the support of these steadfastly loyal groups, and by the almost unconditional backing of the U.S. policy in the Middle East, militant Zionist leaders of Israel have succeeded in recent years to effectively kill both the Oslo Peace Accord and the so-called Road Map to Peace put forth by the United States. Instead, they have resolved to redouble the "necessary" efforts to achieve the goal of securing the "promised land." Indeed, they embarked on this uncompromising path while their political opponents, headed by the late Yitzhak Rabin, were still (surreptitiously) negotiating possibilities of peace with the Palestinians in the late 1980s and early 1990s. In opposing Rabin's idea of negotiation with the Palestinians, they acknowledged that, for the time being, certain conditions (such as the important friendly relations between the United States and a number of Arab states, the large Palestinian population in the occupied territories, and world public opinion) were not favorable to achieving the goal of capturing the "promised land." But they argued that some of those conditions could be changed, including geographic boundaries and territorial configurations of a number of countries in the region. Specifically, the hard-liners "called for Israel to bring about the dissolution and fragmentation of the Arab states into a mosaic of ethnic groupings. Thinking along these lines, Ariel Sharon stated on March 24, 1988, that if the Palestinian uprising continued, Israel would have to make war on her Arab neighbors. The war, he stated, would provide 'the circumstances' for the removal of the entire Palestinian population from the West Bank and Gaza and even from inside Israel proper."[42]

Ariel Sharon's idea that "war would provide the circumstances" for the removal of the Palestinian people is an unmistakable reminder of David Ben-Gurion's view (quoted earlier) that "revolutionary times" provide opportunities for the expulsion of Palestinians—an idea that lies at the heart of the hard-line Zionists' agenda of establishing a Jewish state in the "promised land." The notion that war would "provide the circumstances" for the removal of Palestinians from the occupied territories was (and continues to be) premised on the expectation that the United States would go along with the idea and would, therefore, support Zionist expansionism in the event of the contemplated war.

But as long as the Soviet Union existed as a countervailing world power to the United States, this expectation remained unrealistic. Under the bipolar world of the Cold War era, where the world in general and the Middle East region in particular were divided into East-West spheres of influence, the United States simply could not afford to abandon or antagonize its Arab/Muslim allies in the region by supporting the Zionist plan of another overhaul of the geography of the region. The collapse of the Soviet Union, however, removed a major obstacle to the fulfillment of that plan.

The Demise of the Soviet Union, the Convergence of Interests on War, and the Unholy Alliance

In pursuit of their goal of establishing a Jewish state in the "land of Israel," Zionist leaders have always tried to portray their interests as coinciding or synergetic with the interests of imperialist powers, first with those of Great Britain and then with those of the United States. By the same token, they have also always tried to portray opponents of their territorial ambitions not only as the enemies of Israel but also of those powers. But, as just noted, such attempts at manipulation were not very effective during the Cold War atmosphere. In the aftermath of the Cold War era, however, those strategies began to become more effective; not because Zionist strategists suddenly became smarter, or U.S. policy makers suddenly became more susceptible to Zionist influence, but because some powerful interests in the United States, the military-industrial interests, now converged more closely with those of hard-line Zionists in instigating war and convulsion in the Middle East.

As noted earlier, the demise of the Soviet Union and the end of the Cold War prompted calls in the United States for "peace dividends," that is, for the curtailment and conversion of part of the military budget to civilian use. The idea behind demands for "peace dividends" was simple: since in the aftermath of the collapse of the Soviet Union the United States no longer needed the colossal military apparatus of the Cold War era, part of the military budget could now safely be reallocated toward civilian uses. Frightened by the specter of peace and/or peace dividends, beneficiaries of military spending frantically sought to invent and substitute "new threats" for the "communist threat" of the Cold War era, thereby preempting the realization of peace dividends.

In pursuit of this goal, beneficiaries of war and militarism found a strong, well-established network of politically savvy allies: radical Zionist proponents of "greater Israel." Because the interests of these two powerful groups converged over fomenting war and political convulsion in the Middle East, an ominously potent alliance was forged between them— ominous, because the mighty U.S. war machine was now supplemented by the almost unrivaled public relations capabilities of the hard-line pro-Israel lobby in the United States.[43] The alliance is unofficial and de facto; it is subtly forged through an elaborate network of powerful militaristic think tanks such as the American Enterprise Institute, Project for the New American Century, America Israel Public Affairs Committee, Middle East

Media Research Institute, Washington Institute for Near East Policy, Middle East Forum, National Institute for Public Policy, Jewish Institute for National Security Affairs, and Center for Security Policy. The neoconservative militarists in and around the Bush administration serve primarily the interests of this alliance.

The interests of the military-industrial complex and those of militant Zionism have increasingly become intertwined in more direct and palpable ways:

> After decades of ever-solidifying ties, Israel is now so closely linked to the United States in concrete ways that it is actually a part of the U.S. military-industrial complex. Israel sells military equipment, with our knowledge, to countries to which the U.S. is restricted by law from selling—for instance, to China. So many arms and types of arms are produced in the U.S. for Israel that it has become quite easy for Israel's lobbyists in Washington to go to individual congressmen and point out to them how many jobs in a given district depend on this arms industry and on *not* withholding arms from Israel. In this way, Israel becomes a direct factor in sustaining the U.S. military-industrial complex, in maintaining jobs in the U.S., and in keeping congressmen and other politicians in office.[44]

The convergence and/or interdependence of the interests of the military-industrial complex and those of militant Zionism on war and political convulsion in the Middle East is at the heart of the perpetual cycle of violence in the region: the more the powerful and overlapping lobbies of the military-industrial-Zionist alliance succeed in gearing the U.S. policy in the region to the radical Zionist policies of Israeli leaders, the stronger and bolder Israel becomes, and the more aggressive it will behave in pursuit of its territorial aggrandizement, or in its treatment of the Palestinian people. It is not surprising that, as Bill and Kathleen Christison, former CIA analysts, put it, "Everything Israel does in the Middle East is perceived throughout the world, and accurately so, as having been condoned, encouraged, and enabled by the United States, with the result that any terrorists able to concoct an attack like September 11 will target us before they will target Israel."[45] As the U.S./Israeli policies in the Middle East prompt the frustrated Palestinians and their sympathizers elsewhere to violent reactions, they also provide the U.S. and Israeli policy makers with the pretext they need in order to justify their policies in the region. Such violent reactions to the U.S. and Israeli policies will also make the business of war, the primary concern of the military-industrial complex, more profitable. As noted earlier, as long as the Soviet Union existed as a balancing superpower vis-à-vis the United States, U.S. policy makers in the Middle East were somewhat constrained in their accommodations of territorial ambitions of hard-line Zionism. The demise of the Soviet Union and the end of the Cold War, however, removed such constraints. Not surprisingly, soon after the collapse of the Berlin Wall, representatives of the military-industrial-Likud alliance embarked on a joint offensive against a whole host of long-established international institutions and conventions, arms control treaties and, most importantly, the Oslo peace negotiations between Palestinians and Israelis. Instead of those long-established multilateral treaties and conventions, they now called for aggressive American unilateralism, along with an overhaul of the geopolitical landscape of the Middle East in favor of Israel.

As noted above, the military-industrial-Likud interests promote their views and carry out their plans through an extended but tightly knit web of influential think tanks of militaristic lobbying entities. Some of these lobbying think tanks and their major political players have direct Israeli connections. For example, Colonel Yigal Carmon, formerly of Israeli military intelligence, was a cofounder of the Middle East Media Research Institute (MEMRI). The other cofounder of MEMRI, Meyrav Wurmser, was a member of the Hudson Institute, while her husband, David Wurmser, headed the Middle East Studies Department of the American Enterprise Institute. Richard Perle, a major player in the neoconservative movement, was both a "resident fellow" at the American Enterprise Institute and a trustee of the Hudson Institute.[46] Focusing on two of these influential think tanks, the Jewish Institute for National Security Affairs (JINSA) and Center for Security Policy (CSP), Jason Vest of *The Nation* magazine convincingly unmasked "the close links among the two organizations, right-wing politicians, arms merchants, military men, Jewish billionaires, and Republican administrations."[47]

In the immediate aftermath of the Cold War era, these think tanks and their neoconservative spin doctors published a number of policy papers that clearly and forcefully advocated plans for border change, demographic change, and regime change in the Middle East. For example, in 1996 an influential Israeli think tank, the Institute for Advanced Strategic and Political Studies, sponsored and published a policy document titled "A Clean Break: A New Strategy for Securing the Realm," which argued that the government of Prime Minister Benjamin Netanyahu "should 'make a clean break' with the Oslo peace process and reassert Israel's claim to the West Bank and Gaza. It presented a plan whereby Israel would 'shape its strategic environment,' beginning with the removal of Saddam Hussein and the installation of a Hashemite monarchy in Baghdad, to serve as a first step toward eliminating the anti-Israeli governments of Syria, Lebanon, Saudi Arabia, and Iran."[48]

The document, intended as a political roadmap for the incoming government of Netanyahu, was prepared by a "study group" that included Richard Perle (American Enterprise Institute, study group leader), James Colbert (Jewish Institute for National Security Affairs), Douglas Feith (Feith and Zell Associates at the time), Robert Loewenberg (president, Institute for Advanced Strategic and Political Studies), David Wurmser (Institute for Advanced Strategic and Political Studies), and Meyrav Wurmser (Johns Hopkins University). The dual role that a number of these individuals play is remarkable: serving as advisor both to the Likud party/government and to President Bush's administration. (Perle is now a member of the Defense Policy Board; Feith is an assistant secretary of Defense; and Wurmser is special assistant to State Department chief arms control negotiator John Bolton.)

In an "Open Letter to the President" (Clinton), dated February 19, 1998, a number of these lobbyists, along with a number of their cohorts in the Committee for Peace and Security in the Gulf, recommended "a comprehensive political and military strategy for bringing down Saddam and his regime." The letter further proposed: "It will not be easy—and the course of action we favor is not without its problems and perils. But we believe the vital national interests of our country require the United States to [adopt such a strategy]." Among the letter's signers were the following current Bush administration officials and their cohorts: Elliott Abrams (National Security Council), Richard Armitage (State Department), John Bolton (State Department), Douglas Feith (Defense Department), Fred Ikle (Defense Policy Board), Zalmay Khalilzad (ambassador to Afghanistan), Peter Rodman (Defense Department), Paul Wolfowitz (Defense Department), David Wurmser (State Department), Dov Zakheim (Defense Department), Richard Perle (Defense Policy Board), Donald Rumsfeld (secretary of defense), William Kristol (editor, the *Weekly Standard*), Frank Gaffney (director, Center for Security Policy), Joshua Muravchik (American Enterprise Institute), Martin Peretz (editor in chief, *The New Republic*), Leon Wieseltier (*The New Republic*), and former congressman Stephen Solarz (Democrat—New York).[49]

Similarities between the recommendations made in this 1998 letter to President Clinton and those made in the 1996 report to the Likud government of Benjamin Netanyahu are unmistakable. The only difference is that whereas the 1996 report stressed the "national interests" of Israel the 1998 letter stressed the "national interests" of the United States.[50] This is an indication of the fact that the loyalties of a number of key handlers of the U.S. foreign policy are woefully divided. Unsurprisingly, many of these neoconservative political players have come to be "called in diplomatic and political circles the 'Israeli-firsters,' meaning that they would always put Israeli policy, or even their perception of it, above anything else."[51]

In September 2000, another think tank of the war-mongering cabal of neoconservatives, Project for the New American Century (PNAC), issued a report, "Rebuilding America's Defenses: Strategy, Forces and Resources for a New Century," which explicitly projected an imperial role for the United States the world over. The report specifically proposed an expanded U.S. presence in the Middle East region, using the claims against Saddam Hussein's regime as a pretext: "The United States has for decades sought to play a more permanent role in Gulf regional security. While the unresolved conflict with Iraq provides the immediate justification, the need for a substantial American force presence in the Gulf transcends the issue of the regime of Saddam Hussein." The sponsors of the report included Richard Cheney (vice president), Donald Rumsfeld (secretary of Defense), Paul Wolfowitz (deputy secretary of defense), and Lewis Libby (Cheney's chief of staff). William Kristol, editor of the *Weekly Standard*, was also a coauthor of the report.[52]

This sample evidence clearly shows that the civilian militarists, representing the military-industrial-Likud interests, had intended to invade Iraq and recast the geopolitical landscape of the Middle East long before the criminal attacks of 9/11. Indeed, evidence indicates that, aside from its triggering effect, those attacks had very little to do with such plans. The cabal of neoconservative warmongers, as shown above, had drawn up such plans long before the 9/11 atrocities. But the cabal needed pretexts and opportunities for carrying out its plans. The 9/11 atrocities provided just such an opportunity.[53] On the one hand, the attacks provided beneficiaries of war dividends with the substitute they were seeking for the "communist threat" of the Cold War era in order to justify continued increases of the Pentagon budget. On the other hand, they provided militant Zionism with the "convulsive circumstances" that would avail them of the opportunities to demolish Palestinian houses, to expropriate their land, and to expand Jewish settlements. As Stephen J. Sniegoski points out,

> In the eyes of Israel's leaders, the September 11 attacks had joined the United States and Israel together against a common enemy. And that enemy was not in far-off Afghanistan but was geographically close to Israel. Israel's traditional enemies would now become America's as well. And Israel would have a better chance of dealing with the Palestinians under the cover of a "war on terrorism."[54]

Not surprisingly, immediately after the 9/11 attacks, representatives of the military-industrial-Likud alliance began calling for war not just on Osama Bin Laden and Al Qaedeh but also on a number of countries in the Middle East. Thus, "In the hours following the September 11, 2001, attacks, Secretary of Defense Donald Rumsfeld asked for an immediate assault on Iraq. The following day, in a cabinet meeting at the White House, Rumsfeld again insisted that Iraq should be 'a principal target of the first round in the war against terrorism.'"[55] On September 20, 2001, only nine days after the attacks, the neoconservative strategists of the Project for the New American Century (PNAC) sent a letter to President Bush arguing that the "war on terrorism" must also include punitive measures against Iraq, Iran, and Syria:

> It may be that the Iraqi government provided assistance in some form to the recent attack [of 9/11] on the United States. But even if evidence does not link Iraq directly to the attack, any strategy aiming at the eradication of terrorism and its sponsors must include a determined effort to remove Saddam Hussein from power in Iraq. Failure to undertake such an effort will constitute an early and perhaps decisive surrender in the war on international terrorism. . . . We believe the administration should demand that Iran and Syria immediately cease all military, financial, and political support for Hezbollah and its operations. Should Iran and Syria refuse to comply, the administration should consider appropriate measures of retaliation against these known state sponsors of terrorism.[56]

The letter's signatories included William Kristol, Gary Bauer, Eliot Cohen, Midge Decter, Francis Fukuyama, Frank Gaffney, Eli Jacobs, Michael Joyce, Donald Kagan, Jeane Kirkpatrick, Charles Krauthammer, Richard Perle, Martin Peretz, Norman Podhoretz, Randy Scheunemann, Stephen J. Solars, Leon Wieseltier, and Marshall Wittmann.

In the October 29, 2002 issue of the *Weekly Standard*, William Kristol and Robert Kagan, two of the leading figures of the neoconservative cabal, revealed more of the cabal's plan of changing regimes and establishing a new world order:

> When all is said and done, the conflict in Afghanistan will be to the war on terrorism what the North Africa campaign was to World War II: an essential beginning on the path to victory. But compared with what looms over the horizon—a wide-ranging war in locales from Central Asia to the Middle East and, unfortunately, back again to the United States—Afghanistan will prove but an opening battle. . . . But this war will not end in Afghanistan. It is going to spread and engulf a number of countries in conflicts of varying intensity. It could well require the use of American military power in multiple places simultaneously.[57]

World War IV

This ominous projection of another world war was made more explicit by Eliot A. Cohen three weeks later in a *Wall Street Journal* article titled "World War IV":

> Osama bin Laden's War? . . . A less palatable but more accurate name is World War IV. The Cold War was World War III. . . . The enemy in this war is not "terrorism," . . . but militant Islam. The enemy has an ideology, and an hour spent surfing the Web will give the average citizen at least the kind of insights that he might have found during World Wars II and III by reading "Mein Kampf" or the writings of Lenin, Stalin or Mao.[58]

After an apparently elaborate argument that "the enemy in this war is not terrorism . . . but militant Islam," Professor Cohen proceeds to suggest that the first battle in this war should start with Iraq: "Iraq is the obvious candidate." Now, even if we assume that the professor is right in claiming that "the enemy is militant Islam," it is not clear why he then suggests that the war against militant Islam, "World War IV," should start with Iraq, because the fact is that not much love was lost between the secular Iraqi regime of Saddam Hussein and militant Islam. Indeed, in its drive to secularize Iraq, Saddam Hussein's Ba'athist party/regime carried out some of the most effective and, at times, brutal policies to curtail the traditional influence of religion in the governance and politics of Iraq. Nor have any ties been found between Saddam's regime and Al-Qaedeh.

Professor Cohen is not alone in this portrayal of radical Islam as the new enemy (in place of Cold War era communism), the "threat to Western values," and the culprit in "the clash of civilizations." His ideological cohorts in crafting this insidious theory include Norman Podhoretz, Bernard Lewis, Daniel Pipes, James Woolsey, Charles Krauthammer, and a whole host of their co-thinkers in the neoconservative circles.[59] Speaking at a UCLA forum, sponsored by "Americans for Victory over Terrorism," former CIA director James Woolsey declared, for example, that "the United States is engaged in World War IV, and it could continue for years." Describing the Cold War as the World War III, he further pointed out, "This fourth world war, I think, will last considerably longer than either World Wars I or II did for us. Hopefully not the full four-plus decades of the Cold War." The enemy in the coming World War IV, according to Woolsey, is the Arab/Muslim world, which he breaks down into three subcategories: the religious rulers of Iran, the "fascists" of Iraq and Syria, and Islamic extremists like Al-Qaedeh. All three enemies have waged war against the United States for several years, but the United States has just "finally noticed."[60]

Although Eliot Cohen was the original author of the concept of World War IV, Norman Podhoretz has been the major popularizer of the concept. In a 30,000-word article in the September 2004 issue of *Commentary*, "World War IV: How It Started, What It Means, and Why We Have to Win," he sets out to explain both the rationale for the projected World War IV and the strategies to win it. To explain the looming world conflagration that is allegedly predicated on the conduct of militant Islam, he begins by asserting that "the malignant force of radical Islamism" has as its objective "to conquer our land" and to destroy "everything good for which America stands." After a long and discursive detailing of how and why Islam is incompatible with modernization, and how it therefore poses a serious threat to Western values, he then argues that, to fend off the menace of militant Islam, the United States needs to resolutely engage in a long, drawn-out war in the Muslim world that can be called World War IV.[61] In an earlier article entitled "How to Win World War IV," Podhoretz had written,

> Consider: the campaign against al Qaeda required us to topple the Taliban regime, and we may willy-nilly find ourselves forced by the same political and military logic to topple five or six or seven more tyrannies in the Islamic world (including that other sponsor of terrorism, Yasir Arafat's Palestinian Authority). I can even go along with David Pryce-Jones in imagining the turmoil of this war leading to some new species of an imperial mission for America, whose purpose would be to oversee the emergence of successor governments in the region more amenable to reform and modernization than the despotisms now in place.[62]

Like most of his neoconservative cohorts in and around the Bush administration, Podhoretz markets his prescription for changing a number of regimes in the Middle East as the United States' duty to bring truth, light, democracy, and American virtues to the region. He argues that historical progress is frozen in the soil of Islam, and that democracy cannot grow in a gradual or spontaneous fashion in the Muslim world. But modernization and democracy, he avers, could be injected into this world from without, that is, by the United States. "This, in turn, would finally give adherents of Islam a chance to set feet on the path of greater freedom and greater prosperity—and, not so incidentally, to make their peace with the existence of Israel."[63]

In his September 2004 *Commentary* essay, Podhoretz gives his assurances that "the obstacles to a benevolent transformation of the Middle East—whether military, political, or religious—are not insuperable. . . . There can be no question that we possess the power and the means." The only question is whether we have "the stomach to do what will be required." Indeed, as Paul Craig Roberts points out in a critical review of the theory of World War IV, "To make sure that we have the stomach, Podhoretz blames the 9/11 terrorist attack on American cowardice. He argues that four U.S. presidents (Carter, Reagan, Bush I, and Clinton) spent 24 years convincing Muslims that America is a wimp. . . . First, Carter wimped out on Iran. Then Reagan let Islamic terrorists blow us out of Lebanon. Bush I followed in Reagan's wimp footsteps and refused to finish the job in Iraq. Clinton continued the wimp tradition for two more terms."[64]

Luckily, points out Podhoretz, "America was saved from weakness by President George W. Bush (Bush II), who like Harry Truman unexpectedly turned up with a vision." Bush II's vision is basically the same as that of the champions and beneficiaries of World War IV, the neoconservative militarists who represent the military-industrial-Likud interests, and who have succeeded in crafting the president's policies and shaping his mind. The essence of "the vision," Roberts points out, "is to knock off Iraq, Iran and Syria, the countries that could get in the way of Israel expelling the Palestinians to Jordan and grabbing Lebanon as well. This *is what World War IV is all about*" (original emphasis).[65]

Acknowledgment of these facts is often branded as anti-Semitism by supporters of militant Zionism. For example, Podhoretz is outraged that Susan Sontag actually said that 9/11 was an attack "undertaken as a consequence of specific American alliances and actions." He also tries to tar Mickey Kaus for agreeing with Pat Buchanan that mistreatment of the

Palestinians is part of the problem. And he is horrified that Michael Kinsley agrees with Buchanan that it is an affront to the Constitution to fight undeclared wars.[66]

The weakness of the anti-Semitic smear tactic is that there are distinguished thinkers, many of them Jewish, who cannot be charged with anti-Semitism for disagreeing with Podhoretz and his neoconservative cohorts. The publication last year of *The Politics of Anti-Semitism*, a powerful collection of essays, many written by Jews, has taken the sting from the charge by showing that it is a tactic used to prevent debate. Many of the alleged anti-Semites are Jews' and/or Israel's friends who are concerned that Israel's colonization of Palestine, and its alliance with U.S. military-industrial imperialism in pursuit of "greater Israel," might not be in the long-term interest of the Jewish people. Thus, writes Uri Avnery, for example, "I would not want my country, Israel, to be identified with such an America [a la George W. Bush]. Any advantage we can derive from it may well turn out to be short-term, the damage long-lasting, and perhaps irreversible."[67]

Sadly, however, the zeal with which radical Zionists pursue their goal of "securing the land of Israel," and the weakness of their arguments and policies in pursuit of this goal, seem to compel them to ignore the difference between the friendly and the hostile, truly anti-Semitic, critics of Israel's policies in the Middle East, and paint them all with the same broad brush of anti-Semitism. So, with rare exceptions, virtually everyone in the United States ignores both the reality of the Israeli-Palestinian relationship and the fact that many of the neoconservative militarists are unquestioning supporters of radical Zionism. Not only corporate media and political pundits, but also many of the left/liberal politicians and political activists shy away from mentioning the facts of that relationship lest they might be branded as anti-Semites. In actuality, however, it is impossible to get around the fact that most of the neoconservatives in and around the Bush administration, who wield a great deal of influence over U.S. foreign policy, have long been active supporters of Israel's right-wing politicians and/or leaders. It is also impossible to get around the fact that many of the neoconservative figures happen to be Jewish.

It does not follow, however, that, as some critics argue, the U.S.–Israeli relationship represents a case of "tail wagging the dog," that is, the U.S. foreign policy in the Middle East is shaped by the Israeli/Zionist leaders. Nor do I subscribe to the hoary anti-Semitic canards that are used to put forth a specious case for Jews trying to run the world. While, no doubt, the powerful Jewish lobby exerts considerable influence over U.S. foreign policy in the Middle East, the efficacy and the extent of that influence depend, ultimately, on the real economic and geopolitical interests of U.S. foreign policy makers. In other words, U.S. policy makers in the Middle East would go along with the demands of the radical Zionist lobby only if such demands also tend to serve the special interests that those policy makers represent or serve—not necessarily the interests of the American people, or collective U.S. "national interests" in general. The fact that, as pointed out earlier, U.S. foreign policy during the Cold War era was less accommodating to the territorial desires of militant Zionism than in the post–Cold War period is an indication of this point. Another corroborating indication of the point is that as the military-industrial complex has been gaining more and more influence over U.S. foreign policy, that policy has, accordingly, been more and more geared to the wishes of hard-line Zionism because, as has been frequently pointed out in this chapter, the interests of the U.S. military establishment converge with those of militant Zionism over war and political convulsion in the Middle East.

Some friendly critics attribute the aggressive militaristic policies of militant Zionism to the traumatic memories of fascism and the attendant brutalities that were committed against Jewish people. Thus, political commentator Jim Lobe, for example, writes that "the horrific experience of European Jewry in the twentieth century, culminating as it did with the Nazi Holocaust, is critical to understanding the neoconservative mindset." Lobe further adds, "It is that experience, and the failure of the international community to do anything about it that helps explain the good-and-evil moral categories, the obsession with military force, the disdain for multilateral institutions and international law and, ultimately, the necessity for the United States to be permanently engaged against foreign enemies lest it withdraw into isolationism which, like appeasement, helped pave the way for Hitler and the Holocaust, that make up the neoconservative worldview."[68]

While this may explain radical Zionists' and/or neoconservatives' "mindset" and their policies of unilateral militarism, it does not justify their plans of war and "regime change" in the Middle East. Palestinians and other Arab/Muslim people had nothing to do with the Nazi Holocaust. That these people have been subjected to horrendous punishment for the crimes committed by others simply defies logic—let alone any sense of justice.

Champions of war and militarism facilely use terms and adjectives such as *fascist* and Hitler to characterize any "unfriendly" dictatorial ruler in the Middle East in order to justify their agenda of "regime change" in the region. Such opportunistic use of political rhetoric for nefarious political purposes represents a gross misreading of historical categories and developments. It also indicates that the radical Zionist ideologues who sloppily coin such misplaced terminology are sadly misinterpreting fascism and might, therefore, be drawing wrong lessons. Fascism is a specific historical category that evolves out of particular socioeconomic circumstances or structures. It cannot be haphazardly applied to any socioeconomic system that is at odds with the idealized neoconservative market system.

Nor can fascism be reduced to the "sins" of political personas and individual leaders of Nazi Germany, or the pathological problems of Hitler's mind. While simplistic—or perhaps diversionary—judgments of this sort may succeed in dressing in the uniform of Adolf Hitler the horrific acts that the capitalist system can occasionally perform, such reductionist judgments would not be very useful for the purposes of averting social conditions that may lead to the recurrence of fascism. Hitler was not any more responsible for the rise of fascism in Europe than is President George W. Bush for the rise of neoconservative militarists in America, or for the control of U.S. foreign policy by the representatives of the military-industrial-Likud interests.[69]

Defining the President's Mission

As shown earlier in this chapter, the neoconservative militarists set out to place their plans of unilateral aggression and "regime change" on the U.S. foreign policy agenda soon after the demise of the Soviet Union, that is, under presidents Bush Sr. and Clinton. Despite certain accommodations of the demands of the neoconservatives, both presidents stopped short of fully complying with their agenda. With the arrival of their champion Bush Jr. in the White House, however, neoconservative strategists redoubled their efforts to shape U.S. foreign policy in their image. As they competed with the traditional, "realist" approach to foreign policy, favored (sheepishly and ineffectually) by the State Department's Colin Powell, in order to win the president over to their policy of unilateralism, neoconservative strategists began to define foreign policy issues and objectives in religious, missionary, and mythical terms. As James P. Pinkerton (of the *New York Newsday*) puts it, the neoconservatives'

> word-creations, such as "moral clarity," "axis of evil" and "Bush Doctrine," spread far and wide. These word-weavings were repeated over and over again,

in magazines, books and cable news shows. Bush became Winston Churchill, Saddam Hussein became Hitler, the Arabs were ripe for Americanization, and the U.S. military became the sword not only of vengeance, but also of do-gooding and nation-building.[70]

Not accidentally, the strategy of couching foreign policy in missionary or biblical terms worked. As a born-again Christian, and as someone with little patience for nuances and gray areas, the president was energized once he was led to view his presidential responsibilities, especially his foreign policy agenda, as *missions*. As Halper and Clarke argue, the relatively naïve, unread and unformed Bush allowed a small group of neoconservative militarists like Wolfowitz, Rumsfeld, Perle, Feith, Cheney, and others to suddenly have a much more central and active role in shaping American foreign policy.[71] Not only did the sense of a *missionary* president lead George W. Bush to carry out the neoconservatives' long-awaited foreign policy agenda effectively, but it also made him, as Hugh Urban puts it, "the perfect liaison to the Christian Right that the Neocons needed in order to win popular support and promote their vision of American power both at home and abroad." Urban describes the president's religious reawakening as follows:

> The narrative that Bush and his biographers tell is clearly modeled on the parable of the prodigal son—the young man who fritters away his early life on alcohol and sin, only to find God and return to his rightful place in his father's former occupation. As he recounts his own redemption narrative, Bush had been mired in the world of business and overuse of alcohol, and so turned in his darker hours to the study of scripture. The beginning of his conversion occurred during a summer weekend in 1985, when evangelist Billy Graham visited George and Laura at the Bush summer house in Maine. The reverend, with his magnetic presence and warmth, planted a "seed of salvation" in W.'s soul that soon blossomed into a new birth and helped him "recommit [his] heart to Jesus Christ."[72]

This rededication to Christ proved to be not only a spiritual awakening within George W. himself but also an important part of the Republican party's own reconnection with the Christian Right. The senior Bush had actually had a great deal of trouble reaching out to the religious right, which regarded his Episcopalian, aristocratic airs with some suspicion. The younger Bush was far more successful in connecting with the Religious Right: he was "deeply attuned to the nuances of the evangelical subcultures" and "replaced his father's visionless pragmatism with the Manichaean certitudes of Good and Evil." George W. Bush's religiosity became even more explicit, however, once he decided to run for president in the 2000 election. As he confided to James Robinson, he believed that he in fact had been called by God himself to lead the United States: "I feel like God wants me to run for President. I can't explain it, but I sense my country is going to need me. God wants to me to do it."[73]

Although George W. Bush's perception that God wanted him to run for president energized him to actually run for and become the president of the United States, he nonetheless was not sure in the earlier stages of his presidency of what it was that God wanted him to do for his country, or why he should have been chosen to become the president. The 9/11 attacks on the World Trade Center and the Pentagon changed that earlier confusion and uncertainty, as it helped define his responsibilities in simple, biblical terms of fighting forces of evil worldwide: "Our responsibility to history," Bush stated on September 14, 2001, is "to answer these attacks and rid the world of evil." He further declared on September 25, 2002, "I see things this way: The people who did this act on America are evil people. They don't represent an ideology. They're flat evil. That's all they can think about, is evil. As a nation of good folks, we're going to hunt them down and we will bring them to justice." Indeed, shortly after the 9/11 attacks, the president used the word *crusade* to characterize his response to the attacks. Although, because of worldwide condemnation of the invocation of religious crusades, Bush did not repeat the word anymore, nonetheless that is pretty much what he has repeatedly described in his reactions and responses to those criminal attacks.[74]

So impressive was Bush's powerful religious rhetoric that he soon came to be recognized as the new leader of the Christian Right in America. On the day before Christmas 2001, *The Washington Post* reported that "Pat Robertson's resignation this month as President of the Christian Coalition confirmed the ascendance of a new leader of the religious right in America: George W. Bush." In the words of Ralph Reed, the Christian Coalition's former President, "God knew something we didn't. He had a knowledge nobody else had: He knew George Bush had the ability to lead in this compelling way."[75]

Neoconservative representatives of the military-industrial-Likud-Christian Right wasted no time taking advantage of the newly arisen opportunity (of the nonanalytical, evangelical president in the context of the criminal attacks of 9/11) by impressing their agenda upon the president in the guise of powerful biblical language. As Stephen Sniegoski put it, "Neoconservatives have presented the September 11 atrocities as a lightning bolt to make President Bush aware of his destiny: destroying the evil of terrorism." Norman Podhoretz, one of the leading neoconservative strategists, gleefully describes the "transfigured" president:

A transformed—or, more precisely, a transfigured—George W. Bush appeared before us. In an earlier article . . . I suggested, perhaps presumptuously, that out of the blackness of smoke and fiery death let loose by September 11, a kind of revelation, blazing with a very different fire of its own, lit up the recesses of Bush's mind and heart and soul. Which is to say that, having previously been unsure as to why he should have been chosen to become President of the United States, George W. Bush now knew that the God to whom, as a born-again Christian, he had earlier committed himself had put him in the Oval Office for a purpose. He had put him there to lead a war against the evil of terrorism.[76]

Having helped define the president's mission, the military-industrial-Likud-Christian Right interests, working largely through the neoconservative militarists, have taken the most advantage of the thus energized president. By deliberately couching their nefarious objectives in missionary terms, and repeatedly defining their enemies, real or imaginary, in biblical language ("axis of evil, evildoers, good versus evil, day of reckoning," and the like), they have had no difficulty getting the president to carry out their agenda, including the plan to recast the geopolitical map of the Middle East, starting with the invasion of Iraq. In his January 2003 State of the Union Address, in which he made the strongest case for war against Iraq, the president made an explicit appeal to God, divine will and Providence to justify the sacrifice of American lives; for they will be dying not just for the American people, but for freedom which is "God's gift to humanity."

Many people who were alarmed by these crusade-like pronouncements had hoped that the president's disastrous military adventure in Iraq might have taken the winds out of his belligerent sails. But, as Uri Avnery points out, "rulers of this type . . . cannot admit defeat and stop. On the contrary, failure drives [them] on to more extremes, vowing, rather like the captain of the Titanic, 'to stay the course.' There is no way to guess what Bush may perpetrate, now that . . . his ego has been blown up [by his reelection] to giant proportions, reaffirming what the Greek fabulist Aesop said some 27 centuries ago: 'The smaller the mind the greater the conceit.' "[77]

Mr. Bush's unambiguously combative inaugural speech of January 20, 2005, recommitting his administration to the ideals of spreading democracy across the globe and "ending tyranny in our world," made it clear that the fiasco in Iraq had not weakened his determination to take "liberty as God's gift to humanity" to all corners of our planet. In clearly messianic terms he stated, "By our efforts, we have lit . . . a fire in the minds of men. It warms those who feel its power, it burns those who fight its progress, and one day this untamed fire of freedom will reach the darkest corners of our world. . . . History has an ebb and flow of justice, but history also has a visible direction set by liberty and the author of liberty." The suggestion that struggle against oppression was ordained by God was an apparent reference to the ideas enshrined in the U.S. Constitution that all people have God-given rights.

Although the president avoided the use of his familiar "good versus evil" term in the inaugural speech, he repeatedly conveyed the ideas behind that term by contrasting liberty with tyranny, frequently arguing that our planet was consumed by the struggle between these two opposing forces in which the United States would not stand aside: "So it is the policy of the United States to seek and support the growth of democratic movements and institutions in every nation and culture, with the ultimate goal of ending tyranny in our world." The president is here essentially asserting a unilateral right to interfere in the internal affairs of any country or nation his militaristic advisors may expediently deem undemocratic. Socioeconomic systems of such "unfriendly" countries and, therefore, their domestic politics, are now the unabashedly expressed concern of U.S. foreign policy, because if they are not democratic, the president argued, the United States is not secure: "The survival of liberty in our land increasingly depends on the success of liberty in other lands. . . . The best hope for peace in our world is the expansion of freedom in all the world."[78]

President Bush also plans to press and bully unfriendly foreign leaders on the progress they are making, or failing to make, in attaining U.S. standards of "moral choice" and liberty: "We will persistently clarify the choice before every ruler and nation: The moral choice between oppression, which is always wrong, and freedom, which is eternally right. . . . We will encourage reform in other governments by making clear that success in our relations will require the decent treatment of their own peoples."

In a critical remark on this prescription for permanent war, political commentator Patrick J. Buchanan wrote, "Let it be said: This is a formula for endless collisions between this nation [the United States] and every autocratic regime on earth and must inevitably lead to endless wars. And wars are the death of republics."[79]

The fact that U.S. foreign policy makers have almost always used the mask of liberty and pacifism to disguise ulterior objectives behind their aggressive policies of war and militarism is not new. What is new (and very dangerous) in the case of President Bush is that he views that hoary façade of liberation as a "gift from God." This perception, combined with his power as commander in chief of the most powerful military force in the history of the world, make him "the kind of president who," as Llewellyn H. Rockwell puts it, "seems capable of blowing up the world and calling it good."[80]

What compounds the dangers of Mr. Bush's presidency is the fact that he tends to choose not to be informed of the failure of his plans and policies. For example, he calls the bad news on the war front in Iraq "pessimistic" reporting that is designed to discredit or derail his war plans. His sycophantic neoconservative advisors, who have insidiously led him to feel and behave like a king with a mission from God, eagerly accommodate this perverse tendency of the president by deliberately shielding him from "pessimistic" news. But while he tends to willfully remain ignorant of the reality of war and other unpleasant consequences of his policies, he is "cocksure that not only is he doing the right thing, but that God is blessing and directing his every decision, even to the point that he imagines himself to be infallible (or, rather, if he is not infallible, he cannot generate any evidence of fallibility when asked)."[81]

The fact that President Bush remains largely detached from reality is often reflected in much of what he says in his formal statements, speeches, or press conferences. For more than a year after invading Iraq, for example, he refused to call it an occupation; instead, he insisted on referring to it as liberation. But now that he has finally admitted that the United States is militarily occupying Iraq, he complains that those who resist are rejecting "freedom" and "self government." As Rockwell puts it, "This is like the rapist giving sermons on the need to respect the physical integrity and dignity of his victims."[82]

On a personal level, Mr. Bush is a simple, folksy fellow. And that is why, as a private citizen, he is said to be a likeable person. But that is also what makes him dangerous as the president of the most powerful country in the world. It is such personal characteristics (simple, extremist, and out of touch with reality) that have made him susceptible to the treacherous manipulations of the beneficiaries of war and militarism, the neoconservative militarists who have led him to feel and behave like an emperor with a mission—a king and an evangelist combined. As Uri Avnery points out, "This is a dangerous combination. Such people have caused many disasters in human history. Maximilian Robespierre, the French revolutionary who invented the reign of terror, has been called 'the Great Simplifier' because of the terrible simplicity of his views, which he tried to impose with the guillotine."[83]

Had President Bush enjoyed an independent, discerning, *presidential* judgment, he would have apologized to the American people for the needless death and destruction of the unnecessary war on Iraq, and abstained from running for reelection. Short of such an honorable gesture, he would have dismissed his war-mongering advisors who drove him and the nation to war on lies and fabrications. Sadly, expecting such redeeming judgment or behavior from Mr. Bush is like expecting milk from a he-goat. Instead, he ran and got reelected largely by virtue of the tried-and-true scheme of fear generation, on the one hand, and power projection, on the other—all the hypes, exaggerations, and obfuscations about "moral values" notwithstanding. And while retaining and promoting the neoconservative chicken hawks who drove the nation to war on false pretexts, he dismissed those advisors and intelligence personnel who did not wholeheartedly embrace his unilateral policies of aggression. Thus, in an effort to fill the cabinet positions of his administration with ideological allies and faithful followers, he sent home the hapless, pathetic Colin Powell and appointed his loyal personal secretary Condoleezza Rice as the secretary of state. Now, as Uri Avnery writes, "the order is 'clear the deck for action.' On this deck, Bush is a loose cannon, a danger to everyone around. The results of these elections may be viewed by history as a worldwide catastrophe."[84]

Some observers might view warnings of this sort unnecessarily alarmist. They would argue that the reality on the war front—the fact that U.S. armed forces are already overstretched and seem to have been bogged down in Iraq—means that the administration simply cannot carry out its threats of war against Iran or other countries, and that, therefore, President Bush's combative inaugural speech should not be taken very seriously.

While it is true that the reality of U.S. armed forces do not favor another "regime-changing" war, it is also equally true that the president and his administration do not seem to be in touch with reality. As Paul Craig Roberts points out, "It is no protection that their plan is detached from reality. Robespierre was detached from reality, and that did not stop him. . . . People with power in their hands who are detached from reality are the most dangerous people of all. The delusional quality of their rantings disarms people from taking them seriously: 'Oh, they couldn't mean that.' But they do."[85] Hitler was also removed from reality, and that did not stop him either: when his plan to take over England failed, for example, he ordered invasion of the Soviet Union!

While such behavior is obviously bizarre, it has a logical explanation: rulers like Mr. Bush get easily manipulated by powerful, but often submerged, socioeconomic interests into roles whose dynamics sometimes becomes unstoppable. For them admission of failure and military retrenchment is not an option—just like the logic of the proverbial bicyclist who has to keep riding forward out of the fear that he would otherwise fall over. And that is why their way of dealing with the failure of a military adventure, for example, is to embark on new adventures.

Furthermore, from the viewpoint of the beneficiaries of war dividends—the major force behind President Bush's policies of war and militarism—military success or failure, as well as death and destruction, are of secondary concern. Their primary concern, and their measure of success, is the mere act or continuation of war, as this will ensure increased military spending and higher dividends for the business of war. In other words, the standard of success for war profiteers, who operate from behind the façade of neoconservative forces in and around the Bush administration, is based more on market imperatives than on the conventional military success on the battle field. For example, while from a military point of view the war on Iraq has been a fiasco, from the standpoint of the beneficiaries of war dividends it has been a boon.

The president's second inaugural speech makes it clear that his administration would also pursue "greater freedom" at home, by promoting an "ownership society" built on private ownership of homes, private pension schemes, private social security, and health insurance plans: "By making every citizen an agent of his or her own destiny, we will give our fellow Americans greater freedom from want and fear and make our society more prosperous and just and equal."

Calling privatization and/or elimination of government-guaranteed social security and other economic safety net programs "freedom" (presumably from government) is Orwellian through and through. President Bush's speech leaves no doubts that he intends to dilute, if not eliminate, most of the poverty-alleviation programs that were instituted as a result of President Roosevelt's New Deal with the American people. Prompted largely by the Great Depression of the 1930s, the deal was designed to protect the poor and working Americans against the woes, vagaries, and periodic brutalities of market mechanism. Prior to the deal, Americans had to work—that is, if there was work to do—until they dropped dead. And that often meant premature death, due to economic hardship and lack of financial security programs. Although during and in the immediate aftermath of the Great Depression, fervent proponents of economic laissez-faire among the ruling elite grudgingly acceded to the New Deal program (largely out of a fear of social unrest), they have ever since been on the look out for opportunities to reverse or undermine that program. Now that they have their ideal representative in the White House, and the pressure from "below" is all but dissipated—thanks in no small part to heightened war, militarism, and patriotism—they are at it again, so to speak, trying to reverse or whittle down some of the essential parts of the New Deal gains.

The long-cherished American civil liberties are equally threatened by President Bush's agenda, as reflected in his inauguration speech. In the name of "American values," he seems intent on dismantling the cornerstone of the American values: the separation of church and state. Injecting religion into important aspects of both private and social lives, from women's reproductive choice to schools' choice of textbooks, is tantamount to trying to push the society centuries back and hollowing out the constitution.

It is sometimes said that the American nation and/or history has two souls, a good and a bad one. Perhaps that is true for most nations. But in the American context the dichotomy is much more pronounced. There is the America of Thomas Jefferson, Abraham Lincoln, Woodrow Wilson, Franklin Delano Roosevelt, and Dwight Eisenhower, the America of ideals, the Marshall Plan, the New Deal, science and the arts. And there is the America of the genocide perpetrated against the Native Americans, the country of slave traders and the Wild West myth, the America of Hiroshima, of Joe McCarthy, of segregation and of Vietnam, the violent and repressive America. Musing over the disparity between these two Americas on the occasion of President Bush's inaugural speech, Uri Avnery wrote, "During Bush's second term, this second America may reach new depths of ugliness and brutality. It may offer the whole world a model of oppression."[86]

Most of the opponents of President Bush's policies tend to believe that the solution to the threats posed by those policies lies in replacing him with another president. While personal attributes and intellectual capabilities of presidents do make significant differences, the problem seems to go deeper—beyond personalities. After all, President Bush also sounded "compassionate," peaceful, and understanding during his 2000 presidential campaign. (Jimmy Carter also ran for president as a dove and a champion of détente, or tension reduction with the Soviet Union. But, as discussed in chapter 3 of this study, partisans of war and militarism turned him into a Cold War hawk by the time he left the White House.)

So, while replacing Mr. Bush with another president might make a difference, that difference is bound to be temporary, because the sociopolitical mechanism that brought George W. Bush to the White House, and turned him into a king with a mission from God, is bound to nurture and elevate others like him to the presidency. The moral priority is, therefore, to dismantle that mechanism, the warfare state, or the socioeconomic structure that cultivates and elevates the likes of George W. Bush to positions of power. At a minimum, this requires elimination of war profiteering, converting the dynamics of arms production as a lucrative business whose fortunes depend on permanent war. That mechanism "can be smashed effectively," as the late General Smedley D. Butler put it, "only by taking the profit out of war."[87]

Summary

Of the various forces that contribute to the Bush administration's policy of war and militarism in the Middle East, two stand out as major factors behind the invasion of Iraq: the military-industrial complex and the militant Zionist proponents of "greater Israel" in Palestine, stretching from Jordan to the Mediterranean. The interests of both of these forces, real or perceived, tend to converge on the promotion of war and political convulsion in the region. It is this convergence of interests that explains the unofficial, unspoken, de facto alliance between representatives of these two ominously powerful interest groups.

Radical Zionists, striving to capture the "land of Israel," have always tried to portray opponents of their territorial ambitions not only as enemies of Israel but also of the United States. The thrust of this strategy is to enlist American support for Israel's wars of land acquisition. Under the bipolar world of the Cold War era, however, the United States needed its Arab and/or Muslim "allies" in the Middle East in order to counter the influence of the Soviet Union in the region. This meant that, in its support of Israel, the United States could not afford to abandon those allies and fully comply with Zionist demands of regime or border change in the region as long as the Soviet Union existed as a balancing superpower vis-à-vis the United States.

But the collapse of the Soviet Union and the end of the Cold War changed that geopolitical scenario. The demise of the Soviet system prompted the military-industrial complex to seek substitutes for the "communist threat" of the Cold War era in order to maintain continued escalation of the Pentagon budget. And as representatives of the arms industry and related businesses thus sought alternative threats to the Soviet threat of the Cold War period, they found in radical Islam, long promoted by a number of ideological and political leaders of militant Zionism as a major "threat to Western civilization," an apparently plausible candidate. Thereafter, the interests of militant Zionism in fighting "radical Islam" converged with those of the U.S. military-industrial complex—hence, the de facto alliance between the two powerful interests. The cabal of neoconservative militarists in and around the Bush administration largely represents and/or serves these interests.

Once radical Islam was thus portrayed as the "source of international conflicts" and the "menace to Western civilization," preemptive measures to counter such threats followed logically. The neoconservatives' case for "World War IV" (extending beyond Iraq, to Iran and Syria and other targets) rests on this carefully scripted scenario.[88]

What can be done to rein in the dangerously unbridled neoconservative war makers?

There is no doubt that the neoconservatives' adventurous foreign policy is a threat to world peace and stability. There is also no doubt that their policies are unnecessarily costing American lives, menacing U.S. citizens' civil liberties, undermining their social safety net programs, curtailing the working people's rights and opportunities, plundering national resources, and creating a huge fiscal strain. Equally, there is no question that the neoconservatives' pyrrhic success—so far—in shaping U.S. foreign policy, including the invasion of Iraq, has benefited from heavy doses of deception, disinformation, and Machiavellian manipulations.

The question, rather, is how long can the cabal of neoconservatives get away with telling so many lies, committing so much fraud, and doing so much damage—both at home and abroad?

External/international resistance to the neoconservatives' adventures will obviously help. But the crucial, restraining opposition has to come from within, that is, from the American people. Such opposition to neoconservatives' destructive policies is bound to unfold. There are strong indications that as Eric Margolis points out, "[t]he longer U.S. forces stay in Iraq, the uglier the guerrilla war will get. And the more Americans will realize they were led into this needless conflict by a [president] manipulated by a cabal of neoconservatives whose primary loyalty is not" to the U.S. public but to certain nefarious special interest.[89] There is hope that as the American people realize that their sons and daughters are losing their lives because some policy makers lied, or that they are losing their jobs and livelihood because their national resources are squandered on the production of the means of destruction, they will demand the kind of accountability that will go some way to make the perpetrators of war and deception pay for their destructive policies.

CHAPTER 7

Waste, Inefficiency, and the Spoils of Military Spending

The waste, inefficiency, and corruption associated with the Pentagon budget are no longer a secret. The incestuous business relationships within the so-called Iron Triangle (the Pentagon, its major contractors, and the key congressional committees) have developed into a perversely efficient vehicle for the funneling of the lion's share of the public treasure into the coffers of the Pentagon and its major business clients. Through their big monies and influential lobbying entities, beneficiaries of war dividends have managed to shape crucial decisions on both foreign policy and the allocation of national resources in their own favor. Most members of Congress have grown increasingly addicted to generous contributions to their reelection that come from the fortunes of the Pentagon and its contractors. It is not surprising, then, that many elected officials with an input or voting power in the process of the appropriation of the Pentagon budget find themselves in the pocket of defense contractors, so to speak. Neither is it surprising that these dubious relationships should serve as a breeding ground for the near legendary levels of waste, inefficiency, and corruption that surround the Iron Triangle.

Military Spending, Waste, and Inefficiency

You have a black hole at the Pentagon for money and a blind Congress.
—*Danielle Brian, director of the Project on Governmental Oversight*

Studies of the post–World War II military spending in the United States show that, as the late Sidney Lens put it, the Pentagon "wastes the taxpayer's money like the proverbial sailor on a drunken binge." *Congressional Record* (vol. 115, no. 42, p. S2519) reveals that "during the 1950s virtually all large military contractors . . . ultimately involved costs in excess of original contractual estimates of from 300 to 700 percent." More than a decade later, a Congressional Subcommittee on Economy in Government, headed by the late Wisconsin Senator William Proxmire, showed that the situation had not improved since the 1950s and that the Pentagon's perennial tendency toward "excessive costs, burgeoning military budgets, and scandalous performance" continued unabated. "With the help of few people in the Pentagon itself, such as A. E. Fitzgerald, who were ready to talk regardless of personal consequences, Proxmire's subcommittee . . . uncovered a miasma of waste, inefficiency, and probably corruption."[1] Here is a sample of the subcommittee's findings:

> The Minuteman II, which was expected to cost $3.3 billion will actually cost $7 billion, an overrun of almost $4 billion. The C-5A cargo plane, built by Lockheed, was bid at $3 billion but will run at least $2 billion more. Eight hundred Mark IIs were first figured at $610 million but are now expected to cost at least $2.5 billion. The SRAM missiles, estimated at $301 million in January 1968, by December 1968 were expected to cost upward of $636 million. The Navy DSRV—deep submersible rescue vessel—which was supposed to be built for $36.5 million for 12 vessels is now priced at $480 million for 6; and according to Senator Proxmire there is only a single instance in the last 40 years where such a rescue vessel could have been of use.[2]

This was almost 35 years ago. The shocking revelations of waste and inefficiency led many to be believe that the Pentagon and its contractors would henceforth rectify their practice of squandering taxpayers' money. But the Pentagon's financial profligacy continued unabated. Some 15 years later, even more shocking revelations of its abuse of the public money came to light. This was during the 1984 examination of its books by Senator Chuck Grassley's subcommittee, which exposed the scandalous $400 hammers, $640 toilet seats, and $7,600 coffee pots. When asked if the Department of Defense had improved its handling of tax dollars, Senator Grassley replied: "One would think it [his subcommittee's revelation of corruption] would have made a lasting impression at the Pentagon. Apparently, not even being hit figuratively over the head with a $400 hammer knocked enough sense into the bureaucracy. Since then, I've continued to dig up procurement problems at the Pentagon. That includes 'watching the watchdog,' the internal auditors at the Department of Defense who are charged with ferreting out fraud, waste and abuse in the Pentagon."[3]

But while the "comically expensive toilet seats, hammers, and coffee pots have attracted widespread attention," points out Jacques S. Gansler, a former deputy assistant secretary in the Department of Defense, "a much more serious concern is the dizzying rise in the cost of weapon systems. The cost of a single aircraft carrier is now about $3.4 billion, an F-15 fighter aircraft around $38 million, a B-1B bomber well over $200 million, and each new M-1 tank around $2.4 million. If costs continue to rise at the current rate of 7 percent a year in constant dollars, the next generation of systems could cost twice as much."[4]

In an article titled "Military waste under fire: $1 trillion missing," Tom Abate of the *San Francisco Chronicle* reported on May 18, 2003, "The Department of Defense, already infamous for spending $640 for a toilet seat, once again finds itself under intense scrutiny, only this time because it couldn't account for more than a trillion dollars in financial transactions, not to mention dozens of tanks, missiles and planes." A General Accounting Office (GAO) report, continued Abate, "found Defense inventory systems so lax that the U.S. Army lost track of 56 airplanes, 32 tanks, and 36 Javelin missile command launch-units." Abate further indicated that, following these unsavory revelations, the GAO reviewed the progress of a proposed "Corporate Information Management" (CIM) system designed to cut the Pentagon's rampant waste and inefficiency. "The initiative began in 1989 as an attempt to unify more than 2,000 overlapping systems then being used for billing, inventory, personnel and similar functions. But after 'spending about $20 billion, the CIM initiative was eventually abandoned,' the GAO said."[5]

Gregory Kutz, director of the GAO's financial management division and coauthor of the report on Pentagon waste and inefficiency, contrasted the Pentagon's shoddy bookkeeping and inventory controls to the financial control systems at big nonmilitary private corporations: "I've been to Wal-Mart. . . . They were able to tell me how many tubes of toothpaste were in Fairfax, Va., at that given moment. And DoD [Department of Defense] can't find its chem-bio suits." As part of his report for the *San Francisco Chronicle*, Abate also interviewed Danielle Brian, director of the Project on Governmental Oversight, a nonprofit group in Washington, D.C. Paraphrasing Brian, he wrote, "waste has become ingrained in the Defense budget because opposition to defense spending is portrayed as unpatriotic, and legislators are often more concerned about winning Pentagon pork than controlling defense waste." Abate also reported a direct quote from Brian: "You have a black hole at the Pentagon for money and a blind Congress."[6]

Readers of these lines would understandably find it hard to believe that the Pentagon could not have been able to account for one trillion dollars of the tax payers' money—nearly one-tenth of the gross national product, or $3,636 for every man, woman, and child in the United States. It turns out, however, that 21 months earlier Secretary of Defense Donald Rumsfeld had confessed to a much larger sum: "According to some estimates we cannot track $2.3 trillion in transactions," Rumsfeld admitted in a statement to reporters on September 10, 2001. ($2.3 trillion—that's $8,000 for every man, woman, and child in the nation.) Rumsfeld promised change. But the next day's criminal attacks on the World Trade Center and the Pentagon sent the whole monumental fraud into oblivion. Not that he could have untangled the Gordian knot of the Pentagon's financial chaos; but that the attacks helped relieve the Pentagon from having to undergo another long, and most probably inconsequential, inquiry.

To understand how the Pentagon can lose track of trillions, CBS News correspondent Vince Gonzales followed the case of one military accountant, Jim Minnery, who tried to find out what happened to a mere $300 million. "We know it's gone. But we don't know what they spent it on," Minnery told Gonzales. A former Marine turned whistle-blower, Minnery risked his job by speaking out for the first time about the millions he noticed were missing from one defense agency's balance sheets. He tried to follow the money trail, even crisscrossing the country looking for records. "The director looked at me and said 'Why do you care about this stuff?' It took me aback, you know? My supervisor asking me why I care about doing a good job," said Minnery. He was reassigned; and "officials then covered up the problem by just writing it off," he told Gonzales. "They have to cover it up," he said. "That's where the corruption comes in. They have to cover up the fact that they can't do the job." In the course of preparing his report for CBS News, Gonzales also spoke with a number of Defense Department officials and analysts, both present and past. One of those analysts was Franklin C. Spinney, who had 22 years earlier made headlines exposing what he called the "accounting games." Spinney told Gonzales, "Those numbers are pie in the sky. The books are cooked routinely year after year." Another analyst was retired Vice Admiral Jack Shanahan, who commanded the Navy's 2nd Fleet the first time Donald Rumsfeld served as Defense Secretary (1976). According to Shanahan,

"With good financial oversight we could find $48 billion in loose change in that building [the Pentagon], without having to hit the taxpayers."[7]

The Pentagon's waste and inefficiency are not limited to shady bookkeeping and fraudulent accounting; perhaps more importantly, such unsavory practices are even more prevalent in the production or manufacturing of the armaments. There is no dearth of information on the often shoddy, and sometimes comical, products of the Pentagon's arms producing contractors. I cite here only two instances, one from the past and one very recent, so as to show that the waste and inefficiency of Pentagon contractors is a systemic and apparently incorrigible pattern.

Some 35 years ago, the aforementioned congressional subcommittee of Senator William Proxmire revealed that weapons come off the assembly line "two years later than promised," on the average, and fall far below specifications in the contract. It further showed that "of 13 major aircrafts and missile programs with sophisticated electronic systems built for the Air Force and Navy since 1955 at a cost of $40 billion, only four, costing $5 billion, could be relied on to reach a performance level of 75 percent or above of their specifications." Four others, costing $13 billion, "broke down at a performance level which was 75 percent or less than their specifications." Two, for which the taxpayers paid $10 billion, were so poor they had to be scrapped after three years because of "low reliability," and two, costing $2 billion, had to be abandoned.[8]

By all accounts this pattern of inefficiency has not improved since then. Reporting on the perennial and prevalent waste and inefficiency in the arms industry, Julian Borger and David Teather of the London-based *Guardian* newspaper wrote on May 22, 2003, that the F-22, made by Lockheed Martin and Boeing, "has been dogged by technical problems and huge cost over-runs. Each plane is now priced at $257m, more than $50m above estimates only a few years ago." The marines' V-22 Osprey, an experimental tilt-rotor plane made by Boeing, "also gets a further $1bn, despite a series of fatal crashes and delays that have put the project 10 years behind schedule."[9]

Another example: in mid-August 1997, the General Accounting Office (GAO) released a report on the B-2 bomber. The GAO found that the bomber, for which the taxpayers had to pay $45 billion for 21 planes— $2.1 billion per plane—deteriorates in rain, heat, and humidity and "must be sheltered or exposed only to the most benign environments." The "environmentally controlled shelters" in which they must be housed are not available in overseas bases, at which the plane was supposed to be located to quickly penetrate to the Soviet heartland. Because of its fragility and vulnerability to weather, the plane was also found to require up to 124 hours of maintenance time for each hour in the air, which of course made it phenomenally expensive even beyond its staggering capital cost. Another problem with the plane is that, partly because of its great fragility and sensitivity to climate, it doesn't work. The GAO found that the B-2 failed in its trial missions 74 percent of the time and that its radar "could not tell a rain cloud from a mountainside."[10]

Discussions of waste and inefficiency surrounding the Pentagon and its arms producing clients often tend to focus almost exclusively on the economic or financial losses to the tax payers. While this is, of course, important, it overlooks an even more ominous consequence of the arms industry's substandard and inefficient products: death and destruction of innocent lives and targets in countries labeled as "our enemies." There are indications that the Pentagon often embarks on theatrical bombardments and melodramatic military operations that seem to be designed to camouflage and rehabilitate the deficiencies of the military hardware in the plumes of smoke, the blaze of fire, and the blitz of the acquiescent corporate media. To justify their appropriation of the lion's share of the public money, the Pentagon and its major contractors have strong incentives to show that they use taxpayers' money efficiently—often as measured in terms of actual or potential deaths and destruction per dollar. The massive display of high-tech military hardware in Iraq and Afghanistan that has killed or maimed tens of thousands of people is an indication of this cynical military strategy.

A major part of the armaments industry's inefficiency is no doubt due to the monopolistic or oligopolistic structure of the industry. Ironically, most of the leaders of the industry (and their co-thinkers among the proponents of unilateral militarism) purport to be fervent advocates of free enterprise and competitive markets. Yet, their own business or manufacturing practices are based on anything but competition. The major bulk of weapons procurement is done without competitive bidding; it is often done simply through negotiation between Pentagon contractors and a high-ranking military official, a general or a colonel. "The contractor, therefore, makes a low estimate to begin with, so as not to unduly alarm the Secretary of Defense or congressional skeptics, and then goes on to spend two or three times as much, with little fear that the Pentagon will, or can, cancel his order."[11]

Monopolistic enterprises are divided into two categories in formal, textbook economics. The first type, called natural monopoly, acquires a monopolistic status by virtue of its market efficiency. The second type enjoys a monopolistic status not by virtue of its superior productivity or market competitiveness but through legal or political protection. Arms producers are obviously of the latter type. The nonmarket, questionable political and/or business relationships prevailing within the Iron Triangle—the Pentagon, its prime contractors, and the key congressional committees—allow armaments manufacturers to be treated with "regal generosity," as the late Sidney Lens, author of *The Military-Industrial Complex*, put it. They often do business in government-owned land or in government-owned buildings and facilities free of charge. Nor do they pay for the government-owned machinery and equipment or other infrastructural facilities when they use them in their process of production.

Another example of the Pentagon's generosity toward its industrial clients is its patent policy. The government usually finances the arms industry's research and development (R&D) projects, but it "permits contractors to obtain exclusive patent rights, free of charge, on inventions produced in the performance of government contracts." For example, the Boeing 707 commercial plane was essentially an "offshoot" of the KC-135 military jet tanker. "Hundreds of spin-off products, first developed with DoD, NASA, or AEC money, are now being marketed commercially by the corporations, for their own profit." The Pentagon's generosity toward its major contractors is also evident in its policy of advance financing, which is paying for what is to be produced ahead of time. "While they are still fabricating the weapons, contractors may receive substantial 'progress' payments, which in effect are interest-free loans. . . . Any non-defense manufacturer in America would give his left eyetooth for terms so favorable."[12]

Now, how can all this waste, inefficiency, and dubious practice surrounding the Pentagon and its prime contractors be explained? Are they simply instances of unavoidable errors, or innocent mismanagement? These and similar questions are admittedly rhetorical given the extensive public knowledge, or well-founded perceptions, of the disreputable business relationships between the Pentagon, its prime contractors, and the key congressional committees. Let us examine some of these shabby relationships more closely.

The "Revolving Door" Syndrome and the Spoils of Military Spending

As noted above, it is no longer a secret that the dubious business and political relationships between various influential circles of power within the

Iron Triangle are at the heart of the waste, inefficiency, and corruption that has developed around military spending and war industries. What is rather surprising is that, despite all the notoriety surrounding the shady deals within the Triangle, those questionable relationships have kept further expanding and solidifying over time. More than three decades ago, Sidney Lens, author of *The Military-Industrial Complex*, observed: "Many of the same men who negotiated the lush deals with private business when they wore Pentagon hats used their influence and inside knowledge on behalf of defense companies after retirement."[13] That practice of switching positions back and forth between the Pentagon, its prime contractors, and the lobbying think tanks supporting those contractors—a practice or pattern that is sometimes called the "revolving door syndrome"—continues to this day. That fact that today President Bush's national security apparatus is heavily infested with former managers, advisors, or shareholders of weapons contractors is a strong testament to this revolving door phenomenon.

According to William Hartung, author of *How Much Are You Making on the War, Daddy?*, Lockheed Martin, the nation's largest defense contractor, has more connections to the Bush administration than any other major defense contractor—eight current policy makers had direct or indirect ties to the company before joining the administration. Former Lockheed Chief Operating Officer Peter Teets is now Undersecretary of the Air Force and Director of the National Reconnaissance Office, a post that includes making decisions on the acquisition of everything from reconnaissance satellites to space-based elements of missile defense. Lynne Cheney, wife of Vice President Dick Cheney, served on Lockheed's board of directors from 1994 until January 2001, accumulating more than $500,000 in deferred director's fees in the process. Northrop Grumman, the nation's third largest defense contractor, follows closely behind Lockheed with seven former officials, consultants or shareholders in the Bush administration. Northrop's most important link is James Roche, a former company vice president, who became the Secretary of the Air Force. The company's influence within the Air Force is reinforced by the presence of Assistant Secretary of the Air Force for Installations, Environment and Logistics Nelson Gibbs, who served as corporate comptroller at Northrop from 1991 to 1999. Paul Wolfowitz, Deputy Secretary of Defense during President Bush's first term in office and presently the head of the World Bank, Pentagon Comptroller Dov Zakheim, and Undersecretary of Defense Douglas Feith all had consulting contracts or served on paid advisory boards for Northrop prior to joining the administration. Other ties include: Secretary of the Navy Gordon England, a former vice president at General Dynamics, Deputy Secretary of State Richard Armitage, a former member of Raytheon's board of directors and consultant to Boeing, and Karl Rove, senior advisor to the president, who owned between $100,000 and $250,000 in Boeing stock, according to disclosure forms he has filed.[14]

In a "special report" on the ties between the Defense Policy Board, the government-appointed group that advises the Pentagon and Pentagon contractors, André Verlöy and Daniel Politi of The Center for Public Integrity recently showed that "of the 30 members of the Defense Policy Board at least nine have ties to companies that have won more than $76 billion in defense contracts in 2001 and 2002. Four members are registered lobbyists, one of whom represents two of the three largest defense contractors." According to its charter, the board was set up in 1985 to provide the Secretary of Defense "with independent, informed advice and opinion concerning major matters of defense policy." The members are selected by and report to the Under Secretary of Defense for Policy. All members are approved by the Secretary of Defense. "The board, whose list of members reads like a who's who of former high-level government and military officials, focuses on long-term policy issues such as the strategic implications of defense policies and tactical considerations, including what types of weapons the military should develop." Although board members have no official role in policy decisions, and the board was traditionally more bipartisan, "under Rumsfeld, it has become more interested in policy changes." And while board members are required to disclose their business interests annually to the Pentagon, the disclosures are not available to the public. The companies with ties to Defense Policy Board members include major contractors such as Boeing, TRW, Northrop Grumman, Lockheed Martin and Booz Allen Hamilton, as well as smaller contactors such as Symantec Corp., Technology Strategies and Alliance Corp., and Polycom Inc.[15]

Of the nine board members with ties to Pentagon contractors, Richard Perle represents one of the most notorious cases of conflict of interests. He was the chairman of the Defense Policy Board until March 27, 2003, when he had to resign as chair due to blatant cases of conflict of interest emanating from his representing companies with business before the Defense Department. Perle, who was at the forefront of the campaign to invade Iraq, also "reportedly advised clients of Goldman Sachs on investment opportunities in post-war Iraq, and is a director with stock options of the

U.K.-based Autonomy Corp., whose customers include the Defense Department." In a March 24, 2003 letter, which seems to have prompted Perle's resignation three days later, Rep. John Conyers, the ranking Democrat on the House of Representatives Judiciary Committee, "asked the Pentagon's inspector general to investigate Perle's role as a paid adviser to the bankrupt telecommunications company Global Crossing Ltd." The letter also indicated that Perle might have lobbied on behalf of the Hamilton, Bermuda–based, company that "sought approval of its sale of overseas subsidiaries from the Committee on Foreign Investment in the United States, a government panel that can block sales or mergers that conflict with U.S. national security interests. Rumsfeld is a member of the Committee."[16]

Although Perle's became a most notorious case of illicit dealings within the Iron Triangle, he was by no means the only member of the Defense Policy Board with questionable ties to companies that do business with the Pentagon. Verlöy, Politi, and Pilhofer of the Center for Public Integrity disclose similarly dubious relations between the other eight Board members and the Pentagon contractors.

Retired Adm. David Jeremiah, a former vice chairman of the Joint Chiefs of Staff who served over 38 years in the Navy, is a director or advisor of at least five corporations that received more than $10 billion in Pentagon contracts in 2002. Jeremiah also sat on the board of Getronics Government Solutions, a company that was acquired by DigitalNet in December 2002 and is now known as DigitalNet Government Solutions. According to a news report by Bloomberg, Richard Perle is a director of DigitalNet Holdings Inc., which has filed for a $109 million stock sale.

Retired Air Force Gen. Ronald Fogleman sits on the board of directors of companies which received more than $900 million in contracts in 2002. The companies, which all have long-standing business relationships with the Air Force and other Defense Department branches, include Rolls-Royce North America, North American Airlines, AAR Corporation, and the Mitre Corp. In addition to being chief of staff for the Air Force, Fogleman has served as a military advisor to the Secretary of Defense, the National Security Council and the president. He also served as commander in chief of the U.S. Transportation Command, commander of Air Mobility Command, the 7th Air Force, and the Air Component Command of the U.S./ROK Combined Forces Command.

Retired Gen. Jack Sheehan joined Bechtel in 1998 after 35 years in the United States Marine Corp. Bechtel, one of the world's largest engineering-construction firms, is among the companies bidding for contracts to rebuild Iraq. The company had defense contracts worth close to $650 million in 2001 and more than $1 billion in 2002. Sheehan is currently a senior vice president and partner and responsible for the execution and strategy for the region that includes Europe, Africa, the Middle East, and Southwest Asia. The four-star general served as NATO's Supreme Allied Commander Atlantic and commander in chief U.S. Atlantic Command before his retirement in 1997. After leaving active duty, he served as Special Advisor for Central Asia for two secretaries of defense.

Former CIA director James Woolsey is a principal in the Paladin Capital Group, a venture-capital firm that, similar to Perle's Trireme Partners, is soliciting investment for homeland security firms. Woolsey joined consulting firm Booz Allen Hamilton as vice president in July 2002. The company had contracts worth more than $680 million in 2002. Woolsey told the *Wall Street Journal* that he does no lobbying and that none of the companies he has ties to have been discussed during a Defense Policy Board meeting.

William Owens, another former high-level military officer, sits on boards of five companies that received more than $60 million in defense contracts in the year 2002. Previously, he was president, chief operating officer, and vice chair of Science Applications International Corporation (SAIC), among the ten largest defense contractors. One of the companies, Symantec Corp., increased its contracts from $95,000 in 2001 to more than $1 million in 2002. Owens, who served as vice chairman of the Joint Chiefs of Staff, is widely recognized for bringing commercial high technology into the U.S. Department of Defense. He was the architect of the Revolution in Military Affairs (RMA), an advanced systems technology approach to military operations that represents a significant change in the system of requirements, budgets, and technology for the U.S. military since World War II. Owens serves on the boards of directors for several technology companies, including Nortel Networks, ViaSat, and Polycom.

Harold Brown, a former Secretary of Defense under President Jimmy Carter, and James Schlesinger, who has served as CIA director, defense secretary, and energy secretary in the Carter and Nixon administrations, are two others who have ties to defense contractors. Brown, a partner of Warburg Pincus LLC, is a board member of Philip Morris Companies and a trustee of the Rand Corporation, which respectively had contracts worth $146 million and $83 million in 2002. Schlesinger, a senior adviser at Lehman Brothers, chairs the board of trustees of the Mitre Corp., a not-for-profit that provides research and development support for the government. Mitre had defense contracts worth $440 million in 2001 and $474 million in 2002.

Chris Williams is one of four registered lobbyists to serve on the board, and the only one to lobby for defense companies. Williams, who served as a special assistant for policy matters to Defense Secretary Rumsfeld after having been in a similar capacity for Sen. Trent Lott (R-Miss.), joined Johnston & Associates after leaving the Pentagon. Although the firm had represented Lockheed Martin prior to Williams's arrival, the firm picked up two large defense contractors as clients once Williams was on board: Boeing, TRW and Northrop Grumman, for which the firm earned a total of more than $220,000. The firm lobbied exclusively on defense appropriations and related authorization bills for its new clients. Johnston & Associates is more often employed by energy companies; its founder, J. Bennett Johnston, is a former Democratic senator from Louisiana who chaired the Energy Committee.

The board's membership also contains other well-known Washington hands, including some who are registered lobbyists. Richard V. Allen, a former Nixon and Reagan administration official, who is now a senior counselor to APCO Worldwide, registered as a lobbyist for Alliance Aircraft. Thomas S. Foley is a partner at Akin, Gump, Strauss, Hauer & Feld law firm, which he joined in 2001. He was the U.S. ambassador to Japan from 1997 to 2001 and was the Speaker of the House of Representatives from 1989 to 1994, after being a representative since 1965. Foley is a registered lobbyist, but has no defense clients.[17] (Corporate affiliations of Defense Policy Board members are summarized in table 7.1 below.)

These facts and figures paint an unflattering picture of the political and economic relationships between the powers that can make or instigate war and the economic interests that benefit from it, that is, between war makers and war profiteers. The near unity of the two helps explain why critical policy issues such as war and military appropriations are increasingly being made under the sway of the military-industrial complex and/or the Iron Triangle. In light of the strong influence of war profiteers in the making of critical policy decisions, the rising tendency to war and militarism, having reached new heights under President George W. Bush, should come as no surprise.

Beneficiaries of war dividends are, of course, well aware that their lucrative business of war depends primarily on the maintenance or escalation of war and international political tensions. This helps explain why unilateral

Table 7.1 Corporate Affiliations of Defense Policy Board Members

	Position	*Defense Contracts 2001*	*Defense Contractors 2002*
Harold Brown			
Philip Morris Companies	Board Member	$153,388,337	$146,335,573
Rand Corp.	Trustee	$62,423,257	$83,512,278
Ronald R. Fogleman			
AAR Corporation	Board Member	$65,803,654	$87,821,945
DERCO Aerospace	Board Member	$13,883,258	$13,725,437
ICN Pharmaceuticals	Board Member	$30,000	$49,120
The Mitre Corp.	Board Member	$440,641,017	$474,293,940
North American Airlines	Board Member	$4,889,880	$624,385,094
Rolls-Royce North America	Board Member	$345,065,274	$266,433,147
Thales-Raytheon	Board Member	$3,894,808	$115,280,830
World Airways	Board Member	$(692,986)	$(1,110,514)
David Jeremiah			
Alliant Techsystems	Board Member	$493,830,461	$674,013,008
DigitalNet Government Solutions	Board Member	$44,085,906	$54,016,945
ManTech International Corp.	Advisory Board	$166,059,013	$210,213,983
The Mitre Corp.	Trustee	$440,641,017	$474,293,940
Northrop Grumman Corp.	Advisory Board	$5,152,610,683	$8,732,668,154
Technology Strategies and Alliance Corporation	President	$1,304,810	$60,578
Wackenhut Services	Chairman	$3,208,308	$14,056,103
Philip Merrill*			
Johns Hopkins University	Board Member	$267,143,496	$461,776,483
William Owens			
Microvision	Board Member	$7,508,869	$5,470,165
Nortel Networks Corp.	Board Member	$1,680,610	$271,421
Polycom Inc.	Board Member	$365,853	$178,772
Symantec Corp.	Board Member	$95,741	$1,069,086
ViaSat Inc.	Board Member	$27,442,414	$54,623,408
James Schlesinger			
The Mitre Corp.	Trustee	$440,641,017	$474,293,940
Henry M. Jackson Foundation	Trustee	$11,326,982	$12,490,379
Jack Sheehan			
Bechtel	Senior Vice President	$643,633,530	$1,030,847,151

Continued

Table 7.1 Continued

	Position	Defense Contracts 2001	Defense Contractors 2002
Chris Williams			
Boeing	Lobbyist	$13,979,871,122	$17,325,629,858
Northrop Grumman Corp.	Lobbyist	$5,152,610,683	$8,732,668,154
TRW	Lobbyist	$1,903,297,527	$2,026,546,041
R. James Woolsey			
Booz Allen Hamilton	Vice President (Joined 2002)	$435,015,272	$687,553,097

Notes: All contract figures are for parent companies, except Derco Aerospace and Thales-Raytheon, which together add $19 billion to the total.
*Merrill was appointed president and chairman of the Export-Import Bank of the United States in December 2002. He is no longer serving on the Defense Policy Board.
Source: U.S. Department of Defense, as cited by André Verlöy, Daniel Politi, and Aron Pilhofer, "Advisors of Influence: Nine Members of the Defense Policy Board Have Ties to Defense Contractors," The Center for Public Integrity <http://www.publicintegrity.org/report.aspx?aid=91 &sid=200>.

militarist forces of the ruling elite, the so-called neoconservative forces, strongly supported by the military-industrial complex, opposed demands for demobilization and downsizing of the armed forces following the collapse of the Berlin Wall in 1989. To defeat such demands and to stifle the voices that called for "peace dividends" in the immediate aftermath of the Cold War, these forces successfully substituted "new threats to our national security" (rogue states, global terrorism, militant Islam) for the "communist threat" of the Cold War era, thereby maintaining the continued escalation of military spending. This also helps explain why the Bush administration, under the heavy influence of the military-industrial complex, viewed the 9/11 tragedy as an opportunity for remilitarization and war. The monstrous attacks of 9/11 were treated not as crimes—requiring prosecution through police, intelligence, and judicial work and cooperation on an international level—but as war on America.

Once the 9/11 brutalities were thus exploited as opportunities for war and militarism, heightened military spending followed without much opposition. As Michelle Ciarrocca of the Arms Trade Resource Center put it, "President Bush's military budget increase and the war time 'unity' on Capitol Hill have created an environment in which weapons makers can enjoy the best of both worlds—continuing to make money on the weapons systems of the cold war while reaping the benefits of a war time bonanza of new defense contracts." Quoting Loren Thompson, a defense analyst with the Lexington Institute, Ciarrocca further wrote: "The whole mind set of military spending changed on Sept. 11. The most fundamental thing about defense spending is that threats drive defense spending. It's now going to be easier to fund almost anything."[18]

Although prior to 9/11 President Bush had promised big increases in the Pentagon budget, he had also stated that those increases must accompany a reconfiguration of the military apparatus, especially of the procurement's shopping list. At the heart of the projected reconfiguration was the plan to prioritize military spending in favor of high-tech, "futuristic" weaponry: moving beyond the Cold War model (of building a huge arsenal of tanks, planes, ships, and missiles to contain the Soviet Union) and into the "Revolution in Military Affairs" (of giving priority to high-tech warfare such as smart bombs, night-vision instruments, satellites, robot observation planes, highly mobile light armor, and so on). As this threatened the powerful interests that had been deeply vested in the Cold War model since World War II, tensions flared up within the military-industrial establishment. The *New York Times* characterized the skirmishes as a battle "as intense and intemperate as any in recent memory."

But the 9/11 attacks averted the contested prioritization of military spending. It saved the policy makers the pain of reslicing the pie of the Pentagon budget by drastically augmenting the size of the pie. As James Cypher of the California State University at Fresno put it, "It allowed the Pentagon to have its cake and eat it too—continuing major Cold War-era weapons systems and funding the cyber-age 'Revolution in Military Affairs' (RMA)."[19]

The flow of an additional $47 billion, in the form of an "emergency response fund," into the coffers of the Pentagon in the immediate aftermath of September 11 ended the prioritization debate as it filled all the deep pockets of the beneficiaries of the Pentagon budget. This raised military spending for the fiscal year 2002 by nearly $54 billion over the initial 2001 level of $291 billion, an increase of almost 19 percent. In all, the official Pentagon budget has gone up thus far nearly 45 percent under President Bush, from $291 billion in 2001 to almost $420 billion in 2005. This does not include the nearly $300 billion cost (so far) of the wars in Iraq and Afghanistan. The U.S. now spends more each year than the next 20 largest national defense budgets combined; it is responsible for nearly half of the world's military spending. According to President Bush's plans for military spending, by 2007 "defense" spending will be 20 percent higher than average cold war levels.[20]

This heightened tempo of war and militarism under President Bush has been a boon for war industries and related businesses. Manufacturers of fighter planes will receive an astonishing $400 billion in new multiyear contracts. Lockheed Martin will get $225 billion over 12 years to build nearly 3,000 Joint Strike Fighter planes for the Air Force, Marines, and Navy. According to *Business Week*, Lockheed will also be able to earn $175 billion from sales in foreign markets. Almost 50 percent of the world arms market is currently controlled by the United States. "That figure will be on the rise," points out Cypher, "as new weapons are delivered to Pakistan, Uzbekistan, Tajikistan, Oman, the United Arab Emirates, and Egypt." Cypher further points out,

> Looking ahead, the RMA's [Revolution in Military Affairs'] fantastic weaponry—and its enormous costs—are only just beginning to emerge. Northrup Gruman, General Atomics, and Boeing are speeding robot airplanes into production. Other contractors are developing thermal imaging sensors to "see" targets through night, distance, fog, and even rock formations. The Navy is promoting a new destroyer-class warship, the DD-21, loaded with cruise missiles and guns capable of hitting targets 100 miles inland. Known as the "stealth bomber for the ocean," the DD-21 is estimated to cost $24 billion. Cost overruns of over 300 percent are common, however, so there is no telling what taxpayers will ultimately pay.[21]

Spending on "homeland security" has added further profits to the arms manufacturers' hefty windfalls from the Iraq and Afghan wars: "With the new influx of money for homeland defense . . . virtually all of the big defense contractors—Boeing, Lockheed Martin, and Raytheon—have adapted their marketing strategies and are repackaging their products for use in domestic security," points out Michelle Ciarrocca of the Arms Trade Resource Center. "Boeing is looking into how its sensors designed to track enemy missiles could be used to locate and identify hijacked planes. Lockheed is trying to adapt military simulators to train local emergency response teams. And Raytheon is pitching its hand-held thermal-imaging devices, designed for the military, as useful for fire fighters searching through collapsed buildings."[22]

While these giant manufacturers of warfare instruments are profiting handsomely from President Bush's wars, there is also a whole host of new technology wizards, or "homeland security companies," as *Business Week* calls them, that have spun around the recently created Homeland Security apparatus. These smaller companies, too, are "dusting off old domestic security proposals and developing new ones in an attempt to cash in on what they hope will ultimately be hundreds of billions of dollars in new spending on homeland security," according to *The Wall Street Journal*. Air Structures is introducing fortified vinyl domes for quarantining infected communities in the aftermath of a potential bioterror attack, Visionics is looking into designing facial recognition technology, and PointSource Technologies is developing a sensor to detect biological agents in the air or water.[23]

The fact that military industries flourish on war and international political convulsion has also been reflected in the stock prices of war-based industries since the 9/11 attacks and the ensuing wars on Afghanistan and Iraq. The attacks led to the collapse and temporary shut down of the Wall Street stock market. When it reopened several days later, the few companies showing increased value were the giant military contractors. Among the top gainers for the week of September 17–21, 2001, were military and space contractors such as Lockheed Martin (+30 percent), Raytheon (+37 percent), L-3 Communications (+35.8 percent), Alliant Techsystems (+23.5 percent), and Northrop Grumman (+21.2 percent).[24]

While these giant manufacturers of the means of death and destruction are the obvious beneficiaries of the escalating war and militarism, there are also many less visible Pentagon contractors that are just as handsomely benefiting from the expanded military spending. These are the somewhat clandestine, privately contracted companies that operate on the fringes of U.S. foreign policy by training foreign armies and "security forces," or by "fighting terrorism." As Ken Silverstein of *The Nation* magazine points out, "With little public knowledge, or debate, the government has been dispatching private companies—most of them with tight links to the Pentagon and staffed by retired armed forces personnel—to provide military and police training to America's foreign allies."[25] Thus, "When the Pentagon talks about training the new Afghan National Army, it does not mean with its own soldiers. . . . Instead, the Defense Department is drawing up plans to use its commandos to jump-start the Afghan force, then hire private military contractors to finish the job."[26]

Referring to the fierce competition among these private military training companies to win Pentagon contracts, Pete Singer, an Olin Fellow in the Foreign Policy Studies Program at the Brookings Institution in Washington, points out, "This is big business among these companies. They are furiously bidding on involvement in Afghanistan and the war on terrorism. The minute the Pentagon started to use the phrase 'a program to train and equip the Afghan army,' buzzers went off." The Bush administration's open-ended "war on terrorism" promises to be a boon for these companies: "The war on terrorism is the full employment act for these guys," pointed out D. B. Des Roches, spokesman for the Pentagon's Defense Security Cooperation Agency.[27]

As discussed earlier in this chapter, these private military firms are often formed by retired Special Forces personnel seeking to market their military expertise to the Pentagon, the State Department, the CIA, or foreign governments. For example, MPRI, one of the largest and most active of these firms, which "has trained militaries throughout the world under contract to the Pentagon," was founded by the former Army Chief of Staff Carl Vuono and seven other retired generals. It counts 20 former senior military officers on its board of directors. Army Lt. Gen. Harry E. Soyster, an executive at MPRI, boasts: "We have got more generals per square foot here than in the Pentagon." Other major military firms include Vinnell, BDM International Inc., Armor Holdings Inc., DynCorp of Reston, VA, and SAIC. These and a number of the lesser known military training contractors "operate today in more than 40 countries, often under contract to the U.S. government." The fortunes of these private military training contractors, or modern mercenary enterprises, like those of the manufacturers of the military hardware, have skyrocketed in recent years, especially since the arrival of George W. Bush in the White House: "Since Sept. 11 and the Pentagon's launch of the war on terrorism, the stock prices of the publicly traded contractors have soared."[28]

In a May 31, 2004 report, titled "The Other U.S. Military," Spencer Ante and Stan Crock of *Business Week* revealed how military outsourcing, driven by high profits that are guaranteed by taxpayer dollars, "has been spiraling out of control: Like many businesses that have to staff up rapidly, some security contractors have cut corners in the rush to expand. On the ground in Iraq, contractors appear to have operated with little or no supervision. Mercenaries are not choirboys, but some outfits have signed up hired guns trained by repressive regimes. And revelations that civilians are performing sensitive tasks such as interrogation have jolted Congress and the public." Citing Major General Antonio Taguba's investigation of Baghdad's notorious Abu Ghraib prisoner abuse, the report further revealed that "two interrogators-for-hire, one from CACI International Inc. and one from Titan Corp., in conjunction with military officers, 'were either directly or indirectly responsible for the abuses at Abu Ghraib.' Titan says the individual worked for a subcontractor."

It is difficult to establish the extent or the exact magnitude of the private military contracting business because, as Ante and Crock point out, "there is no central register of contracts, and the Defense Dept. sometimes has other agencies do its purchasing. For example, the contract with CACI International Inc. at Abu Ghraib prison was administered by the Interior Dept., according to *The Washington Post*." The *Business Week* report also pointed out that "In a May 4 letter to the House Armed Services Committee, Defense Secretary Donald H. Rumsfeld said that approximately 20,000 private security workers are employed in Iraq. That doesn't include the thousands of civilians reconstructing bridges, roads, and phone lines."

The report further indicated that in the face of the lucrative and expanding business of military outsourcing, "some big defense contractors are scooping up PMCs [private military contractors], many of which— especially in the security sector—are small and privately held. Computer Sciences (CSC) acquired DynCorp, Northrop Grumman (NOC) bought Vinnell, and L-3 Communications nabbed Military Professional Resources Inc." Quoting Deborah D. Avant, a professor at George Washington University who is writing a book about military contractors, the report also indicated that the traditional giant Pentagon contractors "have been buying up these companies like mad. . . . This is where they think the future is."[29]

Merchants of Death and Destruction

> War is a racket. A racket is best described, I believe, as something that is not what it seems to the majority of the people. Only a small "inside" group knows what it is about. It is conducted for the benefit of the very few. . . . Beautiful ideals were painted for our boys who were sent out to die. . . . This was the "war to make the world safe for democracy." No one told them that dollars and cents were the real reason. No one mentioned to them, as they marched away, that their going and their dying would mean huge war profits . . . . They were just told it was to be a "glorious adventure."
> —General Smedley D. Butler

Debates over the pros and cons of military spending frequently tend to focus on such economic effects of military expenditures as job creation, technological innovation, and productivity enhancement. Critics also often point to waste, inefficiency, and corruption that are nurtured by overextended military establishments. While an understanding of such economic consequences of large military apparatuses is, of course, important, it is even more important not to lose sight of the fact that maintaining and/or justifying disproportionately large military budgets tends to be conducive to war and militarism.

What usually gets lost in the debate over the economic effects of military spending by a superpower is the fact that overgrown military establishments (beyond *legitimate* needs of defending one's borders or national sovereignty) breed war and international convulsion; they are often geared to death and destruction as they tend to instigate international tensions and wars in order to justify continued increases in military spending. Of course, wars have almost always been accompanied by war profiteers. Current or contemporary war profiteers in the United States are, however, of a new and different breed—a new variety or pattern that makes them more dangerous than those of the eras of empires past.

For one thing, beneficiaries of war dividends in the United States, the military-industrial complex, have evolved in recent years increasingly as major determinants of U.S. foreign policy, especially of crucial decisions on war and peace. As Howard Swint, Democratic candidate for Congress in West Virginia, put it: "The seat of power for formulating foreign policy and defense strategy is . . . in the Pentagon . . . . The political engineering by special interests on Capitol Hill is so complete that the Pentagon serves as little more than a conduit for defense appropriations."[30]

For another, arms manufacturers of the past empires were not subject to capitalist market imperatives, as are today's U.S. producers of armaments. Arms producing enterprises were often owned and operated by imperial governments, not by market-driven giant corporations. Consequently, as a rule, weapons production was dictated by war requirements, not by market or profit imperatives, which is often the case with today's arms industries of the United States. The combination of private ownership and the market-driven character of the United States' arms industries has drastically modified the conventional relationship between war and the means of warfare: it is now often the supply or profit imperatives of weapons production that drive the demand for arms, hence the need for war. In other words, imperial wars and demand for arms are nowadays precipitated more by sales or profit prerequisites than the other way around, as was the case with imperial powers of the past. It is this built-in propensity to war that makes the U.S. military-industrial complex a menace to world peace and stability, a force of death and destruction. It was also this tendency to war and militarism that prompted the late President Eisenhower to warn against the threat of the complex to the health and sanity of social and economic structures both at home and abroad. As Nick Turse of the Mailman School of Public Health at Columbia University recently put it: "Let's face it, making war is fast superseding sports as the American national pastime." Since 1980, Turse further indicated, the United States has been involved in military actions in Grenada, Libya, Nicaragua, Panama, Iraq, Afghanistan, El Salvador, Haiti, Somalia, Yugoslavia, Liberia, Sudan, the Philippines, Colombia, Haiti (again), Afghanistan (again), and Iraq (again), and that's not even the full list. "It stands to reason when the voracious appetites of the military-corporate complex are in constant need of feeding."[31]

In order to justify continued increases in the Pentagon appropriations, beneficiaries of war dividends have pursued two complimentary strategies: (a) constant invention of "external threats to our national interests/ security," and (b) constant introduction of ever newer, more efficient, and "futuristic" means of death and destruction. Invention or instigation of "external threats" was discussed in some detail in chapter 4 of this study. Here I cite only one instance of how the beneficiaries of the business of war artfully manage to increase Pentagon appropriations by subtly creating "external threats to the interests or security of the Unites States." The example is old, but it is also new in terms of its relevance; it is from General Smedley D. Butler's 1935 classic critique of imperial wars, *War Is a Racket*:

> The swivel-chair admirals of Washington are very adroit lobbyists. And they are smart. They don't shout that "We need a lot of battleships to war on this nation or that nation." Oh, no. First of all, they let it be known that America is menaced by a great naval power. Almost any day, these admirals will tell you, the greatest fleet of this supposed enemy will strike suddenly and annihilate our 125,000,000 people. Just like that. Then they begin to cry for a large navy. For what? To fight the enemy? Oh my, no. Oh, no. For defense purposes only. Then, incidentally, they announce maneuvers in the Pacific. For defense. Uh, huh.[32]

Arms industry's steady supply of new, improved, or upgraded munitions is not dissimilar to the market-driven behavior of other industries in that they all want to boost sales and profits. There are, however, two major differences between military and nonmilitary industries. The first difference is that, contrary to most civilian industries, military industry's profits are usually guaranteed. Not only are arms producers' profits guaranteed, those profits also tend (on average) to be higher than those of their civilian counterparts— especially during times of war and international conflicts: "The normal profit of a business concern in the United States are six, eight, ten, and sometimes even twelve percent. But war time profits—ah! That is another matter—twenty, sixty, one hundred, three hundred, and even eighteen hundred percent—the sky is the limit. All that the traffic can bear. Uncle Sam has the money. Let's get it."[33]

The second, and perhaps more important, difference between military and civilian producers lies in the fact that the quality of arms manufacturers' products is measured in terms of death and destruction. As this wicked (but capitalistically logical) measure of *quality* plays a key role in arms manufacturers' ability to win contracts from the Pentagon, it would, accordingly, serve as a strong incentive for those contractors to become ever more efficient agents of death and destruction. It is hardly surprising, then, as Turse, points out, "the Pentagon and allied corporations are forever planning more effective ways to kill, maim, and inflict pain . . . Whatever the wars of the present, elaborate weapons systems for future wars are already on the drawing boards. Planning for the projected fighter-bombers and laser weapons of the decades from 2030 to 2050 is underway." Meanwhile, "at the Department of Defense's (DoD's) blue-skies research outfit, the Defense Advanced Research Projects Agency (DARPA), even wilder projects—from futuristic exoskeletons to Brain/Machine Interface initiatives—are being explored." After describing some of the "futuristic" weapons systems that are projected by the Pentagon and its prime contractors, Turse concludes: "With all those exotic pain rays, flechettes, super-efficient machine guns, and rounds and rounds of ammunition readied for action . . . more people are sure to die, while others assumedly will experience 'intense pain' from Peps weapons and the like."[34] Such is the market imperative of the war industries' proof of quality and/or efficiency.

CHAPTER 8

The Political Economy of U.S. Military Spending

Prosperity and progress of a people or a nation depends not only on its ability to create wealth but also on its wisdom to allocate it judiciously. Due to the unique ability of the armed forces to appropriate the lion's share of a nation's resources, close scrutiny of the division of those resources between military and civilian spending is of crucial importance. In the debate over military expenditures, the metaphorical *guns versus butter* trade-off is often used to underline the importance of proper allocation of a nation's treasure between military and civilian spending. The importance of a sensible allocation of public funds between military and civilian expenditures goes beyond the immediate or short-term economic impact of such expenditure. Perhaps more importantly, a disproportionately large and escalating military apparatus tends to undermine the socioeconomic and political base that is supposed to sustain that apparatus.

U.S. military spending is now the largest item in the federal budget. (Officially, it is the second highest item after Social Security payments. But Social Security is a self-financing trust fund. So, in reality, military spending is the highest budget item.) Although the official Pentagon budget of $419 billion (for the fiscal year 2005) is obviously an astronomical figure, it nonetheless grossly understates the actual military spending as it does not include major supplemental appropriations for the wars in Iraq and Afghanistan—which are estimated to approach $300 billion by the end of 2005. There is no question that military spending has evolved as a crucial part of the U.S. economy. The question is whether the resulting widespread dependence on military spending by many workers and businesses is a positive development that needs to be maintained, or whether it is an unfortunate development that needs to be reversed or rectified.

In the proverbial *guns versus butter* debate, critics of inordinately large military spending view the massive allocation of national resources to the production of *guns* as an unfortunate outcome of the gradual rise of militarism over the past 55 years that needs to be curtailed in favor of production of more *butter*. While acknowledging the economic effects of military spending on job creation, demand stimulation, and technological innovations, critics argue that such benefits are often not worth their cost in terms of opportunities forgone or sacrificed: drain or curtailment of resources that could (and should) be used for investment in both human capital (such as health and education) and nonmilitary physical capital (such as roads, bridges, mass transit, and schools) that could lead to larger economic gains, especially long-term growth and development. In this view, the unfortunate addiction to the disproportionately large doses of military spending needs to be remedied not only because it produces too many *guns* and too little *butter*, but perhaps more importantly, a top-heavy military establishment will be unviable in the long run as it tends to undermine the economic base it is supposed to nurture. Furthermore, a large military establishment tends to be baleful to democratic values, republican principles, and civil liberties; corrupting politics and policies both at home and abroad. Perhaps more importantly, to the extent that jobs and livelihoods of many U.S. citizens have become dependent on military spending, it represents a regrettable dependence on a business that is geared to war, death, and destruction.[1]

Others, especially the powerful beneficiaries of war dividends and champions of militarism, see nothing wrong or perverse about the gigantic military budget. From the fact that large military spending creates so many jobs and benefits so many businesses, they conclude that, therefore, the Pentagon's appropriation and spending of public money is an effective means of job creation and demand stimulation, and hence of economic growth and prosperity. This view has come to be known as military Keynesianism, after the renowned British economist John Maynard Keynes, who argued that under conditions of inadequate purchasing power the government should spend money in order to jump-start the stagnant economy by stimulating demand. Proponents of this view often cite the experiences of Nazi Germany in the 1930s and the United States in World War II, Korea and Vietnam as evidence of stimulating or beneficial economic effects of military spending. They also defend military spending on long-term, productivity-enhancing grounds: military spending stimulates investment and technical innovation. In addition to job creation, demand management, and technical innovation, military spending is also defended on imperialistic economic grounds: international economic gains or advantages can be achieved through "extra-economic" or military measures such as wars, control of energy resources, control of financial markets, control or influence over economic and security decisions of global economic rivals, and the ability to dictate the terms of economic relations.[2] This chapter examines these claims and counterclaims in some detail. But first we shall take a quick look at the size of the Pentagon budget.

The Magnitude of the Pentagon Budget

The official defense authorization bill for the fiscal year 2004, signed by President Bush on November 24, 2003, stood at $401.3 billion. This figure exceeds the combined expenditures of the other 20 largest military spenders in the world and is about half of the world's total military spending. The figure does not include the costs of wars in Iraq and Afghanistan, which is fast approaching $300 billion.[3] Although the official military budget already eats up the lion's share of the public money (crowding out vital domestic needs), it nonetheless grossly understates the true magnitude of the Pentagon budget. The "real national defense budget," according to Robert Higgs of the Independent Institute, is approximately $754 billion, not $401.3 billion. The reason for this understatement is that the official Department of Defense (DoD) budget excludes not only the cost of wars in Iraq and Afghanistan, but also a number of other major cost items: the Coast Guard and the Department of Homeland Security; nuclear weapons research and development, testing and storage (in the Energy budget); veterans programs (in Veteran's Administration budget); most military retiree payments (in the Treasury budget); foreign military aid in the form of weapons grants for allies (in the State Department budget); interest payments on money borrowed to fund military programs in past years (in the Treasury budget); sales and property taxes at military bases (in local government budgets); and the hidden expenses of tax free food, housing, and combat pay allowances. After adding these disguised and misplaced expenses to the official DoD budget, Higgs concludes, "Thus, the super-grand total in fiscal year 2004 will reach the astonishing amount of nearly $754 billion—or 88 percent more than the much-publicized $401.3 billion—plus, of course, any additional supplemental spending that may be approved before the end of the fiscal year." Higgs further points out, "Therefore, I propose that in considering future defense budgetary costs, a well-founded rule of thumb is to take the Pentagon's (always well-publicized) basic budget total and double it. You may overstate the truth, but if so, you'll not do so by much."[4]

In relative terms, the official DoD budget of $401.3 billion for the fiscal year 2004 represents 18.2 perecent of the total federal budget of $2,200 billion for the year. The "real national defense budget" of $754 billion, on the other hand, represents 34 percent of the total federal budget. But even these inordinately high ratios underrepresent the real share of the defense budget. The reason for this inaccuracy is that the Social Security budget—which is a trust fund, and should be treated independent of the federal budget—is included in the overall federal budget. To the extent that this practice overstates the size of the federal budget, it thereby also understates the share taken by the Pentagon budget. For example, if for the fiscal year 2004 we take the Social Security budget of nearly $495 billion out of the total federal budget of $2,200 billion, the remainder, which is sometimes called the federal funds portion of the federal budget, will be $1,705 billion. On this adjusted basis, the ratio of the official DoD budget of $401.3 billion will be 23.5 percent, up from the 18.2 percent calculated on the basis of the total federal budget. Likewise, the ratio of the "real national defense budget" of $754 billion on the adjusted basis of $1,705 billion will be 44 percent, up from 34 percent.[5]

Perhaps the enormous magnitude of the Pentagon budget can be grasped more clearly through comparison and contrast. For example, as illustrated by figure 8.1 below, in recent years the Pentagon has been spending more money than all other discretionary budget items combined. According to Carlton Meyer, editor of *G2mil: The Magazine of Future Warfare*, "The USA now spends more money in real dollars (inflation adjusted) on its military than at the peak of the Vietnam war when some 500,000 GIs were in combat, and more than during the Cold War when the powerful Soviet Union existed."[6] As noted above, the United States now spends more each year than the next 20 largest national defense budgets combined. According to the Stockholm-based SIPRI Group, "The United States led the world in defence spending [in 2003], accounting for 47 percent of the total, followed by Japan with five percent and

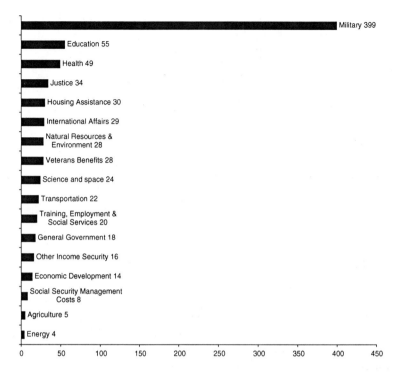

Figure 8.1   Discretionary Budget Items, Fiscal Year 2004 (in $Billion)

Source: Carlton Meyer (Editor), *G2mil: The Magazine of Future Warfare*, October 2003.

Britain, France and China, with four percent each. The figures were in line with estimates by Jane's Information Group, a spokesman from the company's London office told the AP."[7] The 47 percent U.S. share of total world military spending in 2003 has since gone up to nearly 50 percent.

In what it claimed to be the first comprehensive accounting of the costs of the war on the United States, Iraq, and much of the rest of the world, the Institute for Policy Studies (IPS), reported on June 24, 2004, "that the 151.1 billion dollars that will have been spent through this fiscal year could have paid for comprehensive health care for 82 million U.S. children or the salaries of nearly three million elementary school teachers . . . the war and occupation will cost the average U.S. household at least 3,415 dollars through the end of this year." The report further points out, "If spent on international programs, the same sum could have cut world hunger in half and covered HIV/AIDS medicine, childhood immunization, and clean water and sanitation needs of all developing countries for more than two years."[8]

The fact that the Pentagon appropriates and controls more than one-third of the entire federal budget has allowed it to forge the largest constituency and/or dependents nationwide. Tens of thousands of businesses, millions of jobs, and thousands of cities and communities have become dependent on military spending. While a handful of major contractors take the lion's share of military spending, millions more have become dependent on it as the source of their livelihood. As the late Senator William Fulbright observed some 35 years ago, "millions of Americans whose only interest is in making a decent living have acquired a vested interest in an economy geared to war. Those benefits, once obtained, are not easily parted with. Every new weapons system or military installation soon acquires a constituency."[9]

It is not surprising then that not many people are willing to oppose the continuing rise in the Pentagon budget—even if they might philosophically be opposed to militarism and large military spending. Because of the widespread presence of military installations and production sites nationwide, few politicians can afford not to support a continued rise in military spending lest that should hurt their communities or constituencies economically. As Howard Swint, Democratic candidate for Congress in West Virginia put it, "The all-powerful cycle of military appropriations, driven by congressional district-specific military pork as rewarded with campaign contributions, prevents any meaningful effort towards demilitarization."[10] Trade unions seeking to preserve their members' jobs often find themselves supporting military contracts, even though they may not be in principle in favor of large military spending.

Military Spending as Economic Stimulus

... our research suggests that military expenditures are beneficial in the long run to the civilian economy, since much of the additional spending promotes domestic production in our most capital and technology intensive sectors.

—Secretary of Defense Harold Brown, testimony before the U.S. Senate Budget Committee, February 27, 1980. Quoted by De Grasse, Military Expansion, Economic Decline

Military spending represents a major source of demand for the U.S. national product; indeed, it has remained the largest single source of demand since World War II. An increase in military spending is tantamount to injecting purchasing power into the economy, which will then spur production, investment, and employment. This stimulative property of military spending, often invoked by lobbyists and proponents of large military spending during cycles of economic contraction and high unemployment, has come to be known as military Keynesianism, after the renowned British economist John Maynard Keynes. It is also called demand-management: managing demand in the hope of managing the economy.

The essence of demand-management through military spending is that an advanced market economy tends to produce or supply more than it can absorb or demand. "Insufficient" demand, therefore, constitutes a potential source of periodic economic slowdown because the resulting accumulation of inventories will prompt suppliers to cut production, and hence employment. It follows, therefore, that advanced market economies need external sources of demand in order to fend off periodic recessions of "underconsumption." Those external sources of demand can come either from foreign markets, or from deficit government spending, or both. Thus, in the face of weak or insufficient demand and higher rates of unemployment, government spending, military or civilian, can play an important positive role: as it stimulates demand, it will also induce higher levels of production and employment. What is more, the military part of public spending is a more reliable tool of demand-management than the nonmilitary part. This is so not because military spending has a bigger stimulating, or ripple, effect on the economy than civilian spending, but because deficit financing for military purposes passes through political hurdles and policy debates much easier than for nonmilitary or civilian purposes. Policy makers often resist deficit financing, especially during periods of tight budgets. Not so, or as much, when it comes to military spending: they cannot afford to be branded "unpatriotic"; nor can they afford to antagonize or displease the Pentagon. More importantly, their constituencies need the dollars that would come their way as a result of military spending.

Not surprisingly, major beneficiaries of military spending and their lobbyists often defend their desire for continued military buildup on the grounds that military spending stimulates demand, investment, employment, and technical innovation. Expansion of military spending, even if it is deficit spending, becomes especially more facile during times of economic recession. For, during recessionary cycles, the Pentagon's perennially insatiable appetite for continued expansion of its budget converges with the conjunctural needs of economic policy makers to use military spending as a countercyclical, recession-fighting fiscal policy tool in the hope of fending off or ending economic recession. This explains why, in the post–World War II period, some of the most drastic increases in military spending have taken place during periods of economic contraction. For example, when the immediate postwar economic boom of 1947–1948 turned to the 1949–1950 contraction, "and business analysts almost universally predicted that serious recession was imminent," President Truman invoked the Soviet threat and drastically increased military spending.[11]

Likewise, the heightened Cold War hostilities of the late 1970s and early 1980s, which came to be known as the Second Cold War, and the ensuing expansion of military spending were significantly prompted by the need to end the long economic stagnation that had started earlier in the 1970s. A depressed domestic market in the 1970s, combined with powerful competitors in international markets, had seriously threatened industries such as steel, autos, shipbuilding, aerospace, and electronics. Heightened military spending in the late 1970s and early 1980s proved to be a shot in the arm of these and many other anemic industries that benefit, directly or indirectly, from such expenditures. Although expanded military spending began under President Carter in the late 1970s, the more dramatic increase took place under President Reagan. The Pentagon's prime contract awards in 1980 jumped 35 percent over 1979, "while the hard pressed manufacturing sector saw its military contracts increase 48 percent." The impact of President Reagan's drastic increases of military expenditures on national economic recovery can perhaps be gauged by this observation: "In the second quarter of 1980 the Gross National Product fell further. . . . Speculation that the economic situation might duplicate that of 1929 was widespread. Then, almost as suddenly, the recession of 1980 was over. Few noted that one of the major reasons for this reversal was the huge jump of roughly $25 billion in new military contracts issued in fiscal year 1980." Reflecting that close connection between military spending and economic recovery, Casper Weinberger, the secretary of Defense at the time, remarked that arms buildup is "the second half of the administration's program to revitalize America."[12]

A similar connection can be detected between the 2000–2002 recession and the Bush administration's drastic increases in the Pentagon budget. It is true that the increases were approved largely to finance the administration's wars in Iraq and Afghanistan. But the ease with which they were approved was not unrelated to economic policy makers' need to stimulate the economy. It seems that the Bush administration's success in having drastically increased the Pentagon budget was not dissimilar to the proverbial *killing of two birds with one stone*: while satisfying the business needs of the beneficiaries of war dividends, the administration also aimed at stimulating the economy through heightened military spending. Commenting on the economic impact of the $60 billion increase in the Pentagon budget for the fiscal year 2002 (over 2001), James Cypher of the California State University at Fresno wrote, "Much of the new [military] spending will go to new technologies. The information technology sector will probably gain the most . . . according to *Business Week*, electronics and communications components accounted for 40 percent of weapons purchases. So the jump in military spending will function as an industrial policy for the information technology and communications industries, boosting these hard-hit sectors of the U.S. economy."[13] Randall Wray of the Levy Economics Institute of Bard College likewise wrote, ". . . ramped-up government spending on defense from 2001 to 2003 gave a much needed boost to demand (defense spending accounted for 27 percent of economic growth by mid-2003) . . . the growth in the number of government employees helped to turn consumer spending around."[14]

This is why (in addition to short-term demand and/or employment boosting) military spending is also defended on long-term, productivity-enhancing grounds: military spending stimulates investment and technical innovation. The idea here is that military spending enhances productivity through technological spin-off: military spending in research and development and the resulting high technology arms production will be sooner or later transmitted to the civilian sector, thereby leading to economy-wide improvement in productivity. A number of examples are frequently cited in support of this argument. For instance, in an October 1, 2001 article that credited military spending for a lot of post–World War II technological breakthroughs, *Business Week* wrote, "In fact, defense spending on research and development has sparked much innovation. Microchips, radar, lasers, satellite communications, cell phones, GPS, and the Internet all came out of Defense Dept. funding of basic research at the Massachusetts Institute of Technology, Stanford University and national laboratories. There were breakthroughs at IBM and Bell Laboratories, and all were commercialized by Intel Corp., Motorola Inc., and many other corporations."

Few people viewed large military expenditures as a burden on the national economy during the long economic boom of the immediate post–World War II years (1948–1968). On the contrary, many credited the massive military spending with not only having contributed to that economic boom but also for having helped eradicate the destructive effects of the Great Depression of the 1930s. That blind faith in the positive impact of military spending on economic vitality was challenged when that long cycle of the immediate postwar expansion turned into the long cycle of contraction in the 1970s. While the U.S. economy, with its huge military spending, was mired in the protracted recession of the 1970s, the German and Japanese economies, with no or little military spending, enjoyed booming economies and seriously challenged U.S. producers in international markets.

The economic difficulties of the 1970s prompted a heated debate among the U.S. ruling circles over how to remedy those daunting economic problems. In the ensuing deliberations, the globalist or multilateralist faction of the ruling class, which came to be known as Trilateralists, suggested (through the Trilateral Commission) a thaw in American–Soviet relations on the grounds that this would allow a reduction in military spending, and hence a cut in the budget deficit and the national debt. Frightened by this and similar calls for cuts in the Pentagon budget, military strategists came up with their own plans to revitalize the economy. Top among those plans was the so-called MANTECH (Manufacturing Technology) Program. Commenced under the direction of the Air Force System Command (AFSC), the Manufacturing Technology Program sought "to create an industrial revolution in both manufacturing processes and in specific materials—such as the substitution of composites for metals in aircraft production."[15] The military's own description of the Manufacturing Technology Program, as quoted by James Cypher, clearly conveys the ambitious projections of the program:

> The Manufacturing Technology Program is a broad-based, production-oriented program supporting the DoD [Department of Defense] Research, Development and Acquisition Program by providing new/ innovative manufacturing technology which will result in more economical/ timely/reliable production of DoD material. Projects are expected to result in a factory floor application of productivity-enhancing technologies and are viewed as seed money investments necessary to reduce the technical/fiscal risks of follow-on implementation of the results in the defense production base. The MTP is predominantly procurement funded. Most projects are executed by the private sector after competitive selection. Roughly 400/500 individual projects are active at any one time.[16]

Like almost all other military research projects, MANTECH has its own industrial advisory group. A look into the nature and composition of the advisory groups suggests that it is at this locus that the agenda of major Pentagon contractors is transmitted directly to the Pentagon. As James Cypher points out, the corporations that have served in an advisory capacity, either for the MANTECH group or for its subparts, make up a veritable "Who's Who" of U.S. industry: General Dynamics, General Telephone and Electronics, General Motors, Control Data, Lockheed, Caterpillar, and similar Pentagon contractors.[17]

Weak/Dubious Arguments against Military Spending: Military Buildup "Crowds Out" Nonmilitary Private Sector Investment

"Crowding out" is essentially a conservative, neoclassical/neoliberal economic theory that is often invoked in economic policy debates to buttress arguments against social spending. The theory makes two closely linked claims. The first claim, which is sometimes called the "theory of resource diversion,"[18] maintains that public-sector expenditures, military or otherwise, lead to an equal and offsetting decrease in private investment. That is, because there is a direct competition for economic resources (financial, labor, production capacity, etc.) between the public and private sectors, any spending by the public sector is tantamount to an equal amount of lost investment by the private sector. The second argument maintains that for equal amounts of resources spent or invested, the public sector—again, military or civilian—does not generate as many positive economic effects as does nonmilitary private-sector investment. In other words, proponents of this argument do not deny the positive or invigorating economic effects of military spending in terms of job creation, demand or investment stimulation, and technological advancement; what they dispute is that the resources "diverted" from the nonmilitary private sector to public spending do not create as much positive economic effect as would have been created by nonmilitary private investment, that is, public sector investment is not worth its opportunity cost in terms of forgone private-sector investment.[19]

Although the "crowding-out" theory was originally developed by anti-interventionist, conservative economists and politicians in their campaign against public sector spending, it has been adopted in recent years and decades by many of their liberal and/or left-oriented counterparts to argue against large military expenditures. But the "crowding-out" hypotheses, and the arguments against military spending on the basis of these hypotheses, suffer from a number of weaknesses. Let us examine these arguments in some detail.

The first major arguments of the "crowding-out" theory, as pointed out above, is that military spending does not increase aggregate or national investment because it causes an equal and offsetting reduction in nonmilitary private investment. But this argument assumes that the Pentagon and the nonmilitary private investors always compete over a fixed or finite pool of financial resources. This claim implicitly assumes that nonmilitary investors are always short of funds for investment, that they constantly compete with the Pentagon for the same dollars in financial markets, and that, therefore, every dollar borrowed and spent by the Pentagon is a dollar lost in capital markets for nonmilitary investors. Yet, many corporations and businesses often have plenty of internal financial resources as a result of their retained earnings, or undistributed profits; and what they often seek is not so much capital or credit as it is profitable outlets for investing their abundant cash.[20]

The claim that the Pentagon and the nonmilitary private sector always chase a fixed or finite amount of dollars in financial markets may be true during cycles of economic growth and expansion, when businesses tend to expand capacity, but not so during cycles of economic decline or contraction. During periods of economic slowdown or recessionary cycles, many businesses simply opt for retrenchment and downsizing, whether they have cash or not. It is usually during such periods of depressed economic conditions and high unemployment that efforts to increase military spending have been most successful, since under such circumstances military expenditures are viewed as stimulus shots in the arm of the depressed economy. Drastic increases in military spending in the early 1950s, the early 1980s, and the early 2000s all came about on the heels of the respective recessionary cycles of those times. Obviously, the large military expenditures under such economic conditions do not push or "crowd" out nonmilitary industrialists from capital or credit markets.[21] On the contrary, such expenditures might spur them into action by providing both new purchasing power in the market and opportunities for profitable investment outlets.

Furthermore, the "crowding-out" argument implicitly assumes that the overall/national private-sector investment (I) and public-sector spending (G) are strictly limited by the overall/national amounts of savings (S) and tax dollars (T); that is, (I + G) = (S + T). It follows from this assumption that, given total national savings (S + T), if G is increased, I must be decreased accordingly, and vice versa. In this way, a direct trade-off is established between I and G because the combined source of their funding (S + T) is implicitly assumed to be given as a fixed and inflexible amount. But (I + G) = (S + T) is a financing or income-expenditure equilibrium condition (meaning that, ideally, one should not go beyond one's means); it is rarely an actual or real-world state of affairs. In the real world, and in the short- to medium-term, funding sources of I and G are much more flexible than S, T, or (S + T). The credit system, the money supply and, hence, the sources of funding for both I and G are quite flexible in advanced market economies. For example, during periods of expanding business cycles and optimistic economic scenarios investors would not be constrained by the existing pool of national savings, or by the financial resources of the banking system, because during such periods of optimism financial institutions' ability and willingness to extend credit becomes quite flexible—almost unlimited. As one officer of the New York Federal Reserve Bank has put it, "In the real world, banks extend credit . . . and look for reserves later. In one way or another, the Federal Reserve will accommodate them."²² On the other hand, during periods of economic stagnation and pessimism, investors tend to retrench and abstain from expansion even if they are wallowing in cash. As pointed out above, when during periods of economic decline the government embarks on deficit spending, military or civilian, in order to stimulate a stagnant economy it would not necessarily be "crowding-out" private investors because during such recessionary cycles private investors tend to refrain from spending anyway, whether they have capital or not.

The argument that military spending diverts investment resources away from the nonmilitary private sector is dubious on yet another ground: it assumes that increases in the Pentagon appropriations are financed by increases in taxes on corporate profits and/or high incomes (i.e., by taxing the financial resources for investment, or the so-called *investable* funds). Yet, this is not necessarily the case. In fact, increases in U.S. military spending since the early 1980s have been accompanied by decreases in taxes on corporate profits and higher earnings. The U.S. ruling class has diligently made it certain that increases in the Pentagon budget would not divert *investable* resources away from the nonmilitary private sector. Those increases in the Pentagon budget have been financed, instead, by cuts in nonmilitary public spending, by borrowing from the Social Security Trust

Fund, and by plunging the nation into debt and deficit. Indeed, during the last three decades or so, large Pentagon appropriations have been used as a device to strengthen, not weaken, the private sector. As Richard Du Boff aptly points out, "For antigovernment conservatives, military expenditures have acted as a regulatory mechanism, expanding government support for private enterprises and limiting the expansion of the federal government for virtually all non-military purposes."[23]

The second major argument of the "crowding-out" theory, in addition to the "resource diversion" argument, is that the resources diverted from non military private-sector production to military production do not generate as many positive or stimulating economic effects (in terms of employment, economic growth, and technological or productivity enhancement) as would nonmilitary or civilian production. The two arguments are essentially like *two sides of the same coin*, or two hypotheses of the same theory—one would be incomplete, if not pointless, without the other. Robert W. DeGrasse, an exponent of the hypothesis that military production is less productive than civilian production, and the author of *Military Expansion, Economic Decline*, writes, "Since soldiers and arms producers do not create goods and services that can be consumed by others," military spending can be "viewed as an impediment to economic progress."[24] Lloyd J. Dumas, another proponent of this view, likewise writes, "Churches are constructed and bibles are printed not to provide material well-being, but to help fulfill the human need for spiritual guidance. . . . By the same token, battle tanks and missiles do not themselves add to the material standard of living . . . they do not directly contribute to the central purpose of the economy and so do not have any economic value. It is logical, then, to classify activities that result in goods or services that do not have economic value as *economically non-contributive*" (italics in original). Dumas further writes, "There is no question that the production of military goods and services is non-contributive activity. Whatever else may be said for such products, they do not add to the present standard of living as consumer goods do, or to the economy's capacity to produce standard-of-living goods and services in the future, as producer goods do."[25]

A detailed analysis of the theoretical weaknesses of these and other "crowding-out" arguments is beyond our discussion here.[26] Suffice it to say that such weaknesses stem primarily from conceptions of what constitutes productive labor or activities and what constitutes unproductive ones. Arguments (such as Dumas's) that military production is "economically non-contributive," or unproductive, tend to view productive activities in an ahistorical sense; that is, in terms of their general social and economic usefulness. Yet, from a capitalistic point of view—or, more precisely, from the viewpoint of capital—any labor or activity that is profitable is also productive, regardless of what it produces or how its products are used. What defines productive labor under capitalism is *exchange value*, not *use value*, to borrow Karl Marx's felicitous words.[27]

On empirical grounds, too, the hypothesis that economic effects of Pentagon-financed investment are smaller than those of nonmilitary investment has never been conclusively supported by evidence. Research results of econometric studies of the relationship between military spending and economic performance, including both cross-country comparisons and time-series comparisons within the same country, are at best mixed: there are as many studies that tend to reject this hypothesis as those that tend to support it. For example while DeGrasse (1983), Smith and Smith (1983), and Ward and Davis (1992) found negative links between military spending and economic performance, Atesoglu (2002), Nordhaus (2002), and Fordham (1998) found positive links. There are yet other researchers who have found no or negligible links between military spending and economic performance (Gold 2005, Payne and Ross 1992, and Kinsella 1990).

A major part of these mixed results seems to be due to the researchers' choice of the time period, or economic cycle, for their studies. For instance, researchers who focus on the long cycle of economic slowdown of the late 1960s through the early 1980s in the United States tend to attribute the sluggish economic performance of those years to the large U.S. military spending: "Our analysis indicates that America's higher share of gross domestic product (GDP) spent on the military has contributed to the decline in manufacturing competence." By the same token, from the fact that the economies of Germany and Japan, two countries with very small military spending at the time, performed quite strongly during that period, these researchers conclude that there must be a negative correlation between military spending and economic growth, technological progress and productivity enhancement: "Nations with higher military burdens tend to have lower levels of investment and lower productivity growth."[28]

On the other hand, researchers who have focused on the economic performance of these major industrialized countries in the 1980s and 1990s have come to the opposite conclusion because during those decades the United States and United Kingdom, the two countries with large military expenditures, enjoyed stronger economic performance than did Germany and Japan, the two countries with smaller military expenditures. These researchers further invoke the experiences of Nazi Germany in the 1930s and of the United States in World War II, Korea and Vietnam as further evidence that military spending stimulates the economy.[29]

A major claim of the "crowding-out" theory is that, for equal amounts of spending, military production does not create as many jobs as civilian production: ". . . military spending does create employment, but it actually generates fewer jobs for the buck than equivalent civilian expenditures."[30] This argument tends to stand the test of evidence better than other hypotheses of the "crowding-out" theory. For example, a 2002 congressional Budget Office report found that every $10 billion spent on weapons generates 40,000 fewer jobs than $10 billion spent on civilian programs.[31] The main reason that military production creates fewer jobs than the equivalent civilian investment is that military production tends to use relatively more capital or equipment and less labor than most other industries—although not all other industries. A study conducted in the early 1980s by the Employment Research Associates showed that military production created roughly 28,000 jobs per billion dollars of investment. The study also indicated that while (for the same billion dollars) most civilian industries such as public works projects and education services created more jobs, there were also a number of civilian industries such as oil refining and car manufacturing that created fewer jobs. Overall, the 28,000 arms production jobs were only "slightly less than the 30,000 jobs created by the median industry in the Bureau of Labor Statistics' input-output model."[32] (The claim that military production creates "fewer jobs for the buck than the equivalent" nonmilitary production is, of course, relevant only to the part of the Pentagon budget that is spent on its purchases for procurement purposes, the portion that is spent by its contractors for arms production. The argument is irrelevant to the part of the Pentagon budget that goes directly to pay its personnel because government employment created by military spending is comparable to other types of federal employment. Money for civil service workers creates approximately the same number of jobs whether it is spent by the Defense Department or by other departments.)

Two points need to be made about these comparative employment statistics. First, they indicate that, as shown in the next section of this chapter, what military spending crowds out is not so much nonmilitary private-sector investment as it is social or nonmilitary public spending. Second, to the extent that these statistical studies of comparative job creation show that overall, or on the average, military production generates fewer jobs for the same dollars than civilian production, such studies tend to hide as much as they show; they suffer from a dubious assumption that tends to make their statistical results less than reliable. That questionable assumption, as discussed earlier in this section, is that funds invested in arms production always represent deductions from nonmilitary private-sector investment. In other words, implicit in these comparative studies is that there is a jelly-like pool of investable funds that can be spread either in the direction of arms production or of nonmilitary production. In reality, however, this is often not the case. It would have been the case if military spending was financed primarily through taxation on corporate profits or other forms of income from capital (as opposed to labor). But, as was discussed earlier, increases in military spending since the early 1980s have been financed largely by cutting nonmilitary public spending, by drawing down the Social Security Trust Fund, and by debt and deficit creation. Indeed, those increases of the Pentagon budget have been accompanied by drastic tax reductions, not tax hikes, on corporate profits and high incomes.[33]

In brief, the theory that military spending crowds out nonmilitary private-sector investment and/or production and, therefore, impedes economic performance is a weak theory. At best, it is inconclusive and unconvincing; at worst, it is overwhelmed by counterarguments and evidence that military spending is more likely to be stimulating, not impeding, an advanced market economy. Implicitly, the "crowding-out" argument is that, as James Cypher of California State University at Fresno points out, "the U.S. capitalist class and its state managers really do not know how to pursue their own interests."[34] The argument is based on dubious assumptions that tend to downplay the "spin-off" and innovation effects of military spending. It is true that exotica like "star wars" may be diverting high-tech resources, especially the highly skilled labor force such as engineers and scientists, from critical civilian resources. But it should also be remembered, once again, that it was the Cold War era military competition that brought forth the computer, and the space race gave birth to the semiconductor. Likewise, "several other key industries—aircraft and engines, composite materials, communications equipment, scientific instruments—received their initial stimulus and production runs from military contracts."[35] It is important to recall that World War II military spending brought the U.S. economy out of the lingering effects of the

1930s depression. One should likewise keep in mind that the drastic military increases of the early 1950s helped reverse the recessionary cycle of the late 1940s, and the similarly sweeping increases of the Pentagon expenditures of the early 1980s helped end the 1980–1982 recession. But while the claim that military spending crowds out nonmilitary private-sector investment is dubious, there is no question that it crowds out non-military public-sector spending. This will be examined next.

Military Spending Crowds out Public-, not Private-, Sector Spending: A Regulatory Mechanism to Reverse the New Deal

> Every gun that is made, every warship launched, every rocket fired signifies, in the final sense, a theft from those who hunger and are not fed, those who are cold and are not clothed.
>
> —Dwight D. Eisenhower

It follows from the above discussion that what gets crowded out, or forgone, by military spending is often not private-sector investment spending but nonmilitary public spending. This includes both physical capital, or physical infrastructure (such as roads, bridges, mass transit, schools, drinking water, wastewater, dams, solid waste, hazardous waste, navigable waterways, and energy) and human capital, or soft/social infrastructure, such as health and education. In other words, it is often the proverbial *butter* that gets melted away when a disproportionately large share of public money is allocated to the production of *guns*:

> The new military buildup is not likely to "crowd out" private investment, but to stimulate investment and technical innovation. The military buildup will definitely "crowd out," however, spending on public needs, such as a viable rapid rail system, public education, and a national health care system—all of which could greatly enhance productivity. More military spending will focus inordinately on information technology and other high-tech systems. More artificial intelligence technologies, global positioning systems, robot planes and thermal imaging sensors, however, are not going to house, educate, or heal people who lack housing, education, or health care.[36]

Official macroeconomic figures show that, over the past five decades, government spending (at the federal, state, and local levels) as a percentage of

GNP (gross national product) has remained fairly steady—at about 20 percent. Given this nearly constant share of the public sector of GNP, it is not surprising that increases in military spending have almost always been accompanied or followed by compensating decreases in nonmilitary public spending. This is, of course, not fortuitous because, as discussed in the previous section of this chapter, instead of financing through progressive taxation, such additions to military spending have been increasingly accompanied by tax cuts on the wealthy—which have then forced cuts on nonmilitary public spending in order to limit budget deficits that are thus created. For example, in the early 1980s, as President Reagan drastically increased military spending, he also just as drastically lowered tax rates on higher incomes. The resulting large budget deficits were then paid for by more than a decade of steady cuts on nonmilitary spending. The administration of President George W. Bush seems to be pursuing a similarly sinister strategy: simultaneously heightening military spending and cutting high-income tax rates.

The trade-off between military and civilian components of public spending was also confirmed by the fact that when, for example, by virtue of FDR's New Deal reforms and LBJ's metaphorical War on Poverty, the share of nonmilitary government spending rose significantly the share of military spending declined accordingly. From the mid-1950s to mid-1970s, the share of nonmilitary government spending of GNP rose from 9.2 to 14.3 percent, an increase of 5.1 percent. During that time period, the share of military spending of GNP declined from 10.1 to 5.8 percent, a decline of 4.3 percent. (Of course, this did not mean that military spending declined in absolute terms; it declined only as a ratio of a bigger and bigger GNP, and in relation to social spending.) That trend was reversed when President Reagan took office in 1980.[37]

As Reagan embarked on his "rearming of America," as he put it, and successfully put into effect his notorious *supply-side* tax cuts, he also cut nonmilitary public spending to make up for the resulting budget shortfalls. From 1978 through 1983, real military spending climbed more than 28 percent, from $161 billion to $207 billion. During that period, real federal grants to state and local governments—a major source for investment in public works projects—dropped 25 percent, from $109 billion to $82 billion. From 1983 through 1988, military spending jumped another 27 percent in real terms, while federal grants to state and local governments "were practically unchanged. Thus, in the late 1980s only 13 percent of state and local government spending was going to public capital formation compared with an average of 30 percent in the 1950s and 1960s."[38]

Although President Reagan's military spending hikes and his supply-side tax cuts helped turn the stagnant economy of the 1970s into the expanding cycle of the 1980s, by the same token it also helped create an imbalance in the opposite direction: insufficient investment in, hence insufficient formation of, physical public capital such as highways, bridges, mass transit, waste water facilities, hazardous waste sites, and the like. The resulting imbalance, or gap, between the expanding economy and the shrinking investment in public works/capital "produced a crunch, in the form of an expanding private economy generating greater demands for public services that cannot be supplied by a public sector becoming relatively smaller. Its manifestation is the dilapidated state of the public infrastructure—streets and highways, bridges, mass transit and railways."[39]

In March 2001, the American Society of Civil Engineers (ASCE) issued a "Report Card for America's Infrastructure," grading 12 infrastructure categories at a disappointing D+ overall, and estimating the need for a $1.3 trillion investment to bring conditions to acceptable levels. In September 2003, ASCE released a Progress Report that examined trends and assessed the progress and decline of the nation's infrastructure. The Progress Report, prepared by a panel of 20 eminent civil engineers with expertise in a range of practice specialties, examined 12 major categories of infrastructure: roads, bridges, mass transit, aviation, schools, drinking water, wastewater, dams, solid waste, hazardous waste, navigable waterways, and energy. The report concluded, "The condition of our nation's roads, bridges, drinking water systems and other public works have shown little improvement since they were graded an overall D+ in 2001, with some areas sliding toward failing grade." Thomas L. Jackson, ASCE president, pointed out, "Time is working against our nation's infrastructure. . . . Since we graded the infrastructure in 2001, our roads are more congested than ever, the number of unsafe and hazardous dams has increased, and our schools are unable to accommodate the mandated reductions in class size."[40] Commenting on this ominous trend of the nation's infrastructure, Seymour Melman, emeritus professor of industrial engineering at Columbia University, wrote, "All this is an important indicator of the opportunity cost, of what has been forgone, as a consequence of the Permanent War Economy."[41]

Proponents of laissez-faire economics—interchangeably called neoclassical, neoliberal, or supply-side economists—tend to view government spending on public capital as a burden on the economy. Instead of viewing public-sector spending on infrastructure as a long-term investment that will help sustain and promote economic vitality, they view it as an overhead. In other words, they seem to lose sight of the indirect, long-term returns to the tax dollars invested in public capital stock by focusing on the current, short-term balance sheets. Yet, evidence shows that neglect of public capital formation can undermine long-term health of a market economy in terms of productivity enhancement and sustained growth. For example, a 1987 study by the Chicago Federal Reserve Bank concluded that "the rates of return are now higher on public than on private investment." The study pointed out that there had been a drastic decline in public capital formation since the 1960s (an ominous trend that continues to this day): "public investment was as high as 2.3 of GNP in 1965–69, but by 1980–84 it had fallen to a mere 0.4 percent." The study argued that the decline in public capital formation paralleled a decline in the rate of profit on private investment. The reason for this correlation is that as the public investment on infrastructure is cut, private investors find that their costs are higher for transportation, water, and so on. Thus a deficiency of public investment hurts the private sector: "If public capital formation were to return to its 1953–1969 average of 2.1 percent of GNP, private profitability would rise by over 2 percentage points. The total national capital stock would be higher, and the economy would be more productive."[42]

Continued increase in military spending at the expense of nonmilitary public spending has undermined more than physical infrastructure. Perhaps more importantly, it has also undercut public investment in soft/social infrastructure such as health care, education, nutrition, housing, and the like—investment that would help improve quality of life, human creativity, and labor productivity, thereby also helping to bring about long-term socioeconomic vitality. Investment in human capital—anything that improves human capacity and/or labor force productivity, such as education and health care—is a major source of social health and economic vitality over time.

Sadly, however, public investment in such vitally important areas has been gradually curtailed during the past quarter century or so in favor of steadily rising military spending. Evidence of this regrettable trend is overwhelming. To cite merely a few examples: "The war priorities have depleted medical and education staffs. U.S. medical planning now includes programs to recruit large numbers of nurses from India." And again, "Shortages of housing have caused a swelling of the homeless population in every major city.

State and city governments across the country have become trained to bend to the needs of the military—giving automatic approvals to its spending without limit. The same officials cannot find money for affordable housing."[43] The *New York Times* columnist Bob Herbert reported on February 6, 2003, that, at the time, some 5.5 million young Americans, age 16–24, were undereducated, disconnected from society's mainstream, jobless, restless, unhappy, frustrated, angry, and sad. Commenting on this report, Professor Seymour Melman of Columbia University wrote, "This population, 5.5 million and growing, is the product of America's national politics that has stripped away as too costly the very things that might rescue this abandoned generation and train it for productive work. But that sort of thing is now treated as too costly. So this abandoned generation is now left to perform as fodder for well-budgeted police SWAT teams."[44]

* * *

Although the Great Depression of the 1930s, and the concomitant social pressure from below, forced the New Deal reforms on the ideological opponents of government spending, those opponents of public-sector spending never really reconciled with or accepted the resulting expansion of social expenditures. Not surprisingly, soon after the significant government spending on the New Deal reform programs helped cleanse the economy of the lingering effects of the Great Depression, opponents of nonmilitary public spending set out to systematically undermine those programs. For the first few decades after the depression and the war, however, efforts at curtailing and/or reversing the gains of the New Deal reforms remained subdued as the enthusiasm and optimism that resulted from those reforms continued to remain strong well into the 1950s and 1960s. Furthermore, the "golden economy" of those decades produced sufficient resources to satisfy both the proponents of military and nonmilitary public spending. It was also that golden economy, and its abundant resources to satisfy both the partisans of *guns* and *butter* production, that facilitated the ruling elites' "governing consensus" of the time.

But as the golden economy of the 1950s and 1960s turned into the long contraction of the 1970s, and the policy-making authorities were forced to make spending cuts under the budget constraints of the depressed economy, the "governing consensus" began to unravel. While a faction of the ruling elite, which came to be known as Trilateralists, or globalists, proposed cuts in military spending, the other faction, known as unilateral militarists, suggested cuts in social spending. To curtail military spending, Trilateralists favored tension reduction with the Soviet Union and a negotiated multilateral approach to international geopolitical and economic issues. Unilateralists, on the other hand, opted for increasing, not reducing, tensions with the Soviet Union in order to increase military spending. In the ensuing debate, unilateralist forces successfully outmaneuvered their political opponents by resorting to that old, tried-and-true strategy of militarism: "external threat to U.S. national security/interests." The forces of war and militarism rallied around the "Committee on the Present Danger," embarked on a wholesale campaign of resuscitating anticommunism, and set off an intensified and hostile relationship with the Soviet Union that came to be known (in the late 1970s and early 1980s) as the Second Cold War. As a result, they succeeded not only to avert cuts in the Pentagon budget but, in fact, to increase military spending considerably. President Reagan called the ensuing big jump in the Pentagon budget the "rearming of America."

As noted above, ever since the end of World War II opponents of nonmilitary public spending were on the lookout to undermine the New Deal and other reforms that were put into effect in the 1950s and 1960s as part of what came to be known as the "war on poverty." That opportunity arrived when President Reagan arrived in the White House. As the opponents of social spending began to put into effect their supply-side economic policies through the Reagan administration, it soon became clear that their strategy to roll back the New Deal and other poverty-reducing reforms was not very far from cynical: drastic tax cuts for the wealthy along with drastic hikes in military spending. As this combination created big budget deficits, it forced cuts in nonmilitary public spending as a way to fill the budget gaps that were thereby created. Thus, for example, a frustrated but powerless Senator Ernest Hollings bitterly complained in 1984 that the combination of raising the Pentagon budget and lowering tax rates on high incomes had "intentionally created a deficit so large that we Democrats will never have enough money to build the sort of government programs we want."[45] David Stockman, President Reagan's budget director and one of the main architects of his supply-side tax cuts, implicitly confirmed this cynical policy of simultaneously raising military spending and cutting taxes on the wealthy in order to force cuts in nonmilitary government spending: "Cutting defense had never been my real ideological agenda. My aim had always been to force down the size of the domestic welfare state to the point where it could be adequately funded with the revenues after the tax cut. All my efforts to cut defense had been to provide political lubricant for the other cuts."[46]

With minor exceptions, the trend that was thus set in motion in the early 1980s—sustained increases in military spending financed primarily by sustained cuts in nonmilitary public spending—continues to this day. The resulting steady decline in social spending has had dire consequences: increased economic insecurity for many, further deepening of class divisions, and a considerable slowdown or reversal of the so-called upward social mobility that appeared so promising in the immediate few decades after World War II.

Opponents of social spending tend to justify these policies in terms of market mechanism: that all they want is to keep "government's hands out of people's pocket" and to let the "invisible hand of the market mechanism" regulate the economy. Yet, their twin policy of tax break for the wealthy and lion's share of public money for military industries seems more akin to an iron fist that is designed to redistribute national resources in favor of the wealthy than the invisible hand of market mechanism. Aptly calling this strategy a "regulatory mechanism," Richard Du Boff of Bryn Mawr College, author of *Accumulation & Power*, writes,

> For over four decades now, the "iron triangle"—Congress, the Pentagon, and the prime arms contractors—has kept the double-edged sword of military spending well honed. One edge bolsters aggregate demand and corporate profits in the economy; the other keeps resources away from a potentially vigorous and attractive civilian government sector. For antigovernment conservatives, military expenditures have acted as a regulatory mechanism, expanding government support for private enterprises and limiting the expansion of the federal government for virtually all non-military purposes.[47]

Military Spending as a Redistributive Mechanism of National Resources in Favor of the Wealthy

An ominous—though logical—consequence of the use of the Pentagon appropriations as a redistributing mechanism of national resources in favor of the wealthy has been further exacerbation of economic inequality. Calling this insidious mechanism of resource allocation in favor of the affluent "redistributive militarism," James Cypher of California State University at Fresno wrote, "Redistributive militarism functioned to transfer income from those in the bottom 80 percent of income distribution to those within the top 20 percent through: (1) an expansion in military procurement of unprecedented proportions; (2) increasingly lax procurement practices, which permitted both higher profit margins and a greater volume of business for arms contractors; (3) a substantive increase in the relationship between arms buildups and federal deficits." The last point of this quotation refers to the fact that when military buildup is financed not through progressive taxation but through borrowing, as has been done in the United States since the early 1980s, it serves to transfer increasing amounts of public money to the lenders or bondholders of federal debt "who, overwhelmingly, are to be found within the top 20 percent of the distribution of income." That is, partisans of militarism tend to finance their continued military buildup not by paying their "fair" share of taxes but by lending what they do not pay in taxes to the federal government and, of course, earning interest.[48]

When military spending escalated during World War II, President Franklin D. Roosevelt told the American people, "Not a single war millionaire will be created in the United States as a result of this world disaster."[49] Today, however, war and militarism have become major vehicles to the land of millionaires and billionaires. Major Pentagon contractors and their CEOs are among the richest corporations and individuals nationwide. Today's earnings of the CEOs of major Pentagon contractors, once roughly the same as their counterparts in other industries, are significantly higher. From 2001 to 2002, defense spending rose by 14 percent, but median total compensation of CEOs at the 37 largest publicly traded defense contractors leaped by nearly 79 percent. In 2002, CEOs of major defense contractors raked in an average of $11.3 million—577 times as much as the annual earnings of an Army private of $19,600 risking his or her life in Iraq. These soldiers are obviously not winners, nor are persons in the reserves and National Guard who are called to protracted active duty overseas. The real winners are war industries, their CEOs, and their lobbyists, who are bilking the American taxpayers. This is a clear vindication of President Dwight Eisenhower's prescient warning that the "military-industrial-complex [would] cause military spending to be driven not by national security needs but by a network of weapons makers, lobbyists and elected officials."[50]

Another ominous consequence of the escalating defense appropriations, combined with deep tax cuts for the wealthy, has been fiscal difficulties at all levels of government. At the federal level, budget deficit is fast approaching half a trillion dollars and the national debt (which is essentially accumulated deficit over time) is now over five trillion dollars. This has greatly contributed to the fiscal crises in many state and local governments and forced drastic cuts in social and infrastructural spending. As noted earlier, this is not altogether fortuitous; it is a direct result of the strategy of simultaneously increasing the Pentagon budget while at the same time lowering taxes for the wealthy in order to deliberately create budget deficits and, thereby, force cuts on nonmilitary public spending. Deliberate and cynical or not, the fact is that this fiscal policy has been devastating to tens of millions of poor and working people. It has also placed middle and lower middle classes under financial stress.

Cuts in federal spending have meant a greater burden on state governments to meet their budgetary obligations. And while states are required to make up the shortfalls, they have faced their own greatest fiscal crises in decades—crises that have been caused by reduced federal grants, increased costs for homeland security, the general economic downturn, and federal and state tax cuts. The National Conference of State Legislatures estimated that between 2001 and 2003 states had to close a cumulative budget gap approaching $200 billion. Because many state income tax rates are linked to federal rates, state revenues fell in tandem with the federal cuts. But unlike the federal government that can run large deficits, virtually all states are required either by their constitutions or laws to have balanced budgets. Thus, to make up for the shortfalls, states have been forced to dip into reserve funds, slash basic services, and/or raise taxes and user fees. Typically, states have cut services and shifted the burden onto cities and towns, adding to the urban crisis that already afflicts many of them. Hardest hit by cuts in services are vulnerable populations who are often concentrated in urban areas—families with disabled members, single mothers and their children, the working poor, and the precarious middle class who are one paycheck or unpaid hospital bill away from poverty. Moreover, when state and local budgets are cut, not only are vital programs affected, but so is a major source of employment: state and local governments employ one in seven U.S. workers and have been a major source of job growth.[51]

In the face of the powerful arguments on the grounds of the opportunity cost of military spending in terms of forgone public spending on public capital, both human and physical, beneficiaries of war dividends have in recent decades switched gears in their efforts to justify continued expansion of military buildup. In addition to the traditional "benefits" of military spending, or military Keynesianism (stimulating demand, investment, employment, and technical innovation), these beneficiaries now emphasize what they call "power projection capabilities" of military spending in their rationalization of military buildup: using military muscle for international economic gains, for access to global markets and resources, and for extracting concessions from economic rivals.[52] This claim of the usefulness of military power as an "extra-economic" measure for international economic gains deserves closer scrutiny. (The term "extra-economic" is borrowed from the late Ernest Mandel, who argued that, during normal economic times or expanding economic cycles, the capitalist class flaunts the invisible hand of the market mechanism and preaches laissez-faire philosophy. But when long expanding cycles turn into long contracting cycles—such as, for example, the Great Depression of the 1930s or the protracted recession of the 1970s—the ruling elite roll up their sleeves, so to speak, discard all pretensions of homage to the invisible hand of the market mechanism, and adopt all kinds of extra-economic measures in order to contain or reverse threatening economic crises and to rescue the market system. Such extra-economic measures include policy or political measures, regulatory or juridical alterations, as well as changes in international relations that might lead to or necessitate wars.[53])

Defending Military Spending on Extra-Economic, Imperialistic Grounds: Military Imperialism versus Free Trade Imperialism

Militarism has always tried to disguise its interests as national interests and justify its parasitic role and existentialist military adventures on grounds that such military operations will lead to economic gains for the imperium or the nation as a whole. This despite the fact that military adventures instigated by beneficiaries of the business of war are often costly economic burdens that tend to be at odds not only with the interests of the masses of the poor and working people, but also with those of nonmilitary transnational capitalists who pay taxes to finance such adventures while losing sales in foreign markets to international competition, as well as losing political and economic stability in global markets.

As discussed in the chapter 2 of this study, militarism should not be confused with the military. Although militarism evolves out of the military, the two are different in character. The military is usually a means to meet certain ends: to maintain national security or to gain economic, territorial, or geopolitical advantages. Militarism, on the other hand, represents a bureaucratized permanent military establishment as an end in itself. Likewise, a distinction needs to be made between economic or classic imperialism, on the one hand, and purely militaristic or parasitic imperialism, on the other. Historically, military imperialism has almost always evolved out of a higher stage of economic imperialism: a prolonged reliance on military power as a means for economic, territorial, or geopolitical gains gradually creates a dynamic out of which evolves a large standing military apparatus that tends to perpetuate itself—and to develop into parasitic military imperialism. Accordingly, under military imperialism, military adventures abroad are often prompted not necessarily by a desire to expand the nation or the empire's wealth beyond the existing levels but by a desire to appropriate the lion's share of the existing wealth and treasure for the military establishment. It is at such stages of parasitic growth of the military apparatus that military operations abroad tend to tip the scales in the direction of cost inefficiency and drain a national economy.

Using military power as a means for economic ends, most empires of the past paid for themselves and often ended up with net economic gains as a result of their military operations abroad. The Dutch, Spanish, and British empires all enriched their homelands through military/colonial exploitation, as did U.S. imperialism until recent years/decades. Not so, however, with today's global expansion of the U.S. military apparatus and its adventurous international muscle flexing. Recent U.S. military buildup and its unilateral aggressions abroad have increasingly become economic burdens not only because they devour a disproportionately large share of national resources, but also because such adventurous operations tend to create instability in international markets, subvert long-term global investment, and increase energy or fuel costs. Furthermore, the resentment and hostilities that unprovoked aggressions generate in foreign lands are bound to create backlash at the consumer level. For example, the Iranian-made beverage Zam Zam Cola has in recent years made significant inroads into the traditional markets of the U.S. brands Coca-Cola and Pepsi not only in the Middle East but also in Europe and elsewhere. A *Business Week* report pointed out in the immediate aftermath of the U.S. invasion of Iraq that in the Muslim world, Europe, and elsewhere "there have been calls for boycotts of American brands as well as demonstrations at symbols of U.S. business, such as McDonald's corporation."[54]

A leading Middle East business journal, *AME Info*, reported in its April 8, 2004 issue that in 2000 a number of Arab organizations "asked Muslims to shun goods from America, seen as an enemy of Islam and a supporter of Israel. In Bahrain, the Al-Montazah supermarket chain, for example, boosted sales by pulling about 1,000 US products off its shelves, and other grocers followed suit." Coca-Cola and Pepsi, "sometimes considered unflattering shorthand for the United States, took the brunt of the blow. Coca-Cola admitted that the boycott trimmed some $40 million off profits in the Gulf in 2002." In 2003, Coca-Cola retreated from Bahrain to Athens. "We see that retrenchment as the rise of local brands. Coca-Cola feels they are identified with US regional policy, and there's nothing they can do about it." The report further pointed out that in recent years a number of "Muslim colas" have appeared in the Middle Eastern/Muslim markets. "Don't Drink Stupid, Drink Committed, read the labels of Mecca Cola, from France. . . . Iran's Zam Zam Cola, originally concocted for Arab markets, has spread to countries including France and the United States." The report also indicated that U.S. exports to the Middle East dropped by $31 billion from 1998–2002. Branded, value-added goods—all the stuff easily recognized as American—were hit the hardest. "Our piece of the pie is shrinking," says Grant Smith, director of IRmep, a Washington-based think tank on Middle Eastern affairs, "and it's because of our degraded image."[55]

Evidence shows that the foreign policy-induced loss of market share in global markets goes beyond the Middle East and/or the Muslim world. According to a December 2004 survey of 8,000 international consumers carried out by Global Market Insite (GMI) Inc., one-third of all consumers in Canada, China, France, Germany, Japan, Russia, and the United Kingdom "said that U.S. foreign policy, particularly the 'war on terror' and the occupation of Iraq, constituted their strongest impression of the United States. Brands closely identified with the U.S., such as Marlboro cigarettes, America Online (AOL), McDonald's, American Airlines, and Exxon-Mobil, are particularly at risk." Twenty percent of respondents in Europe and Canada "said they consciously avoided buying U.S. products as a protest against those policies." Commenting on the results of the survey, Dr. Mitchell Eggers, GMI's chief operating officer and chief pollster, pointed out, "Unfortunately, current American foreign policy is viewed by international consumers as a significant negative, when it used to be a positive."[56] Kevin Roberts, chief executive of advertising giant Saatchi & Saatchi, likewise expressed concern about global consumer backlash against militaristic U.S. foreign policy when he told the *Financial Times* that he believed consumers in Europe and Asia are becoming increasingly resistant to having "brand America rammed down their throats." Similarly, Simon Anholt, author of *Brand America*, told the British trade magazine *Marketing Week* that "four more years of Bush's foreign policy could have grave consequences for U.S. companies' international market share."[57]

Despite these damages and threats to global U.S. market share, beneficiaries of war dividends claim that their military operations abroad would yield economic benefits for the nation as a whole because, they claim, such military actions would help spread unhindered market mechanism, remove obstacles to transnational corporations, and keep foreign markets and resources open to their business operations. Recently, such assertions are frequently interspersed with claims of "spreading democracy worldwide." In this fashion, beneficiaries of war and militarism try to disguise the colossal military buildup, which has become an end—indeed, an empire—in itself, as a means for spreading democracy and achieving international economic advantage. Such claims are made both directly through Pentagon policy documents and indirectly through militaristic surrogate think tanks such as the Project for New American Century (PNAC) and the American Enterprise Institute (AEI). In recent years, such allegations are also made through a number of policy papers written by the Bush administration.[58]

Evidence, as well as logic and common sense, suggests, however, that not only are the assertions that continued military buildup would help spread political and economic freedom hollow and disingenuous but that, in fact, war and militarism as strategies to achieve these lofty ideals are counterproductive, especially in the era of integrated and interdependent global markets. Not only is militarism inherently at odds with freedom, but it is also burdensome economically—except, of course, for the beneficiaries of the business of war. Economic liberalism, which has in the last few decades been called neoliberalism, is, in fact, antithetical to militarism; it shuns militarism not only because militarism is costly and wasteful but also because it is disruptive to international economics and would, therefore, undermine global capitalist profitability—again, except for military industries and related businesses. Accordingly, economic liberalism/neoliberalism relies on market (not military) force to maintain international economic superiority.

As this strategy of relying on market efficiency (instead of military power) in pursuit of international economic advantage tends to expose a large military establishment as parasitic and redundant, it also helps explain the inherent conflict between militarism and liberalism/neoliberalism. The strategy further helps explain why beneficiaries of war and militarism, the military establishment and the neoconservative militarists in and around the Bush administration, were so hostile to Bill Clinton and his neoliberal economic policies. In addition, the conflicting interests of militarism and neoliberalism help explain why these beneficiaries stifled the widespread calls for "peace dividends" and military downsizing in the immediate aftermath of the collapse of the Berlin Wall. Perhaps more importantly, the conflicting interests of militarism and those of nonmilitary transnational capital help explicate why representatives of the latter interests have not encouraged or embraced the Bush administration's policy of unilateral militarism. Although nonmilitary transnational interests have not expressed a strong opposition to the administration's drive to war, they have nonetheless shown some tepid wariness toward it. As shown in chapter 6 of this study, even big oil, the major (but largely incidental) beneficiaries of war, did not support the war on Iraq.

This is not to say that the American oil companies and other nonmilitary transnational corporations would not welcome the spoils of war in the form of oil price hikes, or of the acquisition of asset ownership that would result from privatization of previously public industries and enterprises that might ensue from the policy of "regime change" in a country like Iraq. Indeed, there is evidence that, as soon as Iraq came under U.S. occupation, many such corporations from agribusiness, transportation, telecommunications, financial services, and power rushed their representatives to Baghdad to participate in the contracting and privatization bonanza that followed the occupation.[59] Nonetheless, there is no evidence that major oil and other nonmilitary transnational corporations instigated or encouraged the invasion—as did the military-industrial complex and its neoconservative allies and representatives—because nonmilitary transnational capital prefers stability and predictability in global markets to short-term spoils of war.

Representatives of nonmilitary transnational capital prefer multilateral economic policies of neoliberalism to unilateral actions of the Bush administration because they are afraid that war and militarism might subvert international economics and undermine long-term U.S. competitiveness. Expressing such concerns of neoliberalism, *Business Week* carried an article on the eve of the invasion of Iraq that read, "Washington's unilateral tendencies have also created nervousness in global financial markets on which the U.S. has become dependent. It has made the multilateral trade negotiations—in which so many American companies have a huge stake—a secondary priority. . . . Financing foreign wars and boosting homeland security is bound to erode U.S. economic vitality."[60] Three weeks later, in another article titled "How War Will Shape the Economy" the magazine wrote, "The real threat [of the war] is to the rapid productivity growth of the 1990s, which may be tough to sustain in an unsettled and hostile world. New Economy growth depends on globalization and innovation, both of which could be dampened by war and a potentially difficult aftermath." The article further pointed out, "Any slowdown in the free flow of trade, people, and technologies could significantly dampen innovation and growth in the U.S. and abroad. . . . What we do know is that the market-driven growth the U.S. enjoyed in the 1990s thrived on an atmosphere of global peace. . . . The war in Iraq, the tough rebuilding task ahead, and the rise in global tension all signal to an end to that fertile era."[61]

Writing in the October 27, 2003 issue of the *Star Tribune*, Ron Bosrock of the Global Institute of St. John's University likewise expressed anxiety over negative economic consequences that might follow from the Bush administration's policies of unilateral military operations and economic sanctions: "In the meantime, the U.S. economy, in order to grow, will have to continue to expand into the global markets while dealing with this ever-increasing competition [from EU, China, India, and so on]. If this new U.S. foreign policy [of militarism] leads to decades of upheaval, how will U.S. businesses convince their future global partners that they should look to them for stable business opportunities—as opposed to all those new competitors waiting in the wings?"

Concerns of this nature have prompted a broad spectrum of nonmilitary business interests to form coalitions of trade associations that are designed to lobby foreign policy makers against unilateral U.S. military aggressions abroad. One such antimilitarist alliance of American businesses is USA*ENGAGE. It is a coalition of nearly 700 small and large businesses, agriculture groups, and trade associations working to seek alternatives to the proliferation of unilateral U.S. foreign policy actions and to promote the benefits of U.S. engagement abroad. "American values are best advanced," points out the coalition's statement of principles, "by engagement of American business and agriculture in the world, not by ceding markets to foreign competition. Helping train workers, building roads, telephone systems, and power plants in poorer nations, promoting free enterprise—these activities improve the lives of people worldwide and support American values. Unfortunately the real difference made by American companies and workers through such day-to-day activity is lost in the emotion of political debates, where there is pressure to make a symbolic gesture [a unilateral foreign policy action], even if it won't work."[62]

Nonmilitary business interests' anxiety over the Bush administration's unilateral foreign policy measures is, of course, rooted in their negatively-affected financial balance sheets by those actions: "Hundreds of companies blame the Iraq war for poor financial results in 2003, many warning that continued U.S. military involvement there could harm this year's performance," pointed out James Cox of *USA Today*. In a relatively comprehensive survey of the economic impact of the war, published in the July 14, 2004 issue of the paper, Cox further wrote: "In recent regulatory filings at the Securities and Exchange Commission, airlines, home builders, broadcasters, mortgage providers, mutual funds and others say the war was directly to blame for lower revenue and profits last year." Many businesses blamed the war and international political turbulence as a 'risk factor' that threatened their sales: "The war led to sharp decreases in business and leisure travel, say air carriers, travel services, casino operators, restaurant chains and hotel owners."[63] The survey covered a number of airlines including Delta Airlines, JetBlue, Northwest Airlines, and Alaska Airlines, all of which blamed the war for a drop in air travel. Related industries such as travel agencies, hotels, restaurants, and resort and casino operations all suffered losses accordingly.

The mutual funds managers who were interviewed in the *USA Today* survey included David J. Galvan of Wayne Hummer Income Fund who wrote (in a letter to shareholders), "The war in Iraq created a quagmire for corporations." Vintage Mutual Funds likewise concluded that "the price of these commitments [in Iraq and Afghanistan] may be more than the American public had expected or is willing to tolerate." In a SEC (Securities and Exchange Commission) filing, Domenic Colasacco, manager of the Boston Balanced Fund, characterized the ongoing U.S. occupation of Iraq as "sad and increasingly risky." Even technology giants such as Cisco, PeopleSoft, and Hewlett-Packard that tend to benefit from military spending expressed concerns that "hostilities in Iraq hurt results or could harm performance." For example, managers at Hewlett-Packard complained that "potential for future attacks, the national and international responses to attacks or perceived threats to national security, and other actual or potential conflicts or wars, including the ongoing military operations in Iraq, have created many economic and political uncertainties that could adversely affect our business, results of operations and stock price in ways that we cannot presently predict." Other companies that were specifically mentioned in the survey as having complained about the "whiplash from the Iraq conflict" included home builders Hovnanian and Cavalier homes, casino company Mandalay Resort Group, retailer Restoration Hardware, cosmetics giant Estée Lauder, eyewear retailer Cole, Longs Drug Stores, golf club maker Callaway, and H&Q Life Sciences Investors.

But while thousands of nonmilitary businesses have suffered from losses and stagnation due to war and militarism, war-based industries and related business have been reaping the benefits of a war-time bonanza thanks to drastic increases in military spending under President Bush—officially a 45 percent increase in real terms over what he inherited in 2001. For example, the above-cited *USA Today* survey revealed that, as expected, "Several companies have reported a boost from sales to the military or contracts stemming from the Iraqi reconstruction effort. The war has lifted sales of: gas masks from Mine Safety Appliances; bio-weapons detection kits and training from Response Biomedical; air cargo from Atlas Air; port dredging by JDC Soil Management; packaging by TriMas; body armor and vehicle protection kits from Armor Holding; telecom services and communications gear from Globalnet, CopyTele and I-Sector." There are also many less visible Pentagon contractors that are just as handsomely benefiting from military expansion. These are the somewhat surreptitious, private contractors that operate on the periphery of U.S. foreign policy by training foreign "security forces," or by "fighting terrorism." Often these private military firms are formed by retired Special Forces personnel seeking to market their military expertise to the Pentagon, the State Department, the CIA, or foreign governments. For example, MPRI, one of the largest and most active of these firms, which "has trained militaries throughout the world under contract to the Pentagon," was founded by the former Army Chief of Staff Carl Vuono and seven other retired generals. The fortunes of these military training contractors, or "modern-day mercenary companies," like those of the manufacturers of military hardware, have skyrocketed by virtue of heightened war and militarism under President Bush. For example, "The per share price of stocks in L3 Communications, which owns MPRI, has more than doubled."[64]

This brief discussion of the conflicting interests of military and nonmilitary enterprises helps explain the economic roots of foreign policy disagreements between the current neoconservative proponents of war and militarism in and around the Bush administration, on the one hand, and supporters of neoliberalism and multilateralism who dominated the Clinton administration, on the other. In essence, it is a conflict between parasitic military imperialism, which relies on war and international political tension in order to justify the colossal existence of an overextended military-industrial complex, and free trade imperialism, which relies on free trade and technological superiority for international economic gains. The conflict stems from the fact that, in the era of interdependent world markets, military operations abroad often cost non military transnational capital foreign markets; they also cost international political stability, which is crucial to international trade and investment.

Of course, this is not to say that, in the era of integrated and interdependent world markets, free trade imperialism will never resort to military force, as the leading German Social Democrat Karl Kautsky argued in his theory of "ultra-imperialism." Free trade imperialism, or neoliberalism, too would not shy away from using military force, if "necessary," but usually as an option or means of last resort; that is, when the leading world economic powers cannot resolve their competing interests in global markets by peaceful multilateral negotiations. Such instances of the use of military power as a means for economic ends, however, are best characterized as economic imperialism (where military operations abroad are often viewed as investments that tend to pay for themselves and end up with net economic gains) not parasitic military imperialism, where the use of military force tends to be an end in itself and an economic burden—as is the case with today's unilateral military actions of the Bush administration. Disregarding this crucial difference between economically advantageous military operations of an imperial power and those that are burdensome economically (i.e., between an economically expanding imperial power and a stagnant or declining one), neoconservative militarists in and around the Bush administration claim that their military adventures abroad are prompted by a desire not only "to spread democracy across the globe" but also to advance national economic interests. In the face of the onerous costs of the administration's overextended military adventures abroad, however, such claims sound woefully hollow.

A major hallmark of the neoconservative militarists in and around the Bush administration is their oblivion to or contempt for reality. Not surprisingly then, they characteristically tout their unilateral military adventures abroad as beneficial both to the world and U.S. "national interests." For example, during the 2004 Irving Kristol Lecture at the annual dinner of the American Enterprise Institute, columnist Charles Krauthammer, a hard-line member of the neoconservative circles, rhapsodized about the global role of the United States as the history's "designated custodian of the international system." Since the fall of the Berlin Wall, he opined, "something new was born, something utterly new—a unipolar world dominated by a single superpower unchecked by any rival and with decisive reach in every corner of the globe. This is a staggering new development in history, not seen since the fall of Rome. . . . Even Rome is no model for what America is today." Krauthammer is not alone in portraying and celebrating the neoconservatives' military aggressions of recent years as the new Rome. Other leading neoconservative militarists, including some top officials of the Bush administration such as Secretary of Defense Donald Rumsfeld and his deputy Paul Wolfowits, have likewise insinuated unabashedly that the United States of George W. Bush is the new Rome.[65]

The question is why? Why do the leading figures in the neoconservative movement, including some top officials in the Bush administration, so proudly characterize their unilateral policies of aggression as resembling those of the Roman Empire? It is true that neoconservative militarists tend to suffer from delusions and "reality deficit." But I suspect that their eagerness to compare the Bush administration's aggressive foreign policy with the role of a custodian empire like Rome goes beyond hallucinations and wishful thinking. Perhaps more importantly, such comparisons stem from their need to camouflage the special interests that drive their policies of war and militarism—the military-industrial complex and the radical Zionist proponents of "greater Israel" in the Promised Land—behind general or overall national interests. This seems to be another example of the neoconservative strategists' mastery in fraud, fabrication, and disguise: they do not mind having their policies labeled as imperialistic—in fact, as just pointed out, they insinuate that those policies are imperialistic—as long as it implies imperialism in an abstract or general sense, with connotations of national interests, as this would masquerade the real special interests that benefit and drive the war.

To the extent that there may be parallels between the imperialistic posturing of the Bush administration and those of the Roman Empire, such similarities are more akin to the post-Rubicon, late fourth century, or declining Rome than the thriving Rome of earlier stages. The capricious, confused, and costly military adventures of the administration, both in terms of blood and treasure, seem to resemble the historical pattern that characterized the erratic policies of Roman generals after Juliet Caesar crossed the Rubicon—policies that contributed to the eventual collapse of the Empire—not those of the booming empire of the earlier times. This is not to say that U.S. imperialism is headed toward an imminent collapse, but that if the increasingly costly escalation of militarization is not contained, it could undermine America's international economic competitiveness and stint national potential for long-term development and prosperity.

Sadly, however, U.S. policy makers do not seem to be bothered much by the ominous trend of continued expansion of militarism. The question is why? Certainly, they must be aware of the draining impact that disproportionately large military spending is having on the economic base that is supposed to nurture it. They could not be altogether oblivious of the likelihood that the costly trade-off between military and nonmilitary public spending might undermine long-term growth potential of the nation, as it would neglect social and economic infrastructure, limit investment in human capital, and weaken the health and productivity of its labor force. Likewise, they could not be blind to the enormous contributions of the rising military spending to the swelling national debt and deficit and the likelihood that, if this menacing trend is not brought under control, it might debauch the dollar and paralyze financial markets, both nationally and internationally. So, the question, once again, is why do most U.S. policy makers not seem to be worried about the likelihood that the escalating militarization of recent years might not be viable in the long term? And if it is true that, as I have argued in this study, the nonmilitary transnational capital, including big oil, prefers international political stability to the unilateral military adventures of the Bush administration, why, then, do the representatives of nonmilitary transnational interests not stand up to the partisans of war and militarism, and why don't they try to put a leash on the runaway military buildup?

Although militarism's unilateral aggressions abroad often cost nonmilitary transnational capital stability, predictability, and sales markets, such military operations also benefit capitalist interests in other ways. In other words, while there are conflicts of interests between military and nonmilitary capitalists, there are also convergences of their interests—often vis-à-vis the interests of their common class opponents: the poor and working classes. There are a number of areas where military and nonmilitary capitalist interests converge.

To begin with, the war atmosphere and heightened patriotism make it easier for the ruling class to redistribute national resources in favor of capital, or against labor. For example, the atmosphere of war and national security state that the neoconservative militarists in and around the Bush administration have created has made it easier for opponents of social spending to give drastic tax cuts to the wealthy while, at the same time, cutting on the meager but critically needed benefits of the poor and working classes. The huge budget deficit that has been created by increased Pentagon expenditures and decreased taxes on the wealthy "is squeezing public workers at all levels, resulting in wage freezes and elimination of entire departments."[66] The late Reverend Martin Luther King Jr. expressed this ominous correlation between the actual wars abroad and metaphorical wars on the poor and working classes at home quite incisively when he observed (in the context of the Vietnam War) that the bombs raining down on the "enemy" also endanger the future and the livelihoods of people in poor and working-class communities in the United States.

Second, during periods of economic slowdown and sluggish demand, the entire capitalist class, not just the military-based capitalist interests, would favor military spending, as during such times of deficient purchasing power military spending is viewed as a shot in the arm of an anemic economy. During contractionary business cycles and pessimistic economic outlooks, the private sector often tends to retrench and abstain from investment and expansion. As this skittish, pro-cyclical behavior of the private sector tends to aggravate an already lethargic economy, the public sector would loom as a promising (and perhaps the only) source of "jump-starting" the economy through a robust spending program.[67] This is the essence of the so-called demand-management, or Keynesian, economics. It is also what prompted President Roosevelt's New Deal economic policies. But because the ruling class is usually reluctant to increase the civilian component of public spending, military spending wins facile support for expansion as the source of demand enhancement. This helps explain (at least, partially) why the military-industrial complex has been most successful in increasing military spending during recessionary cycles of the economy: the late 1940s–early 1950s, the late 1970s–early 1980s, and the early 2000s. It also helps explain that it is not military spending (or war) per se that helps stimulate the economy. It is, rather, the mere fact of spending, of injecting purchasing power into the economy, that helps bring about economic recovery. Instances of economic recovery credited to wars and military spending could have been achieved just as (or even more) effectively had such government spending hikes been devoted, instead, to nonmilitary public works projects. Indeed, there is evidence that, as discussed earlier in this chapter, civilian public spending would probably not have required as much as what military spending required to achieve the same levels of employment or aggregate demand objectives.[68]

Third, militarism tends to sow the seeds of unquestioned discipline, ideological acquiescence, respect for military-type order, and obedience to hierarchy. It inculcates these "military ways of thinking,"[69] into the civilian culture both through subtle and indirect ways—for example, through educational and political institutions—and direct, militaristic ways such as, for example, the imposition of the "Patriot Act," which legally restricts citizens' civil liberties. The regulatory mechanism of the large military spending operates in a comprehensive or multifaceted fashion. On the one hand, by curtailing nonmilitary public spending, it creates large numbers of "undereducated" and unemployed young individuals, who hail largely from low-income, ethnic and/or racial minorities. On the other, by pouring resources into the deep pockets of the Pentagon, it creates "opportunities" for these individuals who sign up to learn skills, earn money for education, and escape the pains of protracted unemployment—and, at times, of course, also to serve as cannon fodder for the militarists' war machine. As Dan Smith and Ron Smith, authors of *The Economics of Militarism*, describe,

> Militarism has a variety of effects within power relations of capitalist societies. Military spending both sustains and is sustained by an ideology based on perceptions of threat to the established order and the need to respond to it. Promoting military values may help develop feelings of national unity, prestige and discipline, making workers more amenable to accepting the social order and their place within it . . . especially by integrating disparate social and ethnic groups into the social whole. . . . Beyond this, military power is the final guarantor of the state's power in domestic society. . . . If the state's regulation of social relations is in danger of breaking down, it is ultimately the military on which the maintenance of the existing distribution of power and wealth would depend.[70]

An atmosphere of heightened militarism and war-time anxiety helps the capitalist class to discipline and exploit the working class more effectively. As Rodney Ward, a longtime labor activist, points out, "Wars have always had a deep impact on working people. In addition to the slaughter of war, wars have often undermined the strength of working class organizations.

Government repression tied to World War I all but destroyed the Industrial Workers of the World and the Socialist Party." Ward also points out how "Workplace regimentation in World War II played an important role in the long-term bureaucratization of unions, replacing militant shop floor activity with safer routinized grievance and arbitration procedures."[71]

The brunt of the war is placed largely on the shoulders of the poor and working classes. The current U.S. military is formally an all-volunteer force. In truth, however, today's military recruitment strategy is essentially a disguised "poverty draft," as pointed out by the Central Committee for Conscientious Objectors. Oskar Castro of the Youth and Militarism Project of the American Friends Service Committee (AFSC) points out that "most people signed up not because they were gung-ho warriors. Most people signed up for the college money and wonderful career opportunities, leadership skills and respect" that military recruiters offer—attractive promises to a young person whose alternatives are a dead-end job or unemployment. Nearly half of the soldiers in the U.S. military are reservists. In addition to the emotional trauma soldiers and their loved ones experience during a war-time mobilization, reservists also endure significant economic hardships. As they are activated from civilian jobs, many face dramatic pay cuts and disruption of health benefits. Setting aside the risk of war, they take heavy economic blows, often 30–50 percent cuts in pay. One New York City reservist explained, for example, that activation would mean his family would lose their home.[72]

The war tears away at the lives of the working people not only on the war front but also on the home front. While they are risking their lives on the (unnecessary) battle fields, the Bush administration and corporate interests are using the war-time insecurity as a pretext to strip union rights from many workers. For example, the administration has deprived tens of thousands of federal workers in the hurriedly instituted Department of Homeland Security of union rights in the name of "national security." The Department of Defense is developing plans to follow suit. The administration has also called for the privatization and/or outsourcing of as many as 800,000 non-postal federal jobs. If successful, this move would replace large numbers of union jobs with nonunion ones at lower pay and with less accountability; it would strike a huge blow at the strength of public-sector unions. Diane Witiak, an American Federation of Government Employees (AFGE) spokeswoman, describes this union-busting atmosphere or strategy: "If you dare to oppose the administration, you're almost considered a traitor. We resent that the administration considers unionization and patriotism incompatible. In fact, [unionization is] essential. [The administration] will go back to the old cronyism and favoritism that the Civil Service Act corrected. It's only a matter of time before Bush starts with the private sector!"[73]

Due to these considerations, nonmilitary capitalist interests tend to go along with (or, at least, not to seriously resist) the militarization plans of the military-industrial interests, despite the fact that such plans might sometimes jeopardize their trade and investment opportunities abroad. But even when the champions of war and militarism have occasionally faced serious resistance to the escalation of the Pentagon appropriations, they have proven to be quite creative in outmaneuvering advocates of the containment of the Pentagon budget. During the Cold War era this was not a difficult act to perform, as the pretext for continued militarization—the "communist threat"—seemed to conveniently lie at hand. Justification of increased military spending in the post–Cold War period, however, has prompted the military-industrial interests to be even more creative in inventing (or manufacturing, if necessary) "new sources of danger to U.S. interests." These "new sources of threat" are said to stem from the "unpredictable, unreliable regional powers of the Third World," from the so-called rogue states, from a decontextualized "global terrorism" and, more recently, from "Islamic fundamentalism." As discussed in chapter 6 of this study, leading ideologues of war and militarism in and around the Bush administration argue that the United States is involved in a long, protracted war against Islamic fundamentalism, which they call "World War IV"—the Cold War being "World War III."

Since the 2004 reelection of President Bush, partisans of war and militarism have added a new rationale for continued expansion of military buildup: "spreading democracy to all corners of our planet," as the president put it in his second inaugural speech. The claim of spreading democracy is the latest in a series of the administration's alleged reasons for its drive to war: weapons of mass destruction, Al-Qaedeh . . . and now "ending tyranny and establishing democracy." Now that the administration's claims of Saddam Hussein's possession of weapons of mass destruction and his alleged ties to Al-Qaedeh have been proven as fabrications, the war party has come up with its "democracy" excuse: arguing that regardless of one's view on the legitimacy of attacking Afghanistan or Iraq, such U.S.

interventions have brought significant steps toward democracy there and elsewhere in those regions.

Obviously, the administration's democracy argument suffers from mistaking or obfuscating meaningful democracy and liberty with controlled and choreographed ceremonial voting for the election of the handpicked political candidates who would not oppose U.S. dictates or hegemony. While the neoconservative militarists boastfully invoke the massive voter turnout in Iraq on the election day, January 30, 2005, they hardly mention the fact that the impressive—indeed, commendable—enthusiasm for voting was prompted largely by false promises, top among which was sovereignty and the end of U.S. occupation. "Though we praise the courage of Iraqi citizens and the first step of holding an election there," pointed out Marc Pilisuk and Neil Wollman, "to this point what is transpiring in Iraq is not so much democracy as a triumph for leaders of particular factions permitted by the occupying military rulers." Iraq does not have a democracy with power to wrest control from U.S. corporations now feverishly engaged in no-bid, monopolistic contracts and lucrative privatization schemes of public-sector enterprises. Neither can its new government stop the ongoing construction of permanent U.S. military bases in its country, or insist that Iraq's rich resources adequately provide for its citizens traumatized by war. A real democracy in Iraq would reflect majority opinion to end military occupation and stop preferences given to U.S. contractors.[74]

Claims of promoting democracy have almost always colored imperialistic U.S. foreign policies. Thus, popularly chosen leaders such as Mosadegh in Iran, Allende in Chile, Arbenz in Guatemala, and Juan Bosch in the Dominican Republic were all removed by U.S. military and intelligence operations in the name of spreading democracy. These and many other brutal interventions took place because the respective governments dared to ask U.S. transnational corporations for a fair share of the profits they were making in their countries. The history of U.S. foreign policy clearly shows that its promotion of democracy does not necessarily include the right to manage one's economy, to control one's resources, to freely chose one's trading partners, or to challenge foreign corporations. The caricature of democracy that U.S. foreign policy makers are self righteously touting nowadays as the rationale for their unilateral military aggressions can be aptly called the foreign policy of the last resort: as long as the kings, feudal lords, or tribal leaders remain as viable pliant allies, elections are not mentioned. Once history makes such rulers obsolete or unviable, imperialistic

U.S. foreign policy resorts to controlled elections to replace them with equally pliant but now "democratically elected" allies. To the extent that imperialism succeeds in adjusting to or influencing this historical transition, often it is only the form or structure of control that changes, not the essence of it.[75]

CHAPTER 9

Limits of U.S. Militarism

Both economic logic and actual developments indicate that occasional expansion of military spending can serve as an economic stimulus, especially during cycles of high unemployment and insufficient demand. Because the nonmilitary private sector tends to become wary of investing and expanding during such periods of doubt and uncertainty, government spending looms as the substitute or alternative stimulus to inject the badly needed purchasing power into the market in order to jump-start the anemic economy. (It was this necessity of government intervention that gave birth to the 1930s New Deal in the United States, and to Keynesian economics, or demand-management, more generally.)

But because in the absence of social/political pressure from *below* the capitalist class prefers military to civilian public spending, military spending has thus evolved as a major antirecession, or countercyclical, fiscal policy measure in the post–World War II period, especially since the early 1980s. For example, the drastic increase of military spending in the early 1950s is often credited with having helped end the recession of the late 1940s, and the equally sharp increases of the early 1980s is credited with having helped end the long recessionary cycle of the 1970s. Likewise, to the extent that there is an economic recovery from the 2000–2002 recession, the rebounding is partially attributed to President George W. Bush's heightening of military spending. More importantly, it is generally believed that World War II military expenditures helped eradicate the lingering remnants of the Great Depression. Nazi Germany's huge military expenditures in the 1930s and their stimulating economic effects seem to be consistent with this pattern. In his *Late Capitalism*, Ernest Mandel cites a number of other instances from the experiences of England, France, Russia, and Japan of how military expenditures helped stimulate their economies at various historical junctures.[1]

What are the long-term implications of these experiences and the underlying economic logic? Do they imply, as popularly perceived, that war and militarism are conducive to economic prosperity by stimulating aggregate demand and reducing unemployment? More fundamentally, do they mean that, through its countercyclical or antirecession effects, continuous increases in military spending can permanently shield capitalism against wild gyration of market cycles, thereby serving as an insurance policy against periodic recessions of overproduction, or underconsumption? Should military spending hikes be used sparingly, that is, only as short-term or occasional injections of purchasing power, or can they be used on a regular, escalating, and long-term basis? Are there limits to militarism and/or military spending? And if so, what are those limits?

There is a wide range of opinions on these questions. Two major theories, which also seem to be polar opposites of each other, stand out among others. One of these theories, which (for lack of a better term) may be called the theory of imperial militarism à la Old, or post-Rubicon, Rome, maintains that steadily rising military expenditures and permanent arms/war economies are untenable. An escalating and out-of-control militarization of a superpower tends to gradually drive that once-prosperous superpower in the direction of a mismanaged and destructive military-imperial force whose capricious and often purely existential military adventures will eventually become costly both politically and economically. While the top-heavy imperial-military establishment that would thus evolve out of the womb of a corrupt and decadent superpower tends to undermine its economic base, it is also bound to create many enemies abroad while, at the same time, generating a lot of discontent and hostility to the established order at home. Unchecked, a combination of these adverse developments, especially a drained economy and an empty or bankrupt treasury, might eventually lead to the demise of the empire, just as happened to the post-Rubicon, Old Roman Empire. Accordingly, proponents of this theory project that the rising tendency in the United States to military imperialism might be following a similar historical trajectory toward decline and decay.[2] (This theory is discussed in some detail in the second chapter of this study.)

A second, diametrically opposite view—called the theory of permanent arms/war economy, or permanent military Keynesianism—maintains that military spending can be used to boost a weak demand and stimulate a lackluster economy not only on a conjunctural or short-term basis, but also on a regular, long-term, or permanent basis. According to this theory, a well-developed market economy tends to produce more than it can consume or absorb. This tendency to create a gap between supply and demand leads to occasional economic difficulties (at the macro or national level) of underconsumption, or overproduction. It follows that in the face of insufficient demand military spending can serve as the lacking or needed purchasing power to fill the supply-demand gap, thereby helping to contain or turn around a declining or stagnant economy. The late German economist Natalie Moszkowska described this "curative" property of military expenditures as follows:

> The development of civilian industry is increasingly cramped by the absence of monetarily effective demand and by stagnant sales. The development of the war industry knows no such restrictions. Based on the presupposition of war, the armaments industry can develop at a totally different rate and with an impetus never previously known or even suspected. . . . The arms industry does not supply the market nor depend on its capacity to absorb its goods. The state here both provides orders and takes delivery.[3]

Like other proponents of the theory of underconsumption, Moszkowska concluded that, "based on the presupposition of war," and based on the fact that the war industry is immune to supply and demand fluctuations of market mechanism, arms production and military spending can be expanded at will, or as needed; implying that, therefore, continued increases in military spending can provide a permanent solution to the problem of insufficient demand. Not surprisingly, the theory came to be known as the theory of permanent arms (or war) economy.

Both of these theories suffer from extreme or sweeping projections. The dynamics of U.S. militarism and the trajectory of its future developments point to neither of these polar directions: neither the pattern of post-Rubicon Rome nor the likelihood of permanent or uninterrupted military Keynesianism.

The weakness of the theory of post-Rubicon Rome was discussed in some detail in the second chapter of this study. To summarize that discussion, suffice it to point out here that the weakness of this theory stems from what might be called an ahistorical extrapolation: painting a precapitalist or feudalistic future for the highly capitalistic military-industrial complex of the United States. The democratic Republic of Rome was essentially a city-state government. As the city-state republic expanded outward and conquered new provinces and territories, decentralization of power and administration followed accordingly. Since agriculture constituted the economic foundation of the societies of the time, land ownership and control of territory served as a major source of contention among the many local and regional authorities, provincial governors, and military commanders. Inability to resolve conflicting economic interests or territorial claims peacefully often led to violent clashes and armed struggles. Indeed, due to the nature of property ownership (i.e., control or ownership of land), hence, the source of power and prestige, armed civil war and physical defeat or destruction of political or economic adversaries was more often than not the only way to end or to resolve irreconcilable interests or hostilities. This is how, for instance, Roman *imperators* (military commanders), provincial governors, and various other contending sources of power resolved their political and economic claims against each other, or against the Senate and/or nobility that were ensconced in the city-state of Rome, after Julius Caesar illegally crossed the Rubicon and thrust the country into civil war (49 BC).

By contrast, under advanced and well-integrated capitalist economies antagonistic social forces and conflicting interests within the ruling circles tend to avoid violent clashes and military civil wars because, while conflicting, their interests are also vested in a unified market system that is averse to physical violence and armed civil war: if it is disrupted or paralyzed, all the contending factions of the ruling class would lose. The economic imperative of the market mechanism, that is, the need to respect and preserve the health and integrity of the market structure, thus compels all the contending interests within the capitalist ruling class, including military and military-related interests, to play by the rules and requirements of the market system: to fight politically, not physically or militarily, and to resolve their conflicts and differences within the political-juridical framework of *bourgeois* democracy. Indeed, the entire tradition of bourgeois democracy, the parliamentary system of government, and the need for the appearance of the majority will through periodic voting ceremonies evolved in response to market imperatives.

The implication for the future of the military establishment of the United States is that (a) contrary to most precapitalist imperial military structures, the U.S. military-industrial complex is an integral part of the national economic and political establishment; (b) despite its enormous political influence and economic impact, control and management of the military-industrial complex (e.g., expanding the complex and sending armed forces off to war or "streamlining" the apparatus when necessary) is part and parcel of the overall socioeconomic and political control and management on a national level; (c) the fate or the future of the military establishment is thus organically intertwined with the future of U.S. capitalism; and (d) barring a radical social upheaval from below, decline or contraction of the U.S. military-imperial power, once reached its limits and exhausted, is more likely to follow the pattern of Old Europe (e.g., the British Empire) than that of Old Rome (for more on this please see chapter 2).

As noted, the rival theory of permanent arms economy also has its own shortcomings. An obvious weakness of this theory is that it implicitly assumes that the funding or financial sources of military spending are unlimited. Such an assumption is, of course, unrealistic. In reality, military financing is tantamount to a redistribution of resources away from the nonmilitary or civilian sectors to the military sector. Those resources are, of course, limited by the public treasure, or the economy's taxation capacity. Obviously, the capacity of the civilian or nonmilitary industries, and the ability of taxpayers in general, to finance military expenditures are not unlimited. Once that capacity is exhausted, that is, once the tax burden on the civilian capital tends to outweigh the economic benefits of military expenditures, the ruling class is bound to take the necessary steps to curtail further expansion of the Pentagon appropriations.

Despite its colossal magnitude since World War II, however, military spending in the United States does not seem to have ever really tested or exhausted that capacity. Military financing in the immediate postwar period was not difficult, as the "golden economy" of the time easily provided for abundant public spending on both *guns and butter*. But even in the aftermath of the golden economy large military spending has not really been burdensome to the nonmilitary or civilian capital because, since the late 1970s and early 1980s, massive military expenditures have been accommodated largely by cutting the civilian part of public spending and by borrowing. Indeed, during the last three decades or so, military spending has been used as a regulatory mechanism to redistribute national resources in favor of the rich: drastic tax cuts for the wealthy combined with large military expenditures have created wide budget gaps that have, then, forced cuts on social spending.

How long the beneficiaries of militarism and war dividends can continue this strategy of expanding the Pentagon appropriations at the expense of the middle, lower middle, poor and working classes, as well as at the expense of future generations, depends on a number of factors. One such factor is the capacity of the Americans who bear the brunt of war and militarism, that is, the low income, poor, and working people who shoulder most of the burden of war and militarism that costs them blood at the war front and social safety net programs at home. Another factor is how much debt and deficit the national economy is capable of enduring before it reaches the abyss of bankruptcy and the collapse of the dollar. A third factor is how much tax the non military capitalist interests are willing and able to pay for military spending. A fourth factor is the state of the economy: economic growth would increase government revenue and reduce its debt and deficit, and vice versa. An important fifth factor is the reaction of global markets against U.S. policies of war and militarism; that is, whether aggressive militaristic policies of the United States would generate a serious *blowback* against the sale of U.S. products abroad or not. In addition, there are human or personnel limits, as evidenced, for example, by the recent recruitment difficulties facing various branches of the U.S. armed forces. Any, all, or a combination of these factors can test the limits of militarism, precipitate dire, intolerable and, therefore, threatening socioeconomic and political circumstances, and trigger ruling-class efforts at containing or curtailing military spending.

As noted above, the U.S. ruling class has so far successfully evaded paying its share of the costs by borrowing and/or cutting civilian public spending and borrowing. The fact that the enormous military expenditures have so far not been very burdensome to corporate America means that beneficiaries of war dividends and partisans of military expansion still have considerable maneuvering room for further expansion. Such an insidious and irresponsible strategy of financing militarism and wars, however, cannot be continued indefinitely, as it could eventually precipitate widespread social protest, treasury bankruptcy, and financial or dollar collapse. Sooner or later, big business and the wealthy will have to either share the costs of expanding militarism, that is, to restore some of the huge tax breaks they have enjoyed since the early 1980s, or contain and streamline the military establishment. That seems to define the ultimate economic limit of U.S. militarism. And that is where the conflict between military and civilian capitalist interests would probably become most acute.

Nevertheless, it is unlikely that, contrary to the cases of precapitalist empires, the conflicting interests within the U.S. ruling class, having once reached such an economic limit, would lead to violent clashes or military civil wars—as happened, for example, between the heirs of Julius Caesar. For, as pointed out earlier, the common interests of the capitalist ruling circles, vested organically in the integrity and continuity of the market system, cannot afford to embark on violent methods of conflict resolution that might disrupt or paralyze the market, as this would be tantamount to economic suicide. Instead, those common interests of the ruling class tend at such critical points to overshadow their conflicting interests and induce or compel them to compromise within the bounds of the legal and institutional framework of the established order. When the ruling class as a whole feels the economic pinch or burden of escalating military spending, that is, when they find further military expansion cost-inefficient even from their own point of view, they would find ways to compromise over a "restructuring" plan that would "streamline" or slow down the growth of the military machine. The specific institutional framework within which such plans and compromises could be worked out has long been in place; it is sometimes called the Iron Triangle, where all the major ruling interests are represented: the military bureaucracy and/or commanders through the Pentagon, arms industries and related businesses through the Pentagon contractors, and nonmilitary corporate interests through the Congress, or its key committees. There is, of course, a systemic element to this mechanism: it is not because the ruling elite of capitalist imperialism is more intelligent than their counterparts of precapitalist empires; but it is because, as pointed out above, the interests and ambitions of military establishments under advanced capitalism become so organically ingrained and integrated into the market system that those interests would be better served by preserving the health and integrity of the market structure than disrupting or paralyzing that structure.

Restructurings thus imposed on military expansion by the objective limits of financial resources are more likely to be temporary than permanent, representing an ebb in a cyclical pattern of ebbs and flows. Leaving aside exogenous factors such as a large-scale and out-of-control international war, or a widespread and radical social upheaval from below, the size and duration of such economizing retrenchments would depend, among other factors, on the overall state of the economy. During periods of economic expansion and prosperity military spending is usually not a serious problem as during such expansionary cycles financial constraints tend to ease up. Furthermore, during periods of high economic growth social, political, and economic tensions will likewise be reduced both at home and internationally, meaning that there will be less need for military expansion. On the other hand, during cycles of persistent economic contraction both domestic and international circumstances tend to call for military expansion. Domestically, expansion of military spending would be touted as an employment or demand-boosting fiscal policy measure, as the U.S. ruling class is increasingly reluctant to expand non-military public spending. Internationally, as sluggish economic times tend to heighten conflict and competition in global markets, military powers would accordingly tend to flex military muscle and expand arms expenditures.

To say that within certain economic limits—and in the absence of a serious class struggle that could torpedo the status quo—the growth of U.S. military spending will follow a cyclical pattern of ebbs and flows that is shaped largely by the overall market imperatives is not to imply that, therefore, within those manageable limits a large military apparatus is harmless—far from it. The fact is that those potential limits to militarization are often fairly broad and extensive; at times, they can be stretched very widely at high costs to many people and to many cherished values. Within those impending but somewhat fluid limits, an overextended military-industrial apparatus can cost valuable investment in human and physical public capital, curtail civil liberties, subvert republican principle, and instigate ("controlled") wars and international political convulsions. Indeed, almost all of the many post–World War II U.S. military operations abroad have taken place within the bounds of *controlled* militarism.

Nor does the judgment that, left to its own making, the U.S. ruling class is capable of control and management of the military-industrial class is designed to argue or imply that, therefore, there is no end to the imperial-military power of the United States. It is, rather, to argue that the arms industry is, of course, only part of the larger U.S. economy; that the military establishment is an integral part of the overall U.S. establishment; and that, barring *exogenous* factors such as a large-scale international war or radical social revolutions, the U.S. ruling class is capable of controlling and managing military affairs as part of the overall national socioeconomic control and management. Whether or when the U.S. imperial military establishment will decline or decay depends on a more complex constellation of factors than just military spending; it is integrally dependent on the fate or future of U.S. capitalism.

Discussions about the future of capitalism usually tend to revolve around two polar views: first, the almost fetishistic view that capitalism is eternal, the so-called *end-of-history* thesis à la Francis Fukuyama of Johns Hopkins University; and second, the deterministic view, often mistakenly attributed to Marxism, that capitalism will somehow collapse of its own accord. Both views are analytically wrong—as well as nonoperative for any policy purposes. The capitalist system is much more resilient than the proponents of the so-called theory of "automatic collapse" imagine; but it is highly doubtful that it can escape the ultimate fate of precapitalist formations, or modes of production.

A judgment on the future of capitalism, of course, requires an understanding of how it works. A basic property of capitalist development is that it grows in erratic and contradictory ways: as it expands it also creates conditions for contraction and recession. It is during long recessionary periods of economic crises that the system becomes most vulnerable, and its future least certain. During such periods, business and government leaders dispel all pretensions of deferring the economic affairs to Adam Smith's "invisible hand" and rush to the rescue of the system with all kinds of crisis-management, or restructuring, schemes. Those restructuring measures—or "extra-economic factors," as the late Ernest Mandel put it—are usually comprised of the steps or policies deemed necessary by business and government leaders for containing a long cycle of economic contraction and turning it to expansion.[4] They include deregulation of industries, dilution of workplace safety standards, whittling down labor and environmental standards, weakening social safety net programs, corporate and wealthy tax breaks, and the like. They are, in essence, economic, legal, political, institutional, and, at times, military instruments of class struggle that are employed by business and government leaders in order to buttress corporate profitability and prop up the market system. The question of the future of capitalism, and therefore of the U.S. imperial military power, ultimately boils down to the balance of social forces and the outcome of class struggle.

In brief, barring an effective social pressure from *below* or a large-scale international war, the limits of military expansion are largely determined by the politics of public finance, that is, by the budgetary decision-making processes, or by the balance of political power over allocation of national resources. How much of essential social and infrastructural public spending would be sacrificed and, therefore, how much of fundamental social and/or public needs would go unmet, or how much debt and deficit would be accumulated in order to satisfy the profitability needs of the business of war and militarism depend, in the last analysis, on the balance of social forces and the control of political power, that is, on class struggle. Viewed in this light, militaristic tendencies and the drive to wars abroad are often reflections of the metaphorical domestic wars over allocation of national resources.

Important political and policy implications follow from this perspective for the social-political forces and movements that oppose war and militarism, that is, for the social strata that bear most of the brunt of war and militarism. It follows that these social forces can significantly narrow the limits of military expansion if they can (a) force big business and the wealthy to share the escalating costs of military expenditures, that is, if they can systematically resist and successfully block curtailment of the nonmilitary public spending that is used to finance military spending; and (b) bring pressure to bear on policy makers to block deficit financing for war and militarism. If successful, the combined effects of these two measures will force the rich and powerful interests to either pay their "fair" share of taxes, that is, to roll back some of the enormous tax breaks they have enjoyed since the early 1980s, to finance their imperialistic wars, or to curtail further military expansion. In addition to having to share the financial costs of war and militarism, the ruling class should also be forced to share the costs of their wars in terms of blood; that is, their sons and daughters should not be exempted (under the pretext of the so-called all volunteer army) from fighting wars and giving blood. These are by no means revolutionary or outlandish demands; they simply call for an equitable sharing of the costs of war and militarism in terms of blood and treasure. Of course, opponents of war and militarism cannot (and should not) limit their antiwar demands to an equitable distribution of the burden or costs of war. More importantly, they have the mighty reservoir of moral force to draw upon in the face of an unjust and unjustifiable war of aggression.

While persistent demands of this nature, along with the corresponding political or protest actions by the opponents of war and military expansion, might somewhat narrow the limits of militarism, they are unlikely to reduce the colossal military-industrial complex to the levels necessary for purely defensive purposes. That would be possible, as the late General Smedley D. Butler pondered, only when profits are taken out of war and arms production.[5]

Notes

Introduction

1. These include Paul Kennedy, *The Rise and Fall of the Great Powers* (New York: Vintage Books, 1989); Chalmers Johnson, *The Sorrows of Empire* (New York: Metropolitan Books, 2004); Sidney Lens, *The Military-Industrial Complex* (Kansas City, MO: Pilgrim Press and the National Catholic Reporter, 1970); Alfred Vagts, *A History of Militarism: Civilian and Military* (London: Hollis and Carter, 1959); and Andrew J. Bacevich, *The New American Militarism* (New York: Oxford University Press, 2005).
2. See, e.g., Paul Craig Roberts, "Neo-Jacobins Push for World War IV" <http://www.lewrockwell.com/roberts/roberts8.html>; Gordon Prather, "Neo-Crazy Coup d'Etat" <http://www.antiwar.com/orig/prather.php?articleid= 2343>.
3. William Hartung and Michelle Ciarrocca, "The Military-Industrial-Think Thank Complex," *Multinational Monitor*, 24, nos. 1 and 2 (January/February 2003): <http://multinationalmonitor.org/mm2003/03jan-feb/jan-feb03corp2.html#name>.
4. See, e.g., Bacevich, *The New American Militarism*.
5. See, e.g., Johnson, *The Sorrows of Empire*, chapter 9.

Chapter 1   The Military-Industrial Giant: An Empire in Itself

1. Congress of the United States of America, June 1784, as quoted by Sidney Lens, *The Military-Industrial Complex* (Kansas City, MO: Pilgrim Press and the National Catholic Reporter, 1970), 13.
2. Ibid., 12–13.
3. Chalmers Johnson, "America's Empire of Bases," *tomdispatch.com* (January 15, 2004): <http://www.informationclearinghouse.info/article5537.htm>.
4. James Cypher, "Return of the Iron Triangle: The New Military Buildup," *Dollars & Sense*, no. 239 (January/February 2002): 17.

5. Nicholas Turse, "The Military-Academic Complex: Who's the Real Champion?" *tomdispatch.com* (April 27, 2004): <http:// www.tomdispatch.com/index.mhtml?pid=1385>.

6. Summary Federal Budget Tables, fiscal year 2005: <http://www.whitehouse.gov/ omb/budget/fy2004/tables.html>; Robert Higgs, "The Defense Budget Is Bigger than You Think," *The San Francisco Chronicle* (January 18, 2004): <http://www.independent.org/tii/news/ 031222Higgs.html>.

7. Carlton Meyer, "Slash Military Spending," *G2mil, The Magazine of Future Warfare* (October 2003): <http://www.g2mil.com/Oct2003.htm>.

8. Carlton Meyer, "Freeze the Military Budget," *G2mil, The Magazine of Future Warfare* (March 2004): <http://www.g2mil.com/Mar2004.htm>.

9. Matt Moore, "Global Military Spending Soars," veteransforpeace.org (June 9, 2004): <http://www.veteransforpeace.org/Global_military_060904.htm>.

10. Chalmers Johnson, *The Sorrows of Empire* (New York: Metropolitan Books, 2004), 57.

11. *Congressional Record* (May 20, 1969); as cited by Lens, *The Military-Industrial Complex*, 45–46.

12. "Pentagon Lines up Industry Chiefs for Top Jobs," *Newsday* (June 1, 2001); as cited by Johnson, *The Sorrows of Empire*, 62–63.

13. Kelly Patricia O'Mear, "Rumsfeld Inherits Financial Mess," *Insight-Magazine.com* (August 2001); as cited by Johnson, *The Sorrows of Empire*, 58.

14. William Hartung and Michelle Ciarrocca, "The Military-Industrial-Think Thank Complex," *Multinational Monitor*, 24, nos. 1 and 2 (January/February 2003): <http://multinationalmonitor.org/mm2003/03jan-feb/jan-feb03corp2.html#name>.

15. Alfred Vagts, *A History of Militarism: Civilian and Military* (London: Hollis & Carter, 1959), 463.

16. Johnson, *The Sorrows of Empire*, 61.

17. Greg Palast, "Adventure Capitalism," *tompaine.com* (October 26, 2004): <http://www.tompaine.com/articles/adventure_capitalism.php>.

18. Ibid.

19. Ibid.

20. Ibid.

21. Johnson, *The Sorrows of Empire*, 5.

22. Ibid., 58.

23. In Turse, "The Military-Academic Complex: Who's the Real Champion?"

24. For more on this issue see, for example, Charley Reese, "War Propaganda," *antiwar.com* (May 3, 2004): <http://www.antiwar.com/reese/?articleid=2453>.

25. Ibid.

26. For a relatively elaborate discussion of the many subtle ways through which militarism tries to infuse the civilian culture with military ways of thinking

see, for example, Lens, *The Military-Industrial Complex*, and Vagts, *A History of Militarism*.

27. Turse, *"The Military-Academic Complex: Who's the Real Champion?"*
28. Ibid.
29. Ibid.
30. Lens, *The Military-Industrial Complex*, 13.

Chapter 2   Imperial Militarisms: Past and Present

1. Chalmers Johnson, *The Sorrows of Empire* (New York: Metropolitan Books, 2004), 23–24.
2. In Carlton Meyer, "Freeze the Military Budget," *G2mil, The Magazine of Future Warfare* (March 2004): <http://www.g2mil.com/Mar2004.htm>.
3. Johnson, *The Sorrows of Empire*, 16.
4. See, e.g., ibid.; and Andrew J. Bacevich, *The New American Militarism* (New York: Oxford University Press, 2005).
5. Michael Hudson, *Trade, Development and Foreign Debt* (London: Pluto Press, 1992), 71.
6. Ibid., 91.
7. Timothy Garton Ash, "Stagger on, Weary Titan: The US Is Reeling, Like Imperial Britain after the Boer War," *The Guardian* (Thursday, August 25, 2005): <http://www.guardian.co.uk/usa/story/0,12271,1555820,00.html>.
8. Ibid.

Chapter 3   The Rise of U.S. Militarism

1. It is worth noting here that this was not the first time the U.S. policy makers had addressed the issue of economic nationalism and/or self-sufficiency vis-à-vis international interdependence. They had done so in response to both World War I and the Great Depression. For a detailed and interesting account of those debates see Laurence Shoup and William Minter, *Imperial Brain Trust: The Council of Foreign Relations and the United States Foreign Policy* (New York/London: Monthly Review Press, 1977).
2. Ibid., 125.
3. As cited in ibid., 14–15.
4. Ibid., Table 2–1 (p. 70), Table 2–4 (p. 76), Table 2–5 (p. 79), and Table 3–3 (pp. 97–98).
5. The Soviet Union was not included or discussed in this study because the capitalist world had already excluded it from international trade in retaliation for the Bolshevik revolution in 1917 and for doing away with market mechanism.
6. Shoup and Minter, *Imperial Brain Trust*, 126–128.

7. It is worth noting here that these ideas served as the original bases for the institution of the IMF and the World Bank once the projected U.S.-led Grand Area was revised to include the entire capitalist world.

8. All cited in Shoup and Minter, *Imperial Brain Trust*, 128–130.

9. Council Memorandum E-A 17 (June 14, 1941), as cited in ibid., 135.

10. Council Memorandum E-B19 (October 19, 1940), as cited in ibid., 130.

11. Ibid., 146.

12. Ibid., 146–148.

13. Ibid., 141.

14. As cited in ibid., 163.

15. All cited in ibid., 164–165.

16. Memorandum P-B23 (July 10, 1941), as quoted in ibid., 166.

17. The word pax (from Latin origin) means peace. Accordingly, Pax Americana literally means American Peace, that is, peace imposed/established and maintained by the United States—just as Pax Romana and Pax Britannica denoted the same concept in the context of the Roman and British empires.

18. As quoted in Shoup and Minter, *Imperial Brain Trust*, 171–172.

19. Richard Hofstadter, *American Political Tradition* (New York: Vintage, 1984), 349.

20. Michael Hudson, *Trade, Development and Foreign Debt* (London: Pluto Press, 1992), 91.

21. V. I. Lenin, *Imperialism: the Highest Stage of Capitalism* (Peking: Foreign Language Presses, 1975).

22. Karl Kautsky, "Ultra-Imperialism," *New Left Review*, no. 59 (January/February 1970); cited by Nick Beams, "Lenin, Kautsky and Ultra-Imperialism," *wsws.org* (April 11, 2003): <http://www.wsws.org/articles/2003/apr2003/corr-a11.shtml>.

23. Nick Beams, "Lenin, Kautsky and Ultra-Imperialism."

24. Long waves, or cycles, of economic expansion and contraction are not the same as the usual short business cycles. For a discussion of long cycles see Ernest Mandel, *Long Waves of Capitalist Development* (Cambridge: Cambridge University Press, 1980); Ismael Hossein-zadeh, "Long Waves and the Future of Capitalism," in *Political Economy and Contemporary Capitalism: Radical Perspectives on Economic Theory and Policy*, edited by Ron Baiman, Heather Boushey, and Dawn Saunders (New York: M. E. Sharpe, 2000).

25. Lenin, *Imperialism*, Collected Works, vol. 22, 295; as quoted by Nick Beams, "Lenin, Kautsky and Ultra-imperialism."

26. See, e.g., Michael Hardt and Antonio Negri, *Empire* (Cambridge, MA: Harvard University Press, 2000); David McNally, "Understanding Imperialism: Then and Now," *Against the Current*, 20, no. 3 (July/August 2005): 22–25; Gopal Balakrishnan and Stanley Aronowitz, eds., *Debating*

Empire (New York/London: Verso, 2003); Francis FuKuyama, *The End of History and the Last Man* (New York: Avon Books, 1992).

27. Among the various sources on these policy reversals see, e.g., J. C. Pool and S. C. Stamos, *International Economics: Theory, Policy, and Practice* (Massachusetts/ Toronto: Lexington Books, 1990), chapter 6.

28. For a detailed discussion of this factional split in the U.S. ruling class at the time see Holly Sklare, ed., *Trilateralism* (Boston, MA: South End Press, 1980).

29. C. Fred Bergsten, "The New Economics and U.S. Foreign Policy," *Foreign Affairs*, 50, no. 2 (January 1972): 199–223.

30. C. Fred Bergsten, Robert O. Keohane, and Joseph S. Nye, "International Economics and International Politics: A Framework for Analysis," quoted by Jeff Frieden, "The Trilateral Commission: Economics and Politics in the 1970s," in Holly Sklar, *Trilateralism* (Boston, MA: South End Press, 1980), 68.

31. As quoted in Shoup and Minter, *Imperial Brain Trust*, 255.

32. See, e.g., ibid., chapter 7, 254–284.

33. Ibid., 260.

34. Michael Blumenthal, "The World Economy and Technological Change," *Foreign Affairs*, 66, no. 3 (Winter 1987–1988): 547.

35. Quoted in Shoup and Minter, *Imperial Brain Trust*, 267.

36. For an interesting discussion of the Trilateralists' view of the role of a "world custodian" and of collective management of world economy, see Fred Bergsten, George Berthoin, and Kinhide Mushakoji, *The Reform of International Institutions* (Washington, D.C.: Trilateral Task Force on International Institutions, Trilateral Commission, 1976).

37. As quoted in Shoup and Minter, *Imperial Brain Trust*, 271.

38. Frieden, "The Trilateral Commission: Economics and Politics in the 1970s," 70–71.

39. Ibid., 70–71; Fred Block, "Trilateralism and Inter-Capitalist Conflict," in *Trilateralism*, edited by Holly Sklar (Boston, MA: South End Press, 1980), 519–533.

40. Alan Wolfe, "Trilateralism and the Carter Administration: Changed World vs. Vested Interests," in *Trileralism*, edited by Holly Sklar (Boston, MA: South End Press, 1980), 543.

41. James Cypher, "The Basic Economics of Rearming America," *Monthly Review*, 33, no. 6 (1981): 17. For a thorough discussion of the "Vietnam syndrome," and its consequences for the subsequent rise of U.S. militarism, see Andrew J. Bacevich, *The New American Militarism* (New York: Oxford University Press, 2005).

42. Wolfe, "Trilateralism and the Carter Administration: Changed World vs. Vested Interests," 542.

43. Cypher, "The Basic Economics of Rearming America," 20–21.
44. Ibid., 21–22.
45. Ibid., 22.
46. Ibid., 19.
47. Fred Halliday, *The Making of the Second Cold War* (London/New York: Verso, 1983); Noam Chomsky, *Toward a New Cold War* (New York: Pantheon, 1982), chapters 7 and 8.
48. Officially it was assessed at 16 percent of the Federal budget. But when all the costs of the military, including interest payments on the national debt (third highest item in the budget, after military and social security expenditures), were factored in some analysts like Philip Agee and Gore Vidal put it at one-third to one-half of the budget.
49. Commission on Integrated Long-term Strategy, *Discriminate Deterrence*, p. 2; as quoted by Sheila Ryan, "Power Projection in the Middle East," in *Mobilizing Democracy*, edited by Greg Bates (Monroe, ME: Common Courage Press, 1991), 48; James Cypher, "Military Spending After the Cold War," *Journal of Economic Issues*, 25, no. 2 (1991): 608–609.
50. Ryan, "Power Projection in the Middle East."

Chapter 4   Inventing "Threats to Our National Interests"

1. Chalmers Johnson, *The Sorrows of Empire* (New York: Metropolitan Books, 2004), 56.
2. Sidney Lens, *The Military-Industrial Complex* (Kansas City, MO: Pilgrim Press and the National Catholic Reporter, 1970), 18.
3. Gore Vidal, *Perpetual War for Perpetual Peace: How We Got To Be So Hated* (New York: Thunder's Mouth Press/Nation Books, 2002), 158.
4. D. F. Fleming, *The Cold War and Its Origins* (New York: Double Day, 1961), 436.
5. See, e.g., W. A. Williams, *The Tragedy of American Diplomacy* (Cleveland: World Publishing Company, 1959); David Horowitz, *The Free World Colossus* (New York: Hill and Wang, 1965); Lens, *The Military-Industrial Complex*; Ismael Hossein-zadeh, "Perestroika and the Third World," *Review of Radical Political Economics*, 22, nos. 2 and 3 (1990): 252–275.
6. Lens, *The Military-Industrial Complex*, 19.
7. Fleming, *The Cold War and Its Origins*, 1060; as cited in ibid., 19. On this point also see Johnson, *The Sorrows of Empire*, 33–34.
8. Leon Trotsky, *The Third International After Lenin* (New York: Pathfinder Press, 1970), 66.
9. Lens, *The Military-Industrial Complex*, 19–20.
10. As quoted in ibid., 21; and in Horowitz, *The Free World Colossus*, 85.

11. Williams, *The Tragedy of American Diplomacy*, 166–168; as cited by Lens, *The Military-Industrial Complex*, 22.

12. Lewis Board, *Winston Churchill: A Biography*; as quoted in Lens, *The Military-Industrial Complex*, 24.

13. William Hyland, "America's new course," *Foreign Affairs*, 69, no. 2 (1990): 3.

14. T. Sorenson, "Rethinking national security," *Foreign Affairs*, 69, no. 3 (1990): 1.

15. Sheila Ryan, "Power Projection in the Middle East," in *Mobilizing Democracy*, edited by Greg Bates (Monroe, ME: Common Courage Press, 1991), 45.

16. James Cypher, "Military Spending After the Cold War," *Journal of Economic Issues*, 25, no. 2 (1991).

17. Johnson, *The Sorrows of Empire*, 20.

18. Quoted in Ryan, "Power Projection in the Middle East," 47.

19. A. M. Gray, "Defense Policy for the 1990s," *Marine Corps Gazette*, 74, no. 5 (1990): 19.

20. Ibid.

21. As quoted in Ryan, "Power Projection in the Middle East," 46.

22. Johnson, *The Sorrows of Empire*, 20.

23. As quoted in ibid., 20.

24. Ibid., 20–21.

25. William A. Galston (deputy assistant to President Clinton for domestic policy from 1993 to 1995), "Why a First Strike Will Surely Backfire," *Washington Post* (June 16, 2002), sec. A.

26. Johnson, *The Sorrows of Empire*, 22.

27. Federation of American Scientists, as cited by Vidal, *Perpetual War for Perpetual Peace*, 22–41.

28. Bill Christison, "The Disastrous Foreign Policies of the United States," *Counterpunch.com* (May 9, 2002): <http://www.counterpunch.org/christison 0806.html>.

29. Vidal, *Perpetual War for Perpetual Peace*, 20–21.

30. Johnson, *The Sorrows of Empire*, 64.

31. As cited by Norm Dixon, "How the Bush Gang Seized the 'Opportunity' of 9/11," *Green Left Weekly* (May 5, 2004): <http://www.greenleft.org.au/back/ 2004/581/581p12.htm>.

32. Ron Suskind, *The Price of Loyalty: George W. Bush, the White House, and the Education of Paul O'Neil* (New Jersey: Simon and Schuster, 2004); James Mann, *The Rise of Vulcans: The History of Bush's War Cabinet* (New York: Viking/Penguin Group, 2004); Bob Woodward, *Plan of Attack* (New York: Simon and Schuster, 2004); Richard Clarke, *Against All Enemies: Inside America's War on Terror* (New York: Free Press, 2004).

33. As quoted by Norm Dixon, "How Warmongers Exploit 9/11," *Counterpunch.com* (September 11, 2002): <http://www.counterpunch.org/ dixon0911.html>.

34. As cited by Dixon, "How the Bush Gang Seized the 'Opportunity' of 9/11."
35. Chalmers Johnson, "America's Empire of Bases," *tomdispatch.com* (January 15, 2004): <http://www.informationclearinghouse.info/article5537.htm>.
36. Ronald I. Spiers, "How Do You Know When You Win?" *Vermont Rutland Herald* (June 5, 2004): <http://rutlandherald.com/Archive/Articles/Article/81009>.
37. As cited by Brandon J. Snider, "Manufacturing Terrorism," *antiwar.com* (June 14, 2004): <http://www.antiwar.com/blog/index.php?id=P1050>.
38. Spiers, "How Do You Know When You Win?"
39. Snider, "Manufacturing Terrorism."
40. Lens, *The Military-Industrial Complex*, 82.
41. Snider, "Manufacturing Terrorism."

Chapter 5   Militant Islam, Terrorism, and "Clash of Civilizations"

An earlier and shorter version of this chapter was published in the summer 2005 issue (vol. 27, no. 3) of *Arab Studies Quarterly.*

1. Samuel Huntington, *The Clash of Civilizations and the Remaking of World Order* (New York: Touchstone Books, 1997); Bernard Lewis, *What Went Wrong: Western Impact and Middle Eastern Response* (New York/Oxford: Oxford University Press, 2001); Daniel Pipes, "There Are No Moderates: Dealing with Fundamentalist Islam," *The National Interest* (Fall 1995): <http://www.nationalinterest.org/ ME2/ dirmod.asp?sid=&nm=&type=pub&mod=Publications%3A%3AArticles&mid=8F3A7027421841978F18BE895F87F791&tier =3&aid= 3628086DA65A4EB6BFA5F7D25799F6A0& dtxt=>; Charles Krauthammer, "America's Great Success Story" (interview), *Middle East Quarterly*, 1, no. 4 (1994): <http://www.meforum.org/article/197>; Norman Podhoretz, "World War IV: How It Started, What It Means, and Why We Have to Win," *Commentary* (September 2004): <http://www.commentarymagazine.com/podhoretz.htm>.
2. Samuel Huntington, "The Clash of Civilizations," *Foreign Affairs*, 72, no. 3 (1993): 22.
3. Ibid., 47.
4. Gwynne Dyer, "De-Contextualizing Chechnya," <http://www.gwynnedyer.net/articles/Gwynne%20Dyer%20article_%20%20Russia%20and%20Chechnya. txt>.
5. Karen Armstrong, *Islam: A Short History* (New York: Modern Library, 2000), 149.
6. Ibid., 150.
7. Ibid., 150–151.

8. John Esposito, *The Islamic Threat* (New York: Oxford University Press, 1992), 9.

9. Karen Armstrong, "Ghosts of Our Past," *Modern Maturity* (January/February 2002): 45.

10. Huntington, *The Clash of Civilizations and the Remaking of World Order*; Lewis, *What Went Wrong*; Krauthammer, "America's Great Success Story"; Pipes, "There Are No Moderates: Dealing with Fundamentalist Islam."

11. Robert Heilbroner, *The Worldly Philosophers* (New York: Simon and Schuster, 1972), 35.

12. Armstrong, *Islam: A Short History*, 145.

13. Wu Guiyun, "Middle East: The Roots of Conflict," *Asia Times* (November 22, 2002):<http://www.atimes.com/atimes/Middle_East/DK22Ak05.html>.

14. John O. Voll, *Islam: Continuity and Change in the Modern World*, 2nd ed. (Syracuse: Syracuse University Press, 1994), 94.

15. Ismael Hossein-zadeh, *Soviet Non-Capitalist Development: The Case of Nasser's Egypt* (New York: Praeger, 1989).

16. Hrair Dekmejian, "The Anatomy of Islamic Revival: Legitimacy, Crisis, Ethnic Conflict, and the Search for Islamic Alternatives," *Middle East Journal*, 34, no. 1 (Winter 1980): 3.

17. Voll, *Islam: Continuity and Change in the Modern World*, 379.

18. Maxime Rodinson, *Marxism and the Muslim World* (New York: Monthly Review Press, 1981); Esposito, *The Islamic Threat*; Michael C. Hudson, "Islam and Political Development," in *Islam and Development: Religion and Sociopolitical Change*, by John Esposito (Syracuse: Syracuse University Press, 1980).

19. Lewis, "The Roots of Muslim Rage," *The Atlantic*, 266, no. 3 (September, 1990): 60.

20. Esposito, *The Islamic Threat*, 179.

21. Ibid., 7–8.

22. Ibid.

23. Scott R. Appleby, *Spokesmen for the Despised: Fundamentalist Leaders of the Middle East* (Chicago: University of Chicago Press, 1996); Armstrong, *Islam: A Short History*; Youssef M. Choueiri, *Islamic Fundamentalism* (London: Twayne Publishers, 1990); Martin E. Marty and R. Scott Appleby, eds., *Fundamentalism Comprehended* (Chicago/London: University of Chicago Press, 1995).

24. Voll, *Islam: Continuity and Change in the Modern World*, 377.

25. Armstrong, *Islam: A Short History*, 165.

26. Eric Margolis, "Non-Americans dread Bush," *Toronto Sun* (October 24, 2004):<http://www.canoe.ca/NewsStand/Columnists/Toronto/Eric_Margolis/2004/ 10/24/682899.html>.

27. Uri Avnery, "On the Road to Civil War," *counterpunch.org* (October 25, 2004): <http://www.counterpunch.org/avnery10252004.html>.

28. Corporate media is not a vague, general, subjective slogan, or an abstract, metaphorical expression. It denotes, instead, the fact that not only have the so-called mainstream media enterprises developed into market-driven major corporations, but that they are also often in near incestuous business relationships with other giant corporations. For an interesting study of what corporate media really means see, e.g., Peter Phillips, "Big Media Interlocks with Corporate America," *commondreams.org* (June 24, 2005):<http://www.commondreams.org/views05/0624–25.htm>.

29. Chalmers Johnson, *Blowback: The Costs and Consequences of American Empire* (New York: Henry Holt and Company, 2002), 8–9.

30. John Chuckman, "Of War, Islam, and Israel," *Yellowtimes.org* (April 3, 2002): <http://www.yellowtimes.org/article.php?sid=191>.

31. Ibid.

32. Georgie Anne Geyer, "Separation of Church, State Must Apply to Foreign Policy, Too," *uexpress.com* (October 23, 2003): <http://www.uexpress.com/georgieannegeyer/?uc_full_date=20031023>.

33. Chuckman, "Of War, Islam, and Israel."

34. Voll, *Islam: Continuity and Change in the Modern World*, 376.

35. Susan Harding, "Representing Fundamentalism: The Problem of the Repugnant Cultural Other," *Social Research*, 58, no. 2 (1991): 373–393; Stephen R. Warner, "Theoretical Barriers to the Understanding of the Evangelical Christianity," *Sociological Analysis*, 40, no. 1 (1979): 1–9; Voll, *Islam: Continuity and Change in the Modern World*; R. Robertson and JoAnn Chirico, "Humanity, Globalization, and Worldwide Religious Resurgence: A Theoretical Exploration," *Sociological Analysis*, 46, no. 3 (1985): 219–242.

36. Mahmood Hussein, *Class Conflict in Egypt, 1945–1970* (New York: Monthly Review Press, 1973), 136.

37. Tariq Ali, *The Clash of Fundamentalisms: Crusades, Jihads and Modernity* (London/New York: Verso, 2002), 133.

38. Gore Vidal, *Perpetual War for Perpetual Peace: How We Got To Be So Hated* (New York: Thunder's Mouth Press/Nation Books, 2002), 22–41.

39. Charley Reese, "Islamic Democrats," *counterpunch.com* (July 3, 2004): <http:// www.antiwar.com/reese/?articleid=2930>.

40. Ivan Eland, "Protecting the Homeland: The Best Defense is to Give No Offense," *Policy Analysis*, no. 306 (Washington, D.C.: Cato Institute, 1998).

41. Johnson, *Blowback*, 8–9.

42. Vidal, *Perpetual War for Perpetual Peace*, ix.

Chapter 6   Behind the Invasion of Iraq

An earlier and much shorter version of this chapter, entitled "The Neocon-Zionist Alliance for War," was published in *Against the Current*, 18, no. 5 (November/December 2003).

1. From Paul O'Neill's interview with *Time Magazine*, January 10, 2004. As cited by Norm Dixon, "How the Bush Gang Seized the 'Opportunity' of 9/11," *Green Left Weekly* (May 5, 2004): <http://www.greenleft.org.au/back/ 2004/581/ 581p12.htm>; see also Ron Suskind, *The Price of Loyalty: George W. Bush, the White House, and the Education of Paul O'Neil* (New Jersey: Simon and Schuster, 2004); James Mann, *The Rise of Vulcans: The History of Bush's War Cabinet* (New York: Viking/Penguin Group, 2004); Bob Woodward, *Plan of Attack* (New York: Simon & Schuster, 2004); Richard A. Clarke, *Against All Enemies: Inside America's War on Terror* (New York: Free Press, 2004); James Bamford, *A Pretext for War: 9/11, Iraq, and the Abuse of America's Intelligence Agencies* (New York: Doubleday, 2004).

2. As reported by the Associated Press White House correspondent Ron Fournier in a September 5, 2002 article; quoted by Norm Dixon, "How Warmongers Exploit 9/11," *Counterpunch.com* (September 11, 2002): <http://www.counterpunch.org/ dixon0911.html>.

3. See, e.g., Arianna Huffington, "Holding Dick Cheney Accountable," *AlterNet* (August 5, 2002): <http://www.alternet.org/story/13757>; David Green, "Bush-Connected Company Set Up Offshore Subsidiary," *Baltimore Sun* (August 1, 2002): <http://www.commondreams.org/headlines02/ 0801–01.htm>; Timothy J. Burger, "Bush Co. Went Offshore: Harken Energy set up Caymans Subsidiary in 1998," *New York Daily News* <http://www.nydailynews.com/front/story/ 7310p-6742c.html>.

4. See, e.g., Paul Craig Roberts, "Neo-Jacobins Push for World War IV," <http://www.lewrockwell.com/roberts/roberts8.html>; Gordon Prather, "Neo-Crazy Coup d'Etat," <http://www.antiwar.com/orig/prather.php?articleid= 2343>.

5. William D. Hartung, *How Much Are You Making on the War, Daddy?* (New York: Nation Books, 2003), 101; William Hartung and Michelle Ciarrocca, "The Military-Industrial-Think Thank Complex," *Multinational Monitor* 24, nos. 1 & 2 (January–February 2003): <http://multinationalmonitor.org/ mm2003/ 03jan-feb/janfeb03corp2.html#name>; Mann, *The Rise of Vulcans*; DiLip Hiro, *Secrets and Lies: Operation Iraqi Freedom and After* (New York: Nation Books, 2004).

6. Hartung, *How Much Are You Making on the War, Daddy?* 103–106.

7. Ibid., 109.

8. Ibid., 110–111.

9. Ibid., 113.

10. Hartung and Ciarrocca, "The Military-Industrial-Thin Thank Complex"; see also Mann, *The Rise of Vulcans*; and Hiro, *Secrets and Lies.*

11. Hartung and Ciarrocca, "The Military-Industrial-Thin Thank Complex."

12. See, e.g., Pat McDonnell Twair, "Carl Boggs, Chalmers Johnson Discuss Neocon Ideology and American Empire," *Washington Report on Middle East*

Affairs (June 2004): 18, 21; also on line at <http://www.wrmea.com/archives/June_ 2004/0406018.html>.

13. For a discussion of the theory and history of oil price determination see, Cyrus Bina, "The Rhetoric of Oil and the Dilemma of War and American Hegemony," *Arab Studies Quarterly*, 15, no. 3 (Summer 1993); also Cyrus Bina, "Limits of OPEC Pricing: OPEC Profits and the Nature of Global Oil Accumulation," *OPEC Review*, 14, no. 1 (Spring 1990).

14. Gary S. Becker, "Why War with Iraq Is Not about Oil," *Business Week* (March 17, 2003): 30.

15. Johnathan Nitzan and Shimshon Bichler, *The Global Political Economy of Israel* (London/ Sterling, VA: Pluto Press, 2002).

16. Melinda K. Ruby, "Is Oil the Driving Force to War?" unpublished Senior thesis, Dept. of Economics and Finance, Drake University, Des Moines, Iowa (Spring 2004), 10.

17. As quoted in Ruby, Ibid., p. 13.

18. As cited by Roger Burbach, "Bush Ideologues vs. Big Oil: The Iraq Game Gets Even Stranger," <http://www.counterpunch.org/burbach10032003.html>.

19. Ruby, "Is Oil the Driving Force to War?" pp. 14–15; see also Herman Franssen and Elaine Morton, "A Review of U.S. Unilateral Sanctions Against Iran," *Middle East Economic Survey*, 45, no. 34 (August 26, 2002): D1–D5 (D section contains op eds. as opposed to staff-written articles).

20. Ruby, "Is Oil the Driving Force to War?" pp. 16–17; see also David Ivanovich, "Conoco's Chief Blasts Sanctions," *Houston Chronicle* (February 12, 1997).

21. On this issue see, e.g., Chalmers Johnson, *Blowback: The Costs and Consequences of American Empire* (New York: Henry Holt and Company, 2000), 87–88.

22. The statement was widely reported by many news papers and other media outlets. See, e.g., *The Guardian* (June 4, 2003): <http://www.whatreallyhappened.com/aboutoil.htm>.

23. *Business Week* (April 14, 2003): 3.

24. On this issue see, e.g., Johnson, *Blowback*, 87–88.

25. Stefan Halper and Jonathan Clarke, *America Alone: The Neoconservatives and the Global Order* (Cambridge: Cambridge University Press, 2004); reviewed by Jim Lobe: "New Book Attacks Neo-Cons from the Right," *commondreams.org* (August 8, 2004): <http://www.commondreams.org/headlines04/0805-04.htm>.

26. For a good exposition of the close collaboration—indeed, illicit ties—between some of these think-tanks (especially CSP, AEI, JINSA, NIPP, and PNAC) and arms manufacturers, on the one hand, and the Likud lobby, on the other, see Hartung, *How Much Are You Making on the War, Daddy?* chapter 6.

27. Chalmers Johnson, *The Sorrows of Empire* (New York: Metropolitan Books, 2004), 56.

28. For a rich and interesting discussion of this distinction see, e.g., Paul Kennedy, *The Rise and Fall of the Great Powers* (New York: Vintage Books, 1989).

29. James Mann, "The True Rationale? It's a Decade Old," *Washington Post*, Sunday (March 7, 2004), B02; electronic version: http://www.washingtonpost.com/ ac2/wp-dyn/A35472–2004Mar6?language=printer>.

30. Ibid.

31. David Armstrong, "Dick Cheney's Song of America," *Montanapeaceseekers.org*, <http://www.montanapeaceseekers.org/common/documents/20021010/song.php>.

32. Mann, "The True Rationale? It's a Decade Old." For more information on this see also Mann, *The Rise of Vulcans*; Ibid.

33. Armstrong, "Dick Cheney's Song of America."

34. Ibid.

35. Hartung and Ciarrocca, "The Military-Industrial-Think Tank Complex."

36. Tom Segev, *One Palestine, Complete: Jews and Arabs under the British Mandate* (New York: Metropolitan Books, 2000), 404–405; as quoted in Stephen J. Sniegoski, "The War on Iraq: Conceived in Israel," <http:// www.thornwalker. com:16080/ditch/snieg_conc1.htm>. For a history of Zionist ideas on expulsion see, e.g., Benny Morris, *Righteous Victims* (New York: Random House, 1999); Nur Masalha, *Expulsion of the Palestinians: The Concept of "Transfer" in Zionist Political Thought, 1882–1948* (Washington, D.C.: Institute of Palestine Studies, 1992).

37. John Chuckman, "Israel's Bloody Excesses: Was Einstein Right?" *counterpunch.com* (April 4, 2003): <http://www.counterpunch.org/chuckman04042003.html>.

38. Quoted in Norman Finkelstein, *Image and Reality of the Israel-Palestine Conflict*, Introduction to German edition (July 10, 2002) <http://www.normanfinkelstein. com/id127.htm>.

39. Sniegoski, "The War on Iraq: Conceived in Israel."

40. Nitzan and Bichler, *The Global Political Economy of Israel*, 353–354.

41. Ibid., 354–355.

42. Ralph Schoenman, *The Hidden History of Zionism* (Santa Barbara, CA: Veritas Press, 1988), chapter 12, "Strategy for Conquest," as cited in Sniegoski, "The War on Iraq: Conceived in Israel."

43. For some of the strategies through which the Zionist lobby manipulates the public opinion, especially in the United States, see, e.g., <http://electronicintifada.net/v2/article1395.shtml>.

44. Bill and Kathleen Christison, "The Elephant in the Room of Empire: Israel as Sideshow," *counterpunch.com* (October 12, 2004): <http://www.counterpunch.com/christison10122004.html>.

45. Ibid.

46. The literature on the neoconservative think tanks, their family-like close ties, and their relentless scheming to further the interests of war industries, on the one hand, and of militant Zionism, on the other, is plentiful. Here is a sample: (a) Sniegoski, "The War on Iraq: Conceived in Israel"; (b) Brian Whitaker, "US think tanks give lessons in foreign policy," *The Guardian* (August 19, 2002): <http://www.guardian.co.uk/elsewhere/journalist/story/0,7792,777100,00. html>; (c) Richard H. Curtis, "Israel's Lobby Tries to Widen Net Against Terrorism," *Washington Report on Middle East Affairs* (December 2001): <http://www.wrmea.com/archives/december01/0112026. html>; and (d) Akiva Eldar, "An Unholy Alliance with the Christian Right: Gary Baurer and Likud," *Counterpunch.org* (April 8, 2003): <http://www.counterpunch.org/ eldar04092003.html>.

47. Jason Vest, "The Men from JINSA and CSP," *The Nation* (September 2, 2002):<http://www.thenation.com/doc.mhtml?i=20020902&s=vest&c=1>.

48. Sniegoski, "The War on Iraq: Conceived in Israel." The original document, "A Clean Break: A New Strategy for Securing the Realm," can be viewed at: <http://www.israeleconomy.org/strat1.htm>.

49. "Open Letter to the President," February 19, 1998: <http://www.iraqwatch.org/perspectives/rumsfeld-openletter.htm>; Sniegoski, "The War on Iraq: Conceived in Israel"; Frank Gaffney, "End Saddam's Reign of Terror: Better Late than Never," *National Review Online* (February 21, 2002): <http://www. nationalreview. com/contributors/gaffney022101.shtml>.

50. Contrary to the neoconservatives' claims, their belligerent policies serve neither the interests of the ordinary citizens of the United States, nor the long-term interests of the Jewish people. They serve primarily the interests of the U.S. arms manufacturers and the interests of militant Zionism—as perceived by its (misguided) leaders.

51. Sniegoski, "The War on Iraq: Conceived in Israel."

52. Ibid.

53. See, e.g., Johnson, *The Sorrows of Empire*, 229.

54. Sniegoski, "The War on Iraq: Conceived in Israel."

55. Johnson, *The Sorrows of Empire*, 227.

56. William Kristol et al. "Toward a Comprehensive Strategy: A Letter to the President," September 20, 2001 <http://www.nationalreview.com/document/document092101b.shtml>; also in "Project for the New American Century," <http://www.newamericancentury.org/Bushletter. htm>.

57. Robert Kagan and William Kristol, "The Gathering Storm," the *Weekly Standard* (October 29, 2002): <http://theweeklystandard.com/Content/Public/Articles/ 000/000/000/384thhhq.asp>.

58. Eliot A. Cohen, "World War IV," *The Wall Street Journal* (November 20, 2001): <http://www.opinionjournal.com/editorial/feature.html?id=95001493>.

59. See, e.g. (a) Bernard Lewis, *What Went Wrong: Western Impact and Middle Eastern Response* (Oxford/New York: Oxford University Press, 2001); (b) Samuel Huntington, *The Clash of Civilizations and the Remaking of World Order* (New York: Touchstone Books, 1997); (c) Charles Krauthammer, Interview, *Middle East Quarterly* (December 1994); and (d) Daniel Pipes, "There are no Moderates: Dealing with Fundamentalist Islam," *The National Interest* (Fall 1995): <http://www.nationalinterest.org/ME2/dirmod.asp?sid=&nm=&type=pub&mod=Publications%3A%3AArticles&mid=8F3A7027421841978F18BE895F87F791&tier=3&aid=3628086DA65A4EB6BFA5F7D25799F6A0&dtxt=>.

60. "Ex-CIA Director: U.S. Faces 'World War IV,' " from Charles Feldman and Stan Wilson of CNN, posted on Thursday (April 3, 2003): <http://edition.cnn.com/ 2003/US/04/03/sprj.irq.woolsey.world.war/>.

61. Norman Podhoretz, "World War IV: How It Started, What It Means, and Why We Have to Win," *Commentary* (September 2004): <http://www.commentarymagazine.com/podhoretz.htm>.

62. As quoted by Justin Raimondo, "World War IV: Has it arrived?" *Antiwar.com* (April 4, 2003): <http://www.antiwar.com/justin/j040403.html>.

63. Ibid.

64. Paul Craig Roberts, "A Shabby and Sinister Case for War," *antiwar.com* (September 8, 2004): <http://www.antiwar.com/roberts/?articleid=3519>.

65. Ibid.

66. Ibid.

67. Uri Avnery, "King George: The Coronation Viewed from Israel," *counterpunch.com* (January 24, 2005): <http://www.counterpunch.com/avnery 01242005.html>.

68. Lobe, "New Book Attacks Neo-Cons From the Right."

69. For a most interesting, authoritative, and historical analysis of fascism see Leon Trotsky, *Fascism: What It Is and How to Fight It*, repr. ed. (New York: Pathfinder Press, 1993); see also Daniel Guerin, *Fascism and Big Business*, 2nd ed. (New York: Pathfinder Press, 2001).

70. James P. Pinkerton, "The Iraq War, or America Betrayed," *nynewsday.com* (July 15, 2003): <http://www.nynewsday.com/news/nationworld/nation/ny-vppin 153372005jul15.story>.

71. Halper and Clarke, *America Alone.*

72. Hugh Urban, "Bush, the Neocons and Evangelical Christian Fiction," *counterpunch.com* (November 18, 2004): <http://www.counterpunch.com/urban 11182004.html>.

73. Ibid.

74. Richard Cohen, "America's Ayatollah," *Washintonpost.com* (April 15, 2004), A25; also on line at <http://www.washingtonpost.com/ac2/wp-dyn/A13298–2004 Apr14?language=printer>.

75. Both quotations are in Urban, "Bush, the Neocons and Evangelical Christian Fiction."

76. Norman Podhoretz, "In Praise of the Bush Doctrine," *Commentary* <http://www.ourjerusalem.com/opinion/story/opinion20020904a.html>.

77. Avnery, "King George: The Coronation Viewed from Israel."

78. For a good summary of the president's inaugural speech see Julian Borger, "Smiles for the Family, a Fiery Warning for the World," *The Guardian* (January 21, 2005): <http://www.guardian.co.uk/usa/story/0,12271,1395432,00. html>.

79. Patrick J. Buchanan, "Inaugurating Endless War," *antiwar.com* (January 26, 2005): <http://www.antiwar.com/pat/?articleid=4574>.

80. Llewellyn H. Rockwell, Jr., "The Madness of President Bush," *LewRockwell.com* (April 16, 2004): <http://www.lewrockwell.com/rockwell/madness.html>.

81. Ibid.

82. Ibid.

83. Avnery, "King George: The Coronation Viewed from Israel."

84. Ibid.

85. Paul Craig Roberts, "Wake Up! Bush is Serious," *antiwar.com* (January 26, 2005): <http://www.antiwar.com/roberts/?articleid=4576>.

86. Avnery, "King George: The Coronation Viewed from Israel."

87. Smedley D. Butler, *War Is a Racket* (Los Angeles: Feral House, 1935 [2003]), 39.

88. For a sample of views expressed within the neoconservative handlers of President Bush's foreign policy in favor of "World War IV" see, e.g. (a) Justin Raimondo, "World War IV: Has It Arrived?"; (b) Gail Russell Chaddock, "Tracing the Roots of America's war in Iraq: 'Neocon' Architects of a Muscular US Policy Eye More Regime Changes in the Region," *Christian Science Monitor* (April 9, 2003); also on line at: <http://www.csmonitor.com/2003/0409/p03s01-uspo.html>; (c) *Herald Tribune*, "What's Next? U.S. Set Sights on Iran, North Korea," Special to *World Tribune.com* (April 4, 2003): <http://216.26.163.62/2003/ss_wmd_04_03.html>.

89. Eric Margolis, "U.S. Falling into Bin Laden's Trap," *Toronto Sun* (July 6, 2003): <http://www.canoe.ca/Columnists/margolis_jul6.html>.

Chapter 7   Waste, Inefficiency, and the Spoils of Military Spending

1. All cited by Sidney Lens, *The Military-Industrial Complex* (Kansas City, MO: Pilgrim Press and the National Catholic Reporter, 1970), 4.

2. "The Economics of Military Procurement," *Congressional Record*, 115, no. 42 (May 1969), S2518 ff.; cited in ibid., 5.

3. "The Word On: Pentagon Waste," interview with Senator Chuck Grassley, <http://grassley.senate.gov/won/2004/won04-06-18.htm>.

4. Jacques S. Gansler, "Integrating Civilian and Military Industry," <http://www.issues.org/issues/19.4/updated/gansler.html>.

5. Tom Abate, "Military Waste Under Fire: $1 Trillion Missing," *San Francisco Chronicle* (May 18, 2003): <http://www.sfgate.com/cgi-bin/article.cgi?file=/c/a/2003/05/18/MN251738.DTL>.

6. Ibid.

7. Vince Gonzales, "The War on Waste," *cbsnews.com* (January 29, 2002): <http://www.cbsnews.com/stories/2002/01/29/eveningnews/printable325985.html>.

8. *Congressional Record*, January 31, 1969, S1125; as cited by Lens, *The Military-Industrial Complex*, 6.

9. Julian Borger and David Teather, "So Much for the Peace Dividend: Pentagon Is Winning the Battle for a $400bn Budget," *The Guardian* (May 22, 2003): <http://www.guardian.co.uk/usa/story/0,12271,960922,00.html>.

10. As reported by Edward S. Herman, "Privileged Dependency and Waste: The Military Budget," *zmag.org* (October 1997): <http://www.zmag.org/zmag/articles/nov97herman.htm>.

11. Lens, *The Military-Industrial Complex*, 5.

12. Ibid., 6.

13. Ibid., 8.

14. William D. Hartung and Michelle Ciarrocca, "The Military-Industrial-Think Thank Complex," *Multinational Monitor*, 24, nos. 1 and 2 (January/February 2003):<http://multinationalmonitor.org/mm2003/03jan-feb/jan-feb03corp 2.html#name>; James Mann, *The Rise of Vulcans: The History of Bush's War Cabinet* (New York: Viking/Penguin Group, 2004); DiLip Hiro, *Secrets and Lies: Operation Iraqi Freedom and After* (New York: Nation Books, 2004); See also William D. Hartung, *How Much Are You Making on the War, Daddy?* (New York: Nation Books, 2003).

15. André Verlöy, Daniel Politi, and Aron Pilhofer, "Advisors of Influence: Nine Members of the Defense Policy Board Have Ties to Defense Contractors," The Center for Public Integrity,<http://www.publicintegrity.org/report.aspx?aid=91&sid=200>.

16. Ibid.

17. All the information presented here on the ties between the members of the Defense Policy Board and the Pentagon contractors are from the aforementioned "special report," ibid.

18. Michelle Ciarrocca, "Post-9/11 Economic Windfalls for Arms Manufacturers," *Foreign Policy in Focus*, 7, no. 10 (September 2002): <http://www.fpif.org/briefs/vol7/v7n10arms.html>.

19. James Cypher, "The Iron Triangle: The New Military Buildup," *Dollars & Sense*, no. 239 (January/February 2002): 17.
20. Matt Moore, "Global Military Spending Soars," <http://peaceuk.co.uk. mdlnet.co.uk/archive/modules.php?name=News&file=article&sid=1086>.
21. Cypher, "The Iron Triangle: The New Military Buildup," 18–19.
22. Ciarrocca, "Post-9/11 Economic Windfalls for Arms Manufacturers."
23. Ibid.
24. Ibid.
25. Ken Silverstein, "Privatizing War, How Affairs of State Are Outsourced to Corporations Beyond Public Control," *The Nation* (July 28–August 4, 1997).
26. Esther Schrader, "Companies Capitalize on War on Terror," *Los Angeles Times* (April 14, 2002): <http://www.latimes.com/news/nationworld/nation/la-041402trainers.story>.
27. As quoted by ibid.
28. Ibid.
29. Spencer E. Ante and Stan Crock, "The Other U.S. Military," *Business Week* (May 31, 2004), 76–78; also can be viewed at <http://www.businessweek.com/magazine/content/04_22/b3885116.htm>.
30. Howard Swint, "The Pentagon Ruled by Special Interests," <http://www.swintforcongress.us/Pentagon%20Waste%20Op%20Ed.htm>.
31. Nick Turse, "If You Build It, They Will Kill," *antiwar.com* (April 2, 2005): <http://www.antiwar.com/engelhardt/?articleid=5436>.
32. Smedley D. Butler, *War Is a Racket* (Los Angeles: Feral House, 1935 [2003]), 41.
33. Ibid., 27.
34. Turse, "If You Build It, They Will Kill."

Chapter 8 The Political Economy of U.S. Military Spending

1. For a sample of the critics of large military establishments/expenditures see, e.g., Sidney Lens, *The Military-Industrial Complex* (Kansas City, MO: Pilgrim Press and the National Catholic Reporter, 1970); Smedley D. Butler, *War Is a Racket* (Los Angeles: Feral House, 1935 [2003]); Chalmers Johnson, *The Sorrows of Empire* (New York: Metropolitan Books, 2004); Robert DeGrasse, *Military Expansion, Economic Decline* (New York: Council on Economic Priorities, 1983); Seymour Melman, *Profits Without Production* (New York: Dell Publishing Company, 1983); Lloyd J. Dumas, *The Overburdened Economy* (Berkeley/Los Angeles: University of California Press, 1986). The list also includes Adam Smith, the putative father of modern economics, who viewed military spending as an "unproductive" expenditure that detracted from the "wealth of nations."

2. For a sample of the proponents of this view see, e.g., William D. Nordhaus, "Iraq: The Economic Consequences of War," *New York Review of Books*, 49, no. 19 (December 5, 2002): <http://www.nybooks.com/articles/article-preview? article_id=15850>; James Tobin, "Military Expenditure and Investment in OECD Countries," *Journal of Comparative Economics*, 4, no. 1 (1980), 19–32.

3. Charles Bell et al., "The Permanent War Economy: Real Security or False Promise?" *National Jobs for All Coalition*, Special Report, 4 (January 2004): <http://www.njfac.org/sr4.htm>.

4. Robert Higgs, "The Defense Budget Is Bigger Than You Think," *antiwar.com* (January 25, 2004): <http://www.antiwar.com/orig2/higgs012504.html>.

5. Summary Federal Budget Tables, FY 2004: <http://www.whitehouse.gov/omb/budget/fy2004/tables.html>; ibid.

6. Carlton Meyer, "Freeze the Military Budget," *G2mil, The Magazine of Future Warfare* (March 2004): <http://www.g2mil.com/Mar2004.htm>.

7. Matt Moore, "Global Military Spending Soars," <http://cnews.canoe.ca/CNEWS/World/2004/06/09/pf-492268.html>.

8. Phyllis Bennis et al., "Paying the Price: The Mounting Costs of the Iraq War," *Common Dreams*, Institute for Policy Studies (June 24, 2004): <http://www.com mondreams.org/cgi-bin/print.cgi?file=/headlines04/0624–01.htm>.

9. *Congressional Record* (May 20, 1969); as cited by Lens, *The Military-Industrial Complex*, 45–46.

10. Howard Swint, "The Pentagon Ruled by Special Interests," (October 23, 2005): <http://www.swintforcongress.us/Pentagonpercent20Wastepercent 20Oppercent 20Ed.htm>.

11. James Cypher, "The Basic Economics of Rearming America," *Monthly Review*, 33, no. 6 (1981): 12–13.

12. Ibid., 15.

13. James Cypher, "Return of the Iron Triangle: The New Military Buildup," *Dollars & Sense*, no. 239 (January/February 2002): 19.

14. Randall Wray, "The Case for Rate Hikes: Did the Fed Prematurely Raise Rates?" *The Levy Economics Institute Newsletter*, 14, no. 2 (Spring 2005): 13.

15. James Cypher, "Military Spending, Technical Change, and Economic Growth: A Disguised Form of Industrial Policy?" *Journal of Economic Issues*, 21, no. 1 (1987): 49.

16. Ibid.

17. Ibid.

18. Dumas, *The Overburdened Economy*.

19. See, e.g., D. Smith and R. P. Smith, *The Economics of Militarism* (London: Pluto Press, 1983); Steve Chan and Alex Mintz, *Defense, Welfare and Growth: Perspectives and Evidence* (New York: Routledge, 1992); DeGrasse, *Military Expansion, Economic Decline*; and ibid.

20. See, e.g., Ernest Mandel, *Late Capitalism* (London: New Left Books, 1975), chapter 9.

21. Cypher, "Return of the Iron Triangle: The New Military Buildup"; Martin Wolf, "Outpaced: Why Are the Big Euro-Zone Countries and Japan Doing Worse than English Speaking Nations," *Financial Times* (January 13, 2005); Sonmez H. Atesoglu, "Defense Spending and Investment," *Journal of Post-Keynesian Economics*, 27, no. 1 (2004): 163–169.

22. As quoted in Robert L. Heilbroner and James K. Galbraith, *Understanding Macroeconomics* (Englewood Cliffs, NJ: Prentice Hall, 1990), p. 383.

23. Richard Du Boff, "What Military Spending Really Costs," *Challenge*, 32 (September/October 1989): 10.

24. DeGrasse, *Military Expansion, Economic Decline*, 55.

25. Lloyd J. Dumas, "Bang for the Buck: The Real Effects of Military Spending on Security," paper presented at the Allied Social Sciences Association, Philadelphia, PA, January 8, 2005, 4.

26. For an incisive critique of the "crowding-out" theory see, e.g., James Cypher, "Military Expansion, Economic Decline: The Impact of Military Spending on U.S. Economic Performance," *Journal of Economic Issues*, 19, no. 1 (March 1985): 227–233. This is essentially a review/critique of Robert W. DeGrasse's book of the same title, *Military Expansion, Economic Decline*.

27. For a thorough exposition of the theoretical shortcomings of the "crowding out" arguments see, e.g., Ernest Mandel, *Late Capitalism*, Chapter 9.

28. DeGrasse, *Military Expansion, Economic Decline*, 10.

29. Nordhaus, "Iraq," *New York Review of Books* ; Wolf, "Outpaced: Why Are the Big Euro-Zone Countries and Japan Doing Worse than English Speaking Nations"; Atesoglu, "Defense Spending and Investment."

30. Bell et al. "The Permanent War Economy: Real Security or False Promise?"

31. Cited by David Gold, "Fewer Jobs, Slower Growth: Military Spending Drains the Economy," *Dollars & Sense* (July/August 2002): <http://www.third worldtraveler.com/Military_Budget/MilitaryBudget_Economy.html>.

32. As cited in DeGrasse, *Military Expansion, Economic Decline*, 30, 41.

33. Cypher, "Return of the Iron Triangle: The New Military Buildup"; Wolf, "Outpaced: Why Are the Big Euro-Zone Countries and Japan Doing Worse than English Speaking Nations"; and Atesoglu, "Defense Spending and Investment."

34. Cypher, "Military Expansion, Economic Decline: The Impact of Military Spending on U.S. Economic Performance," 23.

35. Du Boff, "What Military Spending Really Costs," 5.

36. Cypher, "Return of the Iron Triangle: The New Military Buildup," 37.

37. Du Boff, "What Military Spending Really Costs," 6.

38. Ibid., 8.

39. Ibid., 7.

40. "The Lights Go Out on Broadway: What Can Happen if America Fails to Invest in Its Infrastructure? Anything."<http://www.asce.org/reportcard/index.cfm? reaction=news&page=5>. ASCE's main Web site is: <htpp://www.asce.org/reportcard>.

41. Seymour Melman, "They Are All Implicated: In the Grip of Permanent War Economy," *Counterpunch.com* (March 15, 2003): <http://www.counterpunch.org/melman03152003.html>.

42. David Alan Aschauer, "Is the Public Capital Stock Tool Low?" Chicago Fed Letter, October 1987; cited by Heilbroner and Galbraith, *Understanding Macroeconomics*, 299–300.

43. Melman, "They Are All Implicated: In the Grip of Permanent War Economy."

44. Ibid.

45. As quoted in Du Boff, "What Military Spending Really Costs," 10.

46. Ibid.

47. Ibid.

48. James Cypher, "Military Spending after the Cold War," *Journal of Economic Issues*, 25, no. 2 (1991): 609–610.

49. Sidney Ratner, *American Taxation: Its History as a Social Force in Democracy* (NY: W.W. Norton, 1942), 35; quoted in Sam Pizzagati, *The Maximum Wage: A Commonsense Prescription for Revitalizing America-by Taxing the Very Rich* (New York: Apex Press, 1992), 57; quoted in Bell et al. "The Permanent War Economy: Real Security of False Promise."

50. As quoted in ibid.

51. Ibid.

52. Cypher, "Military Spending after the Cold War"; A. M. Gray, "Defense Policy for the 1990s," *Marine Corps Gazette*, 74, no. 5 (1990).

53. Ernest Mandel, *Long Waves of Capitalist Development* (Cambridge: Cambridge University Press, 1980); Ismael Hossein-zadeh, "Long Waves and the Future of Capitalism," in *Political Economy and Contemporary Capitalism: Radical Perspectives on Economic Theory and Policy*, edited by Ron Baiman, Heather Boushey, and Dawn Saunders (New York: M. E. Sharpe, 2000), 78–88.

54. *Business Week* (April 14, 2003): 32.

55. "Coke and Pepsi Battle it Out," *AME Info* (April 8, 2004): <http://www.ameinfo.com/news/Detailed/37492.html>.

56. Jim Lobe, "Poll: War Bad for Business," *antiwar.com* (December 30, 2004): <http://www.antiwar.com/lobe/?articleid=4235>.

57. Ibid.

58. See, e.g., "The National Security Strategy of the United States of America," The White House, September 17, 2002; "Rebuilding America's Defenses: Strategy, Forces and Resources For a New Century," A Report of the Project for the New American Century, September 2000; "Defense Planning

Guidance for the 1994–1999 Fiscal Years," Office of the Secretary of Defense, 1992; "Defense Planning Guidance for the 2004–2009 Fiscal Years," Office of the Secretary of Defense, 2002.

59. See, e.g., Nomi Prins, "Making a Killing in Iraq," *Left Business Observer*, no. 105 (August 2003): 2–3.

60. Geoffrey E. Garten, "Bush's Guns-and-Butter Dillemma," *Business Week* (March 17, 2003): 76–77.

61. Michael J. Mandel et al. "How War Will Shape the Economy," *Business Week* (April 14, 2003): 29–32.

62. <http://www.usaengage.org/about_us/index.html>.

63. James Cox, "Financially Ailing Companies Point to Iraq War," *USA Today* (July 14, 2004): <http://www.usatoday.com/money/companies/2004–06–14-iraq_x.htm?POE=click-refer>.

64. Esther Schrader, "Companies Capitalize on War on Terror," *Los Angeles Times* (April 14, 2002): <http://www.latimes.com/news/nationworld/nation/la-041402trainers.story>.

65. See, e.g., Patrick Buchanan, "The Stillborn Empire," *The American Perspective* (March 13, 2005): <http://amconmag.com/2005_03_14/buchanan.html>. Direct quotations from Krauthammer are cited in this essay of Buchanan.

66. Rodney Ward, "In Harm's Way: The Working Class on the War Front and the Home Front," *Dollars & Sense* (May/June 2003): 13.

67. Cypher, "The Basic Economics of Rearming America," 12–17; Ernest Mandel, *Late Capitalism*, 301–309; and Paul A. Baran and Paul M. Sweezy, *Monopoly Capital* (New York/London: Monthly Review Press, 1966), 207–208.

68. Bell et al., "The Permanent War Economy: Real Security or False Promise?" see also David Gold, "Implications of Ballistic Missile Defense for National Security, Defense Industries, and Labor Markets," in *The Full Costs of Ballistic Missile Defense*, edited by Richard F. Kaufman (Washington, D.C.: Center for Arms Control and Non-Proliferation, and Pearl River, NY: Economists Allied for Arms Reduction, 2003), 96–97; also Smith and Smith, *The Economics of Militarism*.

69. Alfred Vagts, *A History of Militarism: Civilian and Military* (London: Hollis and Carter, 1959).

70. Smith and Smith, *The Economics of Militarism*.

71. Ward, "In Harm's Way: The Working Class on the War Front and the Home Front," 15.

72. As cited in ibid., 12–13.

73. As cited in ibid., 13.

74. Marc Pilisuk and Neil Wollman, "What Democracy? A Brief Look at U.S. Foreign Policy," *CommonDreams.org* (April 12, 2005): <http://www.

commondreams.org/cgi-bin/print.cgi?file=/views05/0412-27.htm>; see also Harvey Wasserman, "Senator Byrd is Correct to Equate Bush with Hitler," *CommonDreams.org* (March 7, 2005): <http://www.commondreams.org/views05/0307-22.htm>.

75. For an insightful essay on the difference between the classical/European-type imperialism and U.S. imperialism see Naomi Klein, "The Rise of Disaster Capitalism," *The Nation* (May 2, 2005): <http://www.thenation.com/docprint.mhtml?i=20050502&s=klein>.

Chapter 9   Limits of U.S. Militarism

1. Ernest Mandel, *Late Capitalism* (London: New Left Books, 1975), chapter 9.
2. See, e.g., Paul Kennedy, *The Rise and Fall of the Great Powers* (New York: Vintage Books, 1989); Chalmers Johnson, *The Sorrows of Empire* (New York: Metropolitan Books, 2004).
3. As quoted in Mandel, *Late Capitalism*, 302.
4. Ernest Mandel, *Long Waves of Capitalist Development* (Cambridge: Cambridge University Press, 1980), see especially pp. 20–22 and 51–52.
5. Smedley D. Butler, *War Is a Racket* (Los Angeles: Feral House, 1935 [2003]), 39.

Bibliography

Alam, Shahid. *Is There An Islamic Problem?* Kuala Lumpur: The Other Press, 2004.

Ali, Tariq. *Bush in Babylon: Recolonizing Iraq.* London/New York: Verso, 2004.

———. *The Clash of Fundamentalisms: Crusades, Jihads and Modernity.* London/New York: Verso, 2002.

Appleby, Scott R. *Spokesmen for the Despised: Fundamentalist Leaders of the Middle East.* Chicago: University of Chicago Press, 1996.

Armstrong, Karen. "Ghosts of Our Past." *Modern Maturity* (January/February 2002): 44–47, 70–71.

———. *Islam: A Short History.* New York: The Modern Library, 2000.

Atesoglu, Sonmez H. "Defense Spending and Investment." *Journal of Post-Keynesian Economics* 27, no. 1 (2004): 163–169.

Atesoglu, Sonmez H. "Defense Spending Promotes Aggregate Output in the United States—Evidence from Cointegration Analysis." *Defense and Peace Economics* 13, no. 1 (February 2002): 55–60.

Bacevich, Andrew. *The New American Militarism.* Oxford University Press, 2005.

Balakrishnan, Gopal, and Stanley Aronowitz, eds. *Debating Empire.* New York/London: Verso, 2003.

Bamford, James. *A Pretext for War: 9/11, Iraq, and the Abuse of America's Intelligence Agencies.* New York: Doubleday, 2004.

Banuazizi, Ali, and Myron Weiner, eds. *The State, Religion, and Ethnic Politics.* Syracuse, NY: Syracuse University Press, 1986.

Baran, Paul A., and Paul M. Sweezy. *Monopoly Capital.* New York/London: Monthly Review Press, 1966.

Bates, Greg, ed. *Mobilizing Democracy.* Monroe, ME: Common Courage Press, 1991.

Bina, Cyrus. "The Rhetoric of Oil and the Dilemma of War and American Hegemony." *Arab Studies Quarterly* 15, no. 3 (1993): 1–20.

Block, Fred. "Trilateralism and Inter-Capitalist Conflict." In *Trilateralism*, edited by Holly Sklar. Boston, MA: South End Press, 1980.

Bovard, James. *Terrorism and Tyranny: Trampling Freedom, Justice, and Peace to Rid the World of Evil*. New York: Palgrave-Macmillan, 2003.

Bowles, Samuel, David Gordon, and Thomas Wiesskopf. "Right-Wing Economics Backfired." *Challenge* 34, no. 1 (January/February 1991): 4–9.

Brightman, Carol. *Total Insecurity: The Myth of American Omnipotence*. London/New York: Verso, 2004.

Butler, Smedley D. *War Is a Racket*. Los Angeles: Feral House, 1935 [2003].

Chan, Steve, and Alex Mintz. *Defense, Welfare and Growth: Perspectives and Evidence*. New York: Routledge, 1992.

Cherry, Robert et al. *The Imperiled Economy*. New York: The Union of Radical Political Economics, 1987.

Chomsky, Noam. *Toward a New Cold War*. New York: Pantheon Books, 1982.

Choueiri, Youssef M. *Islamic Fundamentalism*. London: Twayne Publishers, 1990.

Clarke, Richard A. *Against All Enemies: Inside America's War on Terror*. New York: Free Press, 2004.

Cockburn, Alexander, and Jeffrey St. Clair, eds. *Imperial Crusades: Iraq, Afghanistan and Yugoslavia*. London/New York: Verso, 2004.

———, eds. 2003. *The Politics of Anti-Semitism*. Edinburgh/London/Oakland: AK Press, 2003.

Coulomb, Fanny. "Adam Smith: A Defense Economist." *Defense and Peace Economics* 9, no. 3 (1998): 299–316.

Cypher, James. "The Basic Economics of Rearming America." *Monthly Review* 33, no. 6 (1981): 11–28.

———. "Military Spending, Technical Change, and Economic Growth: A Disguised Form of Industrial Policy?" *Journal of Economic Issues* 21, no. 1 (March 1987): 33–60.

———. "Military Spending after the Cold War." *Journal of Economic Issues* 25, no. 2 (June 1991): 607–615.

———. "Return of the Iron Triangle: The New Military Buildup." *Dollars and Sense*, no. 239 (January/February 2002): 16–19, 37–38.

———. "The War Dividend: Gulf War Pumps Up US Military-Industrial Complex." *Dollars and Sense*, no. 166 (May 1991): 9–11.

Cole, Juan R. I., and Nikki R. Keddie, eds. *Shiism and Social Protest*. New Haven, CT: Yale University Press, 1986.

Davis, Joyce M. *Between Jihad and Salaam: Profiles in Islam*. New York: St. Martin's Press, 1997.

DeGrasse, Robert. *Military Expansion, Economic Decline*. New York: Council on Economic Priorities, 1983.

Dekmejian, Hrair. "The Anatomy of Islamic Revival: Legitimacy, Crisis, Ethnic Conflict, and the Search for Islamic Alternatives." *Middle East Journal* 34, no. 1 (Winter 1980): 1–12.

Du Boff, Richard. *Accumulation & Power: An Economic History of the United States*. New York: M.E. Sharpe, 1989.

————. "What Military Spending Really Costs." *Challenge* 32 (September/October 1989): 4–10.

Dumas, Lloyd J. "Bang for the Buck: The Real Effects of Military Spending on Security." Paper presented at the Allied Social Sciences Association, Philadelphia, PA, January 8, 2005.

————. *The Overburdened Economy*. Berkeley/Los Angeles, CA: University of California Press, 1986.

Eland, Ivan. "Protecting the Homeland: The Best Defense Is to Give No Offense." *Policy Analysis*, no. 306 (May 1998). Washington, D.C.: Cato Institute.

Esposito, John. *Islam and Development: Religion and Sociopolitical Change*. Syracuse, NY: Syracuse University Press, 1980.

————. *The Islamic Threat*. New York: Oxford University Press, 1992.

Fischer, Michael M. J. *Iran: From Religious Discourse to Revolution*. Cambridge, MA: Harvard University Press, 1980.

Flanders, Laura. *Bushwomen: Tales of a Cynical Species*. London/New York: Verso, 2004.

Fleming, Denna F. *The Cold War and Its Origins*. New York: Double Day, 1961.

Fordham, Benjamin O. *Building the Cold War Consensus: The Political Economy of U.S. National Security Policy*. Ann Arbor, MI: Michigan University Press, 1998.

Frieden, Jeff. "The Trilateral Commission: Economics and Politics in the 1970s." In *Trilateralism*, edited by Holly Sklar. Boston, MA: South End Press, 1980.

FuKuyama, Frnacis. *The End of History and the Last Man*. New York: Avon Books, 1992.

Gold, David. "Does Military Spending Stimulate or Retard Economic Performance? Revisiting an Old Debate." Paper presented at the annual meeting of the Allied Social Science Association, Philadelphia, PA, January 8, 2005.

Gordon, David, Richard Edwards, and Michael Reich. *Segmented Work, Divided Workers: The Historical Transformation of Labor in the United States*. New York: Cambridge University Press, 1982.

Guerin, Daniel. *Fascism and Big Business*. 2nd edition. New York: Pathfinder Press, 2001.

Hafez, Kai, ed. *Islam and the West in the Mass Media: Fragmented Images In a Globalizing World*. Cresskill, NJ: Hampton, 2000.

Halliday, Fred. *The Making of the Second Cold War*. London/New York: Verso, 1983.

Halper, Stefan, and Jonathan Clarke. *America Alone: The Neo-Conservatives and the Global Order*. Cambridge, MA: Cambridge University Press, 2004.

Harding, Susan. "Representing Fundamentalism: The Problem of the Repugnant Cultural Other." *Social Research* 58, no. 2 (1991): 373–393.

Hardt, Michael, and Antonio Negri. *Empire*. Cambridge, MA: Harvard University Press, 2000.

Hartung, William D. *How Much Are You Making on the War, Daddy?* New York: Nation Books, 2003.

Harvey, David. *The New Imperialism.* New York: Oxford University Press, 2003.

Heilbroner, Robert. *The Worldly Philosophers.* New York: Simon and Schuster, 1972.

Heilbroner, Robert, and James Galbraith. *Understanding Macroeconomic.* Englewood Cliffs, NJ: Prentice Hall, 1990.

Herzog, Roman. *Preventing the Clash of Civilization: A Peace Strategy for the Twenty First Century.* New York: St. Martin's Press, 1999.

Higgs, Robert, ed. *Arms, Politics, and the Economy.* Oakland, CA: Independent Institute, 1990.

Hiro, DiLip. *Secrets and Lies: Operation Iraqi Freedom and After.* New York: Nation Books, 2004.

Hofstadter, Richard. *American Political Tradition.* New York: Vintage Books, 1984.

Horowitz, David. *The Free World Colossus.* New York: Hill and Wang, 1965.

Hossein-zadeh, Ismael. "Behind the U.S. Rush to War: Justifying the Continued Increase in Military Spending." *Against the Current* 17, no. 6 (January/February 2003): 20–24.

———. "Long Waves and the Future of Capitalism." In *Political Economy and Contemporary Capitalism: Radical Perspectives on Economic Theory and Policy*, edited by Ron Baiman, Heather Boushey, and Dawn Saunders. New York: M. E. Sharpe, 2000, 78–88.

———. "The Military-Industrial Complex and Militant Zionism: An Alliance of Endless War." *Against the Current* 18, no. 5 (November/December 2003): 26–33.

———. "Perestroika and the Third World." *Review of Radical Political Economics* 22, nos. 2 and 3 (1990): 252–275.

———. *Soviet Non-Capitalist Development: The Case of Nasser's Egypt.* New York: Praeger, 1989.

Hudson, Michael. *Trade, Development and Foreign Debt.* London: Pluto Press, 1992.

Hudson, Michael C. "Islam and Political Development." In *Islam and Development: Religion and Sociopolitical Change*, edited by John Esposito. Syracuse, NY: Syracuse University Press, 1980.

Huntington, Samuel. "The Clash of Civilizations." *Foreign Affairs* 72, no. 3 (1993): 22–49.

———. *The Clash of Civilizations and the Remaking of World Order.* New York: Touchstone Books, 1997.

Hussein, Mahmood. *Class Conflict in Egypt, 1945–1970.* New York: Monthly Review Press, 1973.

Johnson, Chalmers. *Blowback: The Costs and Consequences of American Empire.* New York: Henry Holt and Company, 2002.

———. *The Sorrows of Empire.* New York: Metropolitan Books, 2004.

Keddie, Nikki R. *Roots of Revolution: An Interpretive History of Modern Iran.* New Haven, C: Yale University Press, 1981.

———, ed. *Sufis, Saints and Scholars.* Berkeley, CA: University of California Press, 1972.

Kelner, D. *The Persian Gulf TV War.* Boulder, CO: Westview Press, 1992.

Kennedy, Paul. *The Rise and Fall of the Great Powers.* New York: Vintage Books, 1989.

Khalidi, Rashid. *Resurrecting Empire: Western Footprints and America's Perilous Path in the Middle East.* Boston, MA: Beacon Press, 2004.

Kinsella, David. "Defense Spending and Economic Performance in the United States: A Causal Analysis." *Defense Economics* 1, no. 4 (1990): 295–309.

Klare, Michael et al. "Resurgent Militarism." In *Trilateralism,* edited by Holly Sklar. Boston, MA: South End Press, 1987.

Kolko, Gabriel. *The Roots of American Foreign Policy.* Boston, MA: Beacon Press, 1969.

Lens, Sidney. *The Military-Industrial Complex.* Kansas City, MO: Pilgrim Press and the National Catholic Reporter, 1970.

———. *Permanent War.* New York: Schocken Books, 1987.

Lewis, Bernard. "The Roots of Muslim Rage." *The Atlantic* 266, no. 3 (September, 1990): 47–60.

———. *What Went Wrong: Western Impact and Middle Eastern Response.* New York/Oxford: Oxford University Press, 2001.

Mandel, Ernest. *Late Capitalism.* London: New Left Books, 1975.

———. *Long Waves of Capitalist Development.* Cambridge: Cambridge University Press, 1980.

Mann, James. *The Rise of Vulcans: The History of Bush's War Cabinet.* New York: Viking/Penguin Group, 2004.

Markusen, Ann. *From Defense to Development? International Perspectives on Realizing the Peace Dividend.* New York: Routledge, 2003.

Marty, Martin E., and R. Scott Appleby, eds. *Fundamentalism Comprehended.* Chicago/London: University of Chicago Press, 1995.

McNally, David. "Understanding Imperialism: Then and Now." *Against the Current* 20, no. 3 (July/August 2005): 22–25.

Melman, Seymour. *Profits Without Production.* New York: Dell Publishing Company, 1983.

Mutalib, Hussin, and Taj ul-Islam Hashemi, eds. *Islam, Muslims and the Modern State—Case Studies of Muslims in Thirteen Countries.* London: Macmillan, 1996.

Nitzan, Johnathan, and Shimshon Bichler. *The Global Political Economy of Israel*. London/Sterling: Pluto Press, 2002.

Nordhaus, William D. "The Economic Consequences of War in Iraq." *New York Review of Books* 49, no. 19 (December 5, 2002): <http://www.nybooks.com/articles/article-preview?article_id=15850>.

Norton, Augustus R. *AMAL and the Shia: Struggle for the Soul of Lebanon*. Austin, TX: University of Texas Press, 1987.

Payne, James E., and Kevin L. Ross. "Defense Spending and the Macroeconomy." *Defense Economics* 3, no. 2 (1992): 161–168.

Pilger, John. *The New Rulers of the World*. London/New York: Verso, 2002.

Podhoretz, Norman. "World War IV: How It Started, What It Means, and Why We Have to Win." *Commentary* (September 2004): <http://www.commentary-magazine. com/podhoretz.htm>.

Piven, Frances F. and Richard Cloward. *Poor People's Movements*. New York: Vintage Books, 1978.

Pollin, Robert. "Destabilizing Finance Worsened This Recession." *Challenge* (March/April 1992): 17–24.

Prestowitz, Clyde. *Rogue Nation: American Unilateralism and the Failure of Good Intentions*. New York: Basic Books, 2003.

Ridgeway, James., ed. *The March to War*. New York: Four Walls Eight Windows, 1991.

Porter, Bruce D. *War and the Rise of the State: The Military Foundations of Modern Politics*. New York: Free Press, 1994.

Robertson, Ronald, and JoAnn Chirico. "Humanity, Globalization, and Worldwide Religious Resurgence: A Theoretical Exploration." *Sociological Analysis* 46, no. 3 (1985): 219–242.

Rodinson, Maxime. *Europe and the Mystique of Islam*. Seattle: University of Washington Press, 1987.

———. *Marxism and the Muslim World*. New York: Monthly Review Press, 1981.

Ryan, Sheila . "Power Projection in the Middle East." In *Mobilizing Democracy*, edited by Greg Bates. Monroe, ME: Common Courage Press, 1991.

Sandercock, Josie et al. *Peace Under Fire: Israel, Palestine, and the International Solidarity Movement*. London/New York: Verso, 2004.

Shaw, Martin. *War, State and Society*. London: Macmillan, 1984.

Scheuer, Michael. *Imperial Hubris: Why the West Is Losing the War on Terror*. Dulles, VA: Potomac Books, 2004.

Schoenmann, Ralph. *The Hidden History of Zionism*. Santa Barbara, CA: Veritas Press, 1988.

Shoup, Laurence H. "Jimmy Carter and the Trilateralists: Presidential Roots." In *Trilateralism*, edited by Holly Sklar. Boston, MA: South End Press, 1980.

Shoup, Laurence H., and William Minter. *Imperial Brain Trust: The Council of Foreign Relations and the United States Foreign Policy*. New York/London: Monthly Review Press, 1977.

Sklar, Holly., ed. *Trilateralism*. Boston, MA: South End Press, 1980.

Smith, Dan, and Ron Smith. *The Economics of Militarism*. London: Pluto Press, 1983.

Sorenson, Theodore. "Rethinking National Security." *Foreign Affairs* 69, no. 3 (1990): 1–18.

Suskind, Ron. *The Price of Loyalty: George W. Bush, the White House, and the Education of Paul O'Neil*. New Jersey: Simon and Schuster, 2004.

Stowasser, Barbara F., ed. *The Islamic Impulse*. Washington, D.C.: Center for Contemporary Arab Studies, Georgetown University, 1987.

Terkel, Studs. *Hard Times: An Oral History of the Great Depression*. New York: Pantheon Books, 1970.

Tobin, James. "Military Expenditure and Investment in OECD Countries." *Journal of Comparative Economics* 4, no. 1 (1980): 19–32.

Trotsky, Leon. *Fascism: What It Is and How to Fight It*. Reprint edition. New York: Pathfinder Press, 1993.

Vagts, Alfred. *A History of Militarism: Civilian and Military*. London: Hollis and Carter, 1959.

Vidal, Gore. *Perpetual War for Perpetual Peace: How We Got To Be So Hated*. New York: Thunder's Mouth Press/Nation Books, 2002.

Voll, John O. *Islam: Continuity and Change in the Modern World*. 2nd edition. Syracuse, NY: Syracuse University Press, 1994.

Ward, Michael D., and David R. Davis. "Sizing Up the Peace Dividend: Economic Growth and Military Spending in the United States, 1948–1996." *American Political Science Review* 86, no. 3 (September 1992): 748–755.

Ward, Rodney. "On the War Front and the Home Front." *Dollars & Sense* (May/June 2003): 12–15.

Warner, R. Stephen. "Theoretical Barriers to the Understanding of the Evangelical Christianity." *Sociological Analysis* 40, no. 1 (1979): 1–9.

Weinberg, Albert K. *Manifest Destiny*. New York: Quadrangle, 1963.

Williams, William A. *The Tragedy of American Diplomacy*. Cleveland: World Publishing Company, 1959.

Wilson, Joseph. *The Politics of Truth: Inside the Lies that Led to War and Betrayed My Wife's CIA Identity*. New York: Carroll and Graf Publishers, 2004.

Wood, Ellen M. *Empire of Capital*. London/New York: Verso, 2003.

Woodward, Bob. *Plan of Attack*. New York: Simon and Schuster, 2004.

Wolfe, Alan. "Trilateralism and the Carter Administration: Changed World vs. Vested Interests." In *Trileralism*, edited by Holly Sklar. Boston, MA: South End Press, 1980.

Wright, Robin. *Sacred Rage: The Wrath of Militant Islam*. New York: Simon and Schuster, 1985.

Index

Printed in the United States
83569LV00004B/9/A